# A Romany in the Family:

DC Ref

4/07

Durham Clayport Library

FOR REFERENCE ONLY

2 7 NOV 2014

FOR REFERENCE ONLY

2 6 JUN 2017

1 6 DEC 2014

1 2 NOV 2015

2 8 MAY 2016

## DURHAM COUNTY COUNCIL
Culture & Leisure

Please return or renew this item by the last date shown.
Fines will be charged if the book is kept after this date.
Thank you for using your library

100% recycled paper.

Published by Robert Dawson, 2005
188 Alfreton Road, Blackwell,
Alfreton, Derbys. DE55 5JH

ISBN 1-903418-27-5

The rights of Robert Dawson to be identified as the writer of this work, have been asserted in accordance with the Copyright Designs and patents Act 1988. All rights reserved. Other than for review purposes, no part of this publication may be reproduced, transmitted or stored in a retrieval system, in any form by any means, without permission in writing from Robert Dawson.

Printed by 4 Sheets Design and Print
197 Mansfield Road, Nottingham, NG1 3FS

# Contents

| | |
|---|---|
| Introduction | 4 |
| 1. How to Tell | 7 |
| 2. Gypsy/Traveller Surnames | 50 |
| 3. Gypsy/Traveller Forenames | 117 |
| 4. Scottish Sources | 235 |
| 5. Wayside Burials | 248 |
| Bibliography | 277 |
| Useful addresses | 281 |

# Introduction

The series of books, of which this is one, represents parts of 50 years contact with Britain's traditional Travellers, especially Romanies and Scottish Travellers. My aim is to record what I have found or witnessed, but I do so with only the intention of ensuring that it is there for the future. Traveller culture changes constantly, and the past 50 years have seen greater changes, I believe, than at any other point in history. I do not suggest that any of these books are the whole story — far from it — but they are aspects which I have found particularly interesting, or which I believe will be of particular value in a hundred years time. I have tried to keep them accurate, but naturally they also represent the views of others and I cannot always vouch for total accuracy, though to the best of my ability they are so.

This particular volume is on Gypsy genealogy. The classic book on the subject is Sharon Floate's "My Ancestors Were Gypsies" and there is also Alan McGowan's excellent "On the Gypsy Trail" (see Bibliography for details of both). What I wanted to do in this, was to provide information which is hardly or not at all covered by these but which incorporates more of the 'how do I know my ancestors were Romany Gypsies' and 'where does the Gypsy trail lead now' rather than their 'how do I go about it'. Therefore this book should be seen as a supplement to the predecessors and cannot in any way replace either.

The book is divided into five major chapters — How to Tell, Surnames, Forenames, Scottish Sources, and Wayside Burials. Almost all the essays in this book have appeared before in print in one of numerous genealogical or historical publications and journals or specialist booklets.

In presenting this book, I emphasise that it deals especially with the Romany Gypsies of Britain and with Scottish Traditional Travellers (sometimes racially abused as 'Tinkers') and to a much lesser extent Ireland's Travellers.

My use of the word Gypsy may be questioned. I use it here in its proper sense, as a member of an ethnic minority and not in some of the silly modern senses which have evolved from use of the word one with wealth, and that they were from the Tax authorities. They would return, they said, in a day to assess everyone for tax and anyone not paying the tax would have their wagons and horses seized. To cover himself, Joe told them that other than a couple of the horses, the remainder belonged to the rest of the people, thereby worsening the situation. Unthinkingly, and caught on the hop, he told the authorities the correct names of all the people. (I should say at this point that I do not believe these really were tax men. I believe this was just a ruse to panic the Gypsies into leaving.)

When the remainder of the Gypsies returned and heard what had happened, they were very angry with Joe. Their existence — as with almost all Gypsies at that time — was very hand to mouth and the prospect of having their very homes confiscated for wealth they certainly did not have, was very frightening.

The following morning, all but Joe pulled off, and all changed their surnames for a few weeks. Joe remained with his horses until his leg mended, and when the "tax men" returned he told them everyone had gone and that they had left their horses but would be coming back for them. The "tax men" checked his caravan, found nothing of value, and believed him. They left after making him promise he would ring the tax office to report when they came back for their animals.

## History of Gypsy Surnames

When Gypsies first arrived in Britain they mainly adopted local surnames, picking those which were:

1. The names of famous gorjers in order to try to obtain some protection by pseudo-influence. Examples include Gray and Lovell.
2. Very common gorjer names, like Smith and Brown.
3. Names of gorjers with whom they intermarried, such as Sandys and Roberts.
4. Names created from forenames, like Reynolds and Turpin (Turpin had in fact gone from a gorjer surname to a forename before even that).

5. Names which derived from Gypsy words, such as Romana, and Lawlo.

6. Names made by amending an existing name, such as Finney (from Finn) and Leatherhead (from Leatherlund).

7. Names said to have been created from incidents within Gypsy history, such as Lock and Boss.

8. Names which derived from misunderstandings of an existing name, such as Kilthorpe (really Chilcott), Oadley (originally Hoadley).

9. Local names to make it seem that the family had always lived there such as Morton and Brooksbank.

10. Aka names from jokes, like Trees (for Wood) and Minj (Romany word for female private parts).

11. Aka names from something happening at that moment such as Carrot and Babe.

12. Nicknames which have become surnames, such as Badger and Gray (one branch, from Grey Finneys), not to be confused with the main-stream Gray family.

13. Amalgamations of existing Gypsy surnames, eg Lovelock, Bosley

14. Joke-names at the expense of the enquirer (Orrer, Onrded)

15. New surnames created by amending existing names, such as Buckland /Buckley/Buckle, and Wharton/Whatton/Walton etc

## Abbreviations for place names in the following:

ABD — Aberdeenshire
ABE — Aberconwy
AGY — Anglesey
ARL — Argyllshire
ARM — Armagh
AUS — Australia
AYR — Ayrshire
BAN — Banffshire
BEW — Berwickshire
BFD — Bedfordshire
BKM — Buckinghamshire
BLA — Blaenau Gwent
BOR — The Scottish Borders
BRE — Breconshire
BRK — Berkshire
CAE — Caernarvonshire
CAI — Caithness
CAM — Cambridgeshire
CAN — Canada
CAR — Cardiff
CGN — Cardiganshire
CHS — Cheshire
CLY — Clywd
CMN — Carmarthenshire
COL — Colwyn
CON — Cornwall
CUL — Cumberland
DBY — Derbyshire
DEN — Denbighshire
DEV — Devonshire
DFS — Dumfriesshire
DNB — Dunbartonshire
DOR — Dorset
DOW — Down
DUB — Dublin
DUR — Durham
ESS — Essex

FIF — Fifeshire
FLN — Flintshire
FOR — Forfar
GAL — Galway
GLA — Glamorgan
GLS — Gloucestershire
GWN — Gwent
HAM — Hampshire
HEF — Herefordshire
HRT — Hertfordshire
HUN — Huntingdonshire
IoW — Isle of Wight
IRE — Ireland
ISR — Israel
JSY — Jersey
KEN — Kent
KGS — Kings (Offaly, Ireland)
KRS — Kinross-shire
LAN — Lancashire
LDN — London
LEI — Leicestershire
LIN — Lincolnshire
LKS — Lanarkshire
LTH — Lothian
MDX — Middlesex
MER — Merionethshire
MGY — Montgomeryshire
MHN — Monaghan
MLN — Midlothian
MON — Monmouthshire
MOR — Moray
NAM — North America
NBL — Northumberland
NFK — Norfolk
NIR — Northern Ireland
NTH — Northamptonshire
NTT — Nottinghamshire
NZ — New Zealand
OXF — Oxfordshire

PEM — Pembrokeshire
PER — Perthshire
PWY — Powys
RAD — Radnorshire
RFW — Renfrewshire
RHO — Rhondda
ROC — Ross and Cromarty
ROX — Roxburghshire
RUT — Rutland
SAL — Shropshire
SAM — South America
SCT — Scotland
SEL — Selkirkshire
SFK — Suffolk
SOM — Somerset
SRY — Surrey
SSX — Sussex
STF — Staffordshire
STL — Stirlingshire
SUT — Sutherland
SWA — Swansea
TIP — Tipperary
TOR — Torfaen
USA — United States of America
WAL — Wales generally
WAR — Warwickshire
WES — Westmoreland
WIL — Wiltshire
WOR — Worcestershire
WRX — Wrexham
YKS — Yorkshire

## Other Abbreviations

Cp — Compare
E — East
f — female
G — Gypsy
Int — Intermittent — there are major gaps in the years spread during which no trace of the family has been found
m — male
N — North
S — South
W — West

The lists which follow are taken from a variety of sources indicated below. They aim to give the reader the chance of seeking their own surname and, if it is there, seeing its significance as a Gypsy surname and which parts of the country and when it occurred.

## Sources

1. My own extensive notes of material collected over many years:
   a) From Gypsies themselves;
   b) From parish records, IGIs, Quarter Sessions Records, police records in Public Reference Offices;
   c) From numerous non-fiction books about Gypsies
   d) From the Journal of the Gypsy Lore Society
   e) From Romany Routes, the Journal of the Romany and Traveller FHS
   f) From correspondence to myself
   g) From transportation lists since c 1600.

## Notes on the Lists

1. When only one year is stated, it can be assumed that the surname concerned is likely to be that of a very small family, an aka name, or not actually a Gypsy at all (ie a counterfeit Egyptian or people mistaken for Gypsies.)

2. There are few references to some families from certain parts of the country — especially Scotland, and what is now Northern Ireland and Eire. Much more research is needed for those countries.

3. Though these entries are mainly of Romanies with some Scottish and Irish Travellers, a few show people (fairgrounds, circuses) and people who ran lodging houses in which Gypsies appear to have stayed, have been included.

4. End year is the latest which can be proved — it does not imply that the family necessarily ceased at that time. Where a family's era is to *Present* it indicates that the family certainly still exists as Romany/Show family, but it does not necessarily mean they are nomadic. Also, there are probably families who I have not indicated as present day, who are still Romany/Show. This is caused by lack of data.

5. Some of these surnames are very dubiously Gypsy. In such cases, the lack of more data should be taken as implying that though they appeared to be Gypsies, or were thus described or claimed, there is good reason to be doubtful.

6. Surnames should not be seen in isolation but as part of a complex interaction in which names can change and change back with great rapidity and without there being a necessarily sinister motives. Equally, families in the past were sometimes inclined to change their surnames every now and then.

7. In consequence of the above factors, these lists will inevitably contain people who, whilst not Gypsies, were taken as such, and were described in official records as travellers, sojourners, strangers, peregrini, vagrants, vagabonds, poor travelling people, tinkers, itinerants, hawkers and chair menders.

8. Where a name is indicated as *"No information"*, this implies that the name is claimed as being one used by Travellers, but, personally, I have no evidence. This does not imply that evidence does not exist elsewhere. *No further information* similarly shows that this is all the information which I personally have.

9. *Data lost* indicates I have mislaid my original source(s). Apologies for such.

# Gypsy Surnames and the Periods When and Counties Where They Were in Use

**Abbott:** 1881 — 1914 DBY, NFK
**Abel:** 1880 GLS
**Abercrombie:** 1676 SCT
**Ableth:** 1708 NTH
**Abnett:** 1891 LDN
**Abraham:** 1960s Midlands (no further information)
**Ackroyd:** 1891 YKS
**Acome:** BKM
**Adams:** 1726 — 1909 BKM, ESS, GLS, IoW, LAN, LDN, SRY, SSX, STF, WES, WIL, YKS
**Adcock:** 1851 NFK
**Ade:** 1891 SSX
**Agar:** 1777 — 1836 BKM, CAM, YKS
**Agate:** 1891 SSX
**Aimes:** See Hames
**Albone:** 1830s NFK, SFK
**Alderton:** 1660 YKS
**Aldridge:** 1891 BRK, HAM, LDN, OXF
**Alexander/Alexandra:** 1851 GLS, HAM, RFW, WIL, YKS
**Al(l)ford:** 1909 HAM, SSX
**Allard:** LDN(E)
**Allatt:** 1879 NTH
**Allen/Ellen:** 1574 — present AUS, CHS, CMN, CON, CUL, DEV, DBY, DUR, ESS, GLS, KEN, LDN, LIN, MDX, NBL, NFK, NIR, NTH, SRY, SSX, WIL, YKS. Cp Eland
**Alli(n)son:** 1880 — 1950 CAM, CUL, DUR, IRE, LAN, SCO, WAL, YKS
**Ambrose:** 1594 — 1817 (int) ESS, MDX
**Amer:** 1677 — 1914 (int) GLS, KEN, SSX, YKS
**Ames:** See Hames
**Anchorn:** 1785 — 1880 (int) BFD, SSX
**Anderson/Anderton:** 1851 — 1881 ESS, KEN, LAN, LDN, MDX, MLN, ROX, SCO, YKS
**Andrews:** 1540 — 1912 (int) CAM, GLS, MDX, OXF, SCO, SSX, YKS
**Annable:** GLS

**Ansell:** 1833 GLS
**Anstee:** YKS
**Antill:** GLS, LIN
**Appleton:** BKM, BRK
**Archer:** 1847 — 1851 BRK, GLS, NBL, OXF, YKS
**Arkell:** GLS
**Armitage:** 1891 — 1966 KEN, NBL, YKS
**Argus:** 1891 SRY
**Arnett.** 1936 LAN
**Arnfield:** 1827 — 1862 DBY
**Arnold:** 1851 — 1912 BFD, DBY, GLS, HRT, KEN, SSX
**Arrington:** See Harrington
**Arundel:** 1907 SSX
**Ashby/Ashbee:** 1857 GLS
**Ashforth.** 1788 YKS **Ash(l)ington:** 1891 YKS
**Ashmore:** LIN
**Ashton:** DBY
**Aspland:** 1891 DUR, NFK
**Astley:** LDN
**Atkins:** 1728 — 1891 (int) HRT, NBL, NTH
**Atkinson:** 1591 — 1891 (int) GLS, NBL, YKS
**Auger:** OXF
**Austin(s):** 1838 — 1902 GLS
**Averhill:** GLS
**Avery:** 1847 GLS
**Ayres/ Hares/Ayers/ Airs etc:** 1553 — present (int) BRK, DBY, GLS, GWN, HAM, KEN, MDX, NFK, SRY, SSX, WAL, YKS
**Bacon:** 1799 — 1961 DBY, HAM, HRT, MDX, SSX
**Badcock:** DEV, ESS, MDX, SRY
**Badger:** 1994 — present DBY
**Badley:** 1834 DBY
**Baggaley/Bagley:** 1796 — 1811 NTH, OXF, YKS
**Baglin:** 1881 GLS
**Baildon:** 1891 BKM
**Baillie/Bailey/Baylis:** 1542 — 1891 (int) BFD, BKM, BOR, CHS, CUL, DBY, GLS, IRE, LDN, NBL, MDX, NFK, NTH, OXF, SAL, SCO, STF, SUR, SSX, YKS
**Baine(s)** 1611 YKS
**Baird:** 1664 LTH

**Baker:** 1721 — present (int) DBY, DEV, DOR, ESS, GLS, HAM, KEN, LAN, LDN, NFK, SFK,SRY, SSX, STF, WIL, YKS
**Ball:** 1751 — 1985 (int) CAM, DBY, ESS, GLS, HAM, IoW, KEN, LAN, LEI, Midlands(E), SRY, SSX, STF, YKS
**Ballinger:** GLS
**Banantine:** AYR
**Banding:** GLS
**Bankley:** LDN
**Banks:** 1837 — 1881 BFD, DBY, GLS, SRY
**Banning:** WIL
**Bannister:** 1576 — 1785 (int) BKM, ESS, LDN, LEI, OXF, SAL
**Baptist:** 1540 — 1579 LAN, SCO
**Barber:** 1641 — 1913 (int) DEV, SFK, SSX, YKS
**Barker:** 1663 — 1995 BFD, CAM, CHS, DBY, HAM, SSX, YKS
**Barley/Barlow:** 1785 — 1891 LIN, NFK, YKS
**Barnard:** ESS, GLS, KEN, LDN
**Barn(es)/Barney:** 1651-1910 AUS, DBY, DOR, GLS, HAM, KEN, NFK, SRY, SSX
**Barnett:** 1891 ESS, NBL
**Barnsley:** 1873 GLS
**Barras:** 1965 — 2000 NTT
**Barrell:** ESS, SFK
**Barrett/Burrett:** 1865 — present DBY, DUR, ESS, GLS, KEN, LEI, MDX, SSX
**Barringer:** LAN, LDN
**Barrington:** GLS
**Barron:** 1898 — 1914 LDN, SFK
**Barrow(s):** 1691 GLS, YKS
**Barry:** BLA, IRE
**Bartlett:** HAM
**Barton:** 1619 — 1970 (int) BKM, DBY, ESS, GLS, KEN, LDN, OXF, SSX
**Barwick:** LIN
**Barwise:** HAM
**Bass:** 1881 ESS
**Basset(t):** 1891 — 1912 KEN, LDN, MDX, SRY, SSX
**Bastien:** 1576-7 OXF
**Batch:** MDX
**Batchelor:** 1881 SRY

**Bateman:** 1597 DBY, ESS, HAM, NTT
**Bates:** 1721 — 1960s DBY, GLS, NTH
**Bateson:** 1519 — 1811 (int) YKS
**Bath:** 1910 SRY
**Batt:** 1976 — 1981 CHS, GLS, LAN
**Batten:** 1721 NTH
**Batty:** 1785 — 1810 YKS
**Baugh:** 1881 KEN
**Baxter:** 1760 — 1980 (int) BKM, DBY, HAM, KEN, LDN, MDX, NFK, SRY, YKS
**Baylis:** See Bailey
**Beach/ Beich:** 1891 GLS, LDN
**Beam/Beamy:** 1881 DEV, KEN
**Bean/Beaney:** 1673 — 1970 DOR, HAM, IRE, KEN, LDN, MDX, SFK, SRY, SSX, WES
**Bearn:** 1960 DEV
**Beazley:** GLS
**Beaumont:** 1753 YKS
**Becket(t):** 1885 HAM, KEN, SSX
**Beckworth:** KEN
**Beddoes:** 1930s
**Beddesford:** 1930s
**Bedford:** OXF
**Beich:** See Beach
**Beige:** 1540 SCO
**Belcher:** 1830 DEV, GLS, OXF
**Beldam/Beldon/Beldorn:** 1912 — 1923 BKM, BRK, KEN, SRY, SSX
**Belding:** 1891 NFK
**Bell:** 1567 — 1889 DBY, MDX, WIL, YKS
**Bellwood:** 1719 YKS
**Belmonte:** Spain
**Bendell:** HAM
**Benham:** 1898 SSX
**Benn:** 1846 SRY
**Bennett:** 1881 — 1960 DBY, LDN, ESS, KEN, MDX, NFK, PWY, SAL, SSX, STF
**Bennison:** 1767 YKS
**Bent:** 1891 KEN, MDX

**Bentley:** 1816 DBY
**Benton:** 1891 KEN
**Bergo:** 1540 SCO. Cp Virgo
**Berriman:** LDN
**Berry:** 1891 — 1975 KEN, SSX, WOR, YKS
**Bertram:**
**Besford:** SAL
**Best:** 1881 — 1913 CON, SSX
**Beswick:** LDN
**Beswickan:** ESS
**Betterley:** NTT (?Perhaps originally a joke at someone's expense, eg *We're the <u>better Lees</u>*)
**Betts:** 1814 — 1932 BKM
**Bibford:** 1921 SSX
**Bibbury:** 1933 MON
**Bibby:** 1866 — 1954 CAM, ESS, HRT, LAN, SSX, YKS
**Bick:** GLS
**Bidder:** GLS
**Biddle:** 1701 — present (int.) BFD, DEV, GLS, HUN, KEN, LAN, NBL, NTH, OXF, SRY, WAR
**Bierley/Birley:** 1686 — present (int.) BFD, DBY, YKS
**Biggs:** 1891 HAM, HRT, STF
**Bignall:** KEN
**Billings:** 1851 — 1881 HUN, LEI, NTH, NFK
**Bilshaw:** GLS
**Bilston:** 1901 SSX
**Bilton:** 1891 — 1970 SRY, SCT
**Birch/Byrch:** 1732 — 1891 BFD, COR, DEV, GLS, HAM, LDN, NFK, SSX
**Bird:** 1833 — 1929 BFD, BRK, DUR, ESS, GLS, HUN, NFK, SSX, YKS
**Birks:** See Burk
**Birmingham:** 1960 CON, MON, WAR
**Bishop:** GLS, KEN, SRY
**Black:** 1801 — 1930 BRK, DBY, HAM, KEN, SCO, SOM, SRY, SSX, WIL
**Blackham:** Midlands(W)
   **Blackman/Blakeman:** 1850 BRK, HAM, WAR, WIL
**Blake:** 1881 CHS, COR, GLS, IRE, YKS

**Blakey:** 1784 YKS
**Bland:** DOR, HAM, LAN, Midlands
**Bleardall:** 1891 DUR
**Blewer:** DBY
**Blezzard:** 1863 DBY
**Bliss:** 1891 NBL
**Blithe:** See Blyth
**Blood:** 1849 — 1876 DSH
**Bloomfield:** LIN
**Blower:** 1894 DUR
**Bluett/Blewett:** 1696 — 1860 (Int) CUL, DUR, ESS, LIN, NBL, STF, WAR, YKS
**Blyth(e)/Blithe:** 1589 — 1975 (int) BEW, BOR, MLN, NBL, NFK, NTH, SCO, YKS
**Boa:** BOR
**Boddicombe:** 1891 MDX
**Bolan:** 1881 KEN
**Bolton/Boulton:** 1891 WOR, YKS
  **Bond(s):** 1891 — 1908 ESS, GLS, LDN, LIN, NFK, SRY, SSX
**Bonnett:** 1848 — 1935 NFK
**Bonside:** 1891 YKS
**Booler:** 1881 KEN
**Boor:** 1820 NTH
**Booth** 1619 — present (int) BKM, CAM, DEV, DBY, GLS, HEF, KEN, LEI, LIN, NTH, NTT, SAL, SSX, STF, YKS
**Boskett:** 1871 SSX
**Boss:** See Boswell. Although some authorities claim this is a separate surname, I have ample evidence that it was almost always interchangable with Boswell.
**Bostock:** NBL
**Bosup:** 1914 SSX
**Boswell:** 1639 — present. All England, most of Wales, Scots borders. Australia. At one stage, a branch of the Boswells took the name Boss, though the surname continued to be interchangeable with Boswell. The surname Boss is still found, but appears now to be an AKA.
**Bosworth:** LDN. Although this name is sometimes regarded as a family in its own right, I believe it is actually a variation on Boswell.

**Bothwell:** 1891 WIL
**Boulton:** See Bolton
**Boulter:** 1848 NFK
**Bounfellow:** 1617 YKS
**Bourne:** 1881 SSX
**Bowden:** 1814
**Bowels:** 1911 SSX
**Bowen:** 1881 GLA, GLS
**Bower(s):** 1595 — present (int) CHS, DEV, DOR, GLS, HAM, KEN, LDN, MDX, NFK, NTH, NTT, SOM, SRY, SSX, WIL
**Bowker:** 1881 LAN
**Bowler:** 1724 DBY
**Bowling:** 1758. OXF
**Bowls:** 1902 SSX
**Bowman:** 1936 KEN
**Bowmill:** 1881 NFK
**Bownia:** See Bunyan
**Boyce:** 1891 DEV, HAM, SSX
**Boyling:** 1764 — present DBY, LIN, NTH, SAL, STF, YKS
**Braddock/ Braddick:** 1907 — present DBY, LDN, LIN, NTT, SAL, WAL
**Bradford:** 1891 — 1962 LAN, SSX
**Bradley:** 1811 CUL, GLS
**Bradshaw:** 1771- 1881 HUN, IRE, YKS
**Braham:** LIN
**Braithwaite:** CUL
**Bramwell:** 1871 DBY
**Bratton:** 1881 KEN
**Bray:** 1881 KEN
**Brazier:** SSX
**Brazil:** 1825 — 1968 KEN, SSX, LDN, SE Counties
**Brearley:** See Brierley
**Breeds/Breeze:** KEN
**Brett:** 1891 GLS, MDX
**Brewer:** 1653 — 1843 (int) GLS, MDX
**Brewerton:** 1594 MDX
**Brewin:** 1825 YKS
**Bridals:** 1963 COR, DEV, DOR
**Bridge(s):** 1891 — 1904 HEF, KEN, SRY

**Bridgen:** 1891 ESS, NFK
**Brien/Bryan(s):** 1743 — 1906 (int) GLS, IRE, WAR, YKS
**Brierley:** 1881 — 1891 LAN, YKS
**Briggs:** 1891 LDN
**Brimsden:** 1846
**Brines:** 1811 NBD
**Brinkley:** 1834 — 1891 BFD, HRT, HUN, KEN, LIN, LDN, MDX, SRY, WAR, YKS
**Brischah:** 1678 YKS
**Bristow:** 1900 SSX
**Britton:** 1891 — 1899 GLS, SSX, WAR
**Broadway:** 1780 — present (int) COR, DEV, KEN, SOM
**Brocklehurst:** DBY, LIN, STF
**Brockless:** BKM
**Brocksop:** 1751 DBY
**Brokland:** LAN
**Bromage:** WOR
**Bronger:** 1906 SSX
**Brooker:** 1891 SSX
**Brook(s)/Broakes:** 1727 — 1941 ESS, GLS, LIN, NTH, SRY, SSX, WOR, YKS
**Broomhead:** 1881 CHS
**Brotherton:** 1851 YKS
**Brough:** 1891 NBL
**Broughton:** LIN
**Browmane:** 1574 YKS. Cp Brownell
**Brown:** 1541 — present (int) ARM, BFD, BRK, CAM, CHS, DBY, DEV, ESS, GLS, HRT, HUN, KEN, LAN, LDN, LIN, MDX, NFK, OXF, NTH, SCO, SRY, SSX, Wales(S), WIL, WRK, YKS
**Brownell/Brownhill:** 1661 — 1726 (int) YKS. Cp Browmaine.
**Browning:** 1852 — 1860 SSX
**Bruce:** 1616 — 1966 (int)
**Brugman:** 1655 HRT
**Bruton:** 1867 — 1870 GLS
**Bryan.** See Brien
**Bryant:** 1881 — 1891 BFD, MDX
**Buck:** 1656 — present (int) DBY, HAM, YKS
**Buckenham:** 1851 NFK
**Buckland:** 1651 — present. BFD, BKM, BRK, CAN, COR, DBY,

DEN, DEV, GLS, HAM, HUN, LDN, MDX, NTH, OXF, SAM, SOM, SRY, SSX, WAL, WIL, WOR, USA

**Buckley/Burkley:** 1563 — present. BKM, CAM, DBY, DOR, DSH, ESS, GLS, HAM, HUN, IoW, IRE, KEN, LDN, LIN, MDX, NFK, NTT, OXF, SFK, SOM, SRY, SSX, WIL, WOR, YKS

**Buckton:** 1657 — 1669 YKS

**Bud(d):** 1907 HAM, SSX

**Bugg:** 1891- 1908 DEV, HAM, NFK, SSX, WIL

**Bull:** DOR, IoW

**Bullantine:** 1891 DUR

**Bullen/ Bullin:** 1891 LDN, NFK, SRY

**Bullock:** 1648 DBY

**Bunce/Bunts:** 1859 — present BFD, BRK, DBY, HEF, LEI, OXF, WIL

**Bunn:** 1881 LIN

**Bunyan:** 1586 — 1640 COR

**Burberry:** 1891 GLS

**Burden:** BKM, BRK

**Burgess:** 1891 — 1906 SSX, YKS

**Burk/Birks:** 1957 — 1970 DBY, SCO

**Burkley:** See Buckley

**Burnet:** 1827 — 1891 (int) DBY, NFK, SCO

**Burnham:** 1739 NTH

**Burns:** 1697 — 1913 (int) NTH, SSX

**Burnsell:** 1815 NFK

**Burnside/ Burnsdon:** 1816 — present (int) DBY, DUR, GLS, LAN, NBL, WES, YKS

**Burrell:** 1706 YKS

**Burrett:** See Barrett

**Burrow(s)/Burrough(s):** 1735 — 1891 GLS, HAM, YKS

**Burton:** 1631 — present CMN, COR, DBY, DEV, DOR, DBY, DUR, ESS, GLA, GWN, HUN, LAN, LIN, MON, NTH, SFK, SRY, SSX, WAL, WIL, YKS

**Butcher:** 1891 LDN. This is an aka name for Buckland.

**Butler:** 1597 — present (int.) BKM, DEN, BRK, DEV, GLS, HAM, HUN, KEN, LDN, MDX, NFK, NTH, OXF, SRY, SSX, WIL, WAR, WOR, YKS

**Butlin:** 1751 — 1800

**Butt:** 1891 NFK, LDN

**Butteridge:** 1910 KEN
**Buttersmith:** 1881 KEN
**Buttery:** BFD
**Butty:** 1873 IRE
**Buxton:** 1711 DBY
**Byers:** GLS
**Byles:** BKM, GLS, NTH, OXF, RUT, WOR
**Byrch:** See Birch
**Cadman:** 1875 — 1933 DBY, MON
**Cain:** 1870 — 1891 GLS, LDN
**Caird:** 1610 — 1818 (int) DBY, LDN
**Cairns/Kairns:** 1891 DUR
**Calladine:** 1803 — present DBY, DUR, NBL, NTT
**Callaghan:** CUL, IRE
**Calot:** 1570 DBY
**Calver:** SFK
**Calverley:** LDN, YKS
**Cambey:** 1725 YKS
**Cameron:** 1938 — present SCO, STF
**Camfield/Canfield:** ESS, HAM, SSX
**Camp:** 1930 — 1939 CMN
**Campbell:** 1624 — 1891 (int) ESS, LDN, SCO, SSX, YKS
**Campion:** LDN, MDX
**Canfield:** See Camfield
**Canham:** No information
**Cannon:** 1908 — present SSX, YKS
**Carew:** 1744 — 1935 (int) SOM, SSX
**Carey:** 1891 — 1909 HAM, KEN, LDN, SRY, SSX
**Carloman:** 1891 — 1933 DUR, MON
**Carlton/Carton:** 1624 BKM, OXF, YKS
**Carman:** 1881 HUN
**Carn:** 1881 COR
**Carpenter:** 1884 GLS
**Carr:** See Kerr.
**Carrick:** YKS 1635
**Carris(s):** 1891 DUR
**Carroll:** 1891 DUR
**Carter:** 1781 — 1920 BRK, COR, DBY, DEV, HAM, KEN, LDN, MDX, NTH, OXF, SRY, SSX, YKS

**Cartwright:** 1881 STF
**Casey:** 1851 — 1881 IRE, LAN, YKS
**Cash:** 1833 — present DBY, IRE, NTT, YKS
**Cashmore:** LEI, WAR
**Castle:** 1806 — 1909. HAM, MDX, SRY, SFK, SSX
**Cater:** 1635 — 1891 (int). NFK, SSX, YKS
**Cattermole:** 1881 SFK
**Cavander:** LAN
**Cavena:** 1881 CGN
**Cawley:** 1968 — 1970 YKS
**Chadwick:** 1891 KEN
**Chalkley:** 1881 KEN
**Chamberlain:** 1909 GLS
**Chambers:** 1962 KEN, SRY,YKS
**Champion:** KEN, LDN
**Chaplin:** 1607 — 1774 (int) SFK, YKS
**Chapman:** 1865 — 1971 BRK, DEV, DUR, HAM, HRT, KEN, LAN, LDN, LIN, SRY, SSX
**Chappell:** BRK
**Charingold:** KEN
**Charles:** 1881 — 1960 NTH, OXF, SCO, WAR
**Charlotte:** 1775 — 1945 CAM, CGN, DBY, NFK, OXF, SAL, SFK, STF, WAR
**Charlton:** 1881 CHS
**Chater:** 1881 BKM
**Cheeseman:** 1899 — 1901 NFK, SSX
**Cheneler:** 81891 LDN
**Chick:** 1891 LDN
**Chilcott/ Kilthorpe:** 1725 — 1891 AUS, BRK, CHS, ESS, HRT, KEN, LAN, LDN, NFK, OXF, SCO, SRY, SFK, SOM
**Childs:** SRY
**Chilton:** SFK
**Chirn:** 1911 HAM
**Chittenden:** KEN
**Chivers:** 1891 MDX
**Churan:** ESS
**Churcher:** HAM
**Clare:** 1853
**Clargo:** BRK

**Claridge:** WIL
**Clark(e):** 1599 — present (int) BKM, BRK, CAM, DEV, DBY, DUR, ESS, GLS, KEN, LAN, LDN, LIN, MDX, NBL, NTH, SCO, SRY, SSX, YKS
**Clarkson:** 1891 YKS
**Clay:** 1706 DBY
**Claydon:** AUS, ESS, OXF. Claimed by the family as a different name from Clayton, but due to the several references to early Claytons as Claydons, I believe the families were originally the same.
**Clayton:** 1775 — 1965 DBY, HEF, LEI, STF, YKS
**Clearly:** KEN
**Clegg:** 1838 GLS
**Clifton:** 1662 SRY, YKS
**Closs:** SFK
**Clune:** LAN
**Coates:** HRT, KEN, SSX, YKS
**Coffee:** 1853 — 1860 GLS
**Cole/Coil:** 1902 — present BKM, BRK, GLS, HAM, KEN, LDN, SRY, STF, WIL, YKS
**Coleman/Colman:** 1827 — present BKM, CON, DBY, LAN, Midlands, NTT, SAL, WIL, WOR, YKS
**Colley:** KEN
**Collins/Colins:** 1891 — present BKM, Black Country, BRK, DBY, HAM, KEN, LDN, Midlands, SSX, WIL
**Colli(n)son:** 1800 KEN, MDX, SRY, SSX
**Combs:** KEN
**Comford:** SRY
**Connell:** — present IRE, LDN
**Connor:** 1891 WIL
**Constance:** KEN, SSX
**Cook(e):** 1845-1910 BFD, HAM, HRT, IRE, KEN, LDN, SFK, WOR
**Cooper:** 1625 — present BKM, BRK, CAM, CUL, DOR, DUR, ESS, GLS, HAM, HEF, HRT, KEN, LDN, MDX, NBL, NFK, NTT, NZ, SCO, SE Counties, SFK, SRY, SSX, USA, Wales, WIL, YKS
**Copeland:** 1881 LAN

**Coppard:** 1891 SSX
**Corbett:** KEN
**Cordwell:** SSX, WIL
**Corfield:** 1873 IRE
**Corkill:** IoM
**Corsey:** 1891 KEN
**Cosby:** 1881 BFD
**Cosier:** BKM
**Coslin:** 1881 DEV
**Coster:** 1945 — 1975 KEN
**Cotton:** 1738 NTH
**Coulston:** 1891 MDX
**Coultman:** 1891 NBL
**Cowdery:** BRK
**Cowdiddle:** 1610 DBY, LDN
**Cowp:** 1579 DUR, YKS
**Cox:** 1803 — 1891 BFD, CHS, GLS, HAM, KGS, LIN, SSX, YKS
**Coyne:** 1891 SSX
**Crabtree:** 1891 YKS
**Crafts:** 1618 LEI
**Cragg:** 1802 ESS
**Cramp:** ESS, KEN, LDN, WAR
**Crane:** 1843 — 1888 NFK
**Crapp:** 1891 DUR
**Craven:** NTH
**Crawford:** 1727 BRK
**Crawley:** LDN
**Crew:** MON, STF
**Crewdron:** 1881 AGY
**Crighton:** NFK
**Critchley:** 1881 NTH
**Crock:** 1881 DEV
**Crocker/Croker:** 1881 — 1901 COR, DEV, SSX, YKS
**Croft:** KEN
**Crole:** 1891 LDN
**Cronk:** 1891 NFK
**Crook:** LDN, NFK
**Crosby:** 1851 — present DBY, DUR, YKS
**Crosley:** 1609 — 1649 YKS

**Cross(e)/Crosbiter:** 1699 — 1891 (int) CUL, ESS, NTH, OXF
**Crow(e):** 1891 — 1960 NFK
**Crowley:** GLS, IRE
**Crumley:** 1671 SCO
**Crutcher:** ESS, HAM, WIL
**Culline:** DUR 1891
**Cundell/ Cundy:** 1788 — 1851 (int) YKS
**Cunningham:** 1825 — present DBY, NTT, SCO
**Cunnington:** 1879 YKS
**Curl:** 1908 LAN
**Curlit:** CUL
**Curtis:** 1634 — 1888 (int) BFD, BKM, HUN, LDN, NTH, YKS
**Cushway:** ESS, LDN, SRY
**Cuthbert:** BKM, OXF
**Cutts:** 1828 — present (int) DBY, NTT, STF, WOR
**Dabfoot:** 1899 SSX
**Dale:** 1675 — 1881 (int) DBY, KEN, YKS
**Daley/Dailey/Daly:** 1891 DEN, KEN, Wales, YKS
**Dalson/ Dalton:** 1891 ESS, HRT, KEN, LDN
**Dane:** 1881 KEN
**Danner:** 1908 DBY
**Danton:** 1881 KEN
**Darker/Darkins:** HRT, LDN, NTH
**Darnborough:** 1791 MDX
**Dart:** 1891 HEF
**Davenport:** KEN 1881
**Davi(d)son:** 1865 — 1881 LIN, SCT, SOM
**Davis/Davies/Davy:** 1571 — present (int) BRK, CAE, CAM, CHS, DBY, DEN, DOR, ESS, GLS, HAM, HRT, KEN, LDN, Midlands, NFK, NTH, OXF, SFK, SOM, SRY, SSX, WIL, WKS, WOR, WRX, YKS, Wales
**Daw(e)s:** 1891 ESS, HRT
**Dawson:** 1804 — 1908 LAN, LDN, YKS
**Day:** 1699 — present (int) BFD, BRK, CAM, GLS, HAM, HRT, KEN, LDN, NBL, NFK, NTH, OXF, SFK, SSX, YKS
**Deacon/Deaking:** 1881 — 1891 DEV, HAM, IoW, KEN, LDN, SRY, SSX
**Deadman/Dedman:** 1891 DBY, LDN
**Deago:** 1577 BKM

**Dean:** 1731 — 1891 (int) YKS
**Dear:** 1891 DUR
**Dee:** 1614 — 1881 (int) ESS, NFK, YKS
**Deighton:** 1775 — present ESS, KNT, LDN, NFK, WOR
**Delaney:** 1990-present CHS, SRY
**Dell:** HRT, LDN
**Denman:** 1914 SSX
**Dennard/Denerd:** HAM, KEN, LDN, SSX
**Dennett:** 1891 LDN
**Denton:** 1891 DUR
**Denyer/Dennard:** 1923 SRY, SSX
**Derrick:** 1873 SOM
**Deverall/Devall:** 1960 KEN, MDX
**Devine/ Divine:** 1853 KEN, SSX
**Dexter:** KEN
**Dibley:** 1881 KEN
**Dickens:** 1880
**Dickinson:** 1891 KEN
**Diett:** LDN
**Diggins:** 1891 SRY
**Dilkes:** 1891 SRY
**Dimberline:** 1774-1843 YKS
**Dinsmore:** 1840 NIR
**Dinson:** 1891 LDN
**Divine:** See Devine
**Dix:** 1806 WIL
**Dixie/ Dixey:** 1891 KEN, SRY
**Dixon/Dickson:** 1881 — 1947 AUS, BFD, ESS, GLS, HAM,. HRT, LAN, NFK, OXF, SRY, WIL, YKS
**Dobson:** 1639 Midlands, YKS
**Doby/Toby:** HAM
**Docaria:** 1891 NFK
**Docherty/Docerty:** 1840 — 1881 NIR
**Doe:** 1844 — 1945 BKM, BRK, DOR, ESS, HAM, KEN, SCO, SRY, SSX
**Dolan/Dollenye/Dowlan** 1598 — 1891 ESS, NBL, SSX, YKS
**Dolby/Dalby:** 1881 NFK
**Dolson:** 1906 SSX
**Donaldson:** 1996 STF

**Donea:** 1540 — 2 SCO
**Donnelly:** 1769 — 1891 int LAN, NBL
**Dono(g)hue:** 1853 — present GLS, IRE, KEN, SSX
**Donovan:** KEN
**Dooley:** 1891 — present SSX
**Doran:** 1950 — present DBY, IRE, LEI
**Dore:** 1799 — 1822 GLS
**Dormer:** LDN (E)
**Dorrell:** 1872 GLS
**Douglas:** c 1590 — 1930 (int) DUR, LAN, NBL, NFK, SCO, YKS
**Doutch:** 1853 GLS
**Downes:** 1881 BFD
**Doyle:** 1881 — present IRE, LAN
**Drake:** KEN
**Drakeley:** Midlands
**Draper:** 1625 — present BFD, BKM, CAM, ESS, GLS, HAM, HRT, HUN, KEN, LAN, LDN, NFK, NTH, NTT, OXF, SAL, SFK, SRY, SSX, Wales, YKS
**Drawbridge:** 1891 SSX
**Drew:** MON, STF
**Dringo:** 1599 YKS
**Driscoll:** KEN
**Driver:** 1851 YKS
**Druett:** 1625 — 1825
**Drummond:** 1960 SCO
**Dryer:** 1881 LEI
**Duck:** 1891 — present DUR, LDN, NTT
**Duckett:** OXF
**Duddy:** LDN, MDX
**Dudgson:** 1709 YKS
**Duffan:** 1830 NTH
**Duff(e)y/Duff:** 1757 — present (int) HAM, LIN, NTH, SSX, Wales. Often used as Aka name for McFee
**Duffield:** SRY
**Dunbar:** 1881 DEN
**Duncan:** 1664 KEN, SCO, SRY, Wales
**Dundas:** 1891 SRY
**Dunger:** NFK 1851
**Dunham:** 1722 NTH

**Dunn:** 1739 — present IRE, WKS, YKS
**Dunton:** BKM, BRK
**Du Plessis:** 1954 KEN
**Durrant:** 1891 — 1905 France, Hungary, SSX
**Duval/Devall/Dival/Devel:** 1891 KEN, LDN
**Dye:** 1891 ESS
**Dymmock:** 1850
**Dynes/Dines:** 1825 WIL
**Dyson/Dyton:** DBY, HRT
**Eagleton:** 1891 HRT
**Ealer:** 1556 WIL
**Eames:** DBY 1706
**Early:** 1881 LAN
**East:** 1960s Midlands
**Easter:** NTH
**Eastwood:** 1633 — 1970 (int) CHS, ESS, HRT, KEN, LDN, SRY, SSX, YKS
**Eaton:** 1973 — 1976 KEN
**Eaves:** KEN
**Eccles:** 1676 — 1740 YKS
**Ede:** 1902 SSX
**Edgerton/Egerton:** 1928 — present MON, Wales
**Edley:** 1873 JSY
**Edmond(s):** 1881 — 1891 HRT
**Edwards:** 1725 — present CGN, CMN, DBY, DEN, ESS, GLA, GLS, KEN, LDN, MGY, NTH, SAL, SRY, SSX, STF, Wales, generally, YKS
**Efemey:** 1891 HAM, WIL
**Eggins.** See Higgins
**Eglin:** 1673 YKS
**Eland:** NTT. Cp Allen
**Eley:** 1788 — 1898 HAM
**Elfes:** 1891 MDX
**Ellen:** See Allen
**Elliott:** 1815 — 1916 BOR, DBY, KEN, LDN, LIN, MDX, NBD, NTT, SCO, SSX, YKS
**Ellis:** 1851 DBY, KEN, LAN, SSX, YKS
**Elvyn:** 1615 NFK
**Emmett:** KEN, SRY, SSX

**Espigatt:** Basque Country, France, UK
**Evans:** 1775 — present CAR, CGN, CUL, DBY, GLA, GLS, LAN, LDN, MGY, NTH, NTT, SAL, SRY, STF, SWA, Wales
**Everett:** 1779 DBY
**Everton:** KEN
**Eves:** 1881 KEN
**Faa/Faw/Fall:** 1470 — 1900 (int) BFD, DUR, HRT, LDN, NBL, NTT. SAL, SCO, STF, YKS
**Fairchild:** 1726 NTH
**Fairey:** NTH
**Falkad:** 1848 DBY
**Falkenner:** 1834 — 1926 (int) CAM, DBY, NTH, SRY
**Fallard:** 1881 DEV
**Farnfield:** SRY
**Farrow:** 1930 — present CUL, YKS
**Favel:** BFD
**Fawcett:-** 1739 YKS
**Fayett:** 1891 NFK
**Fearne/Fearnside:** 1598 — 1641
**Feary:** See Fury
**Featherstone:** 1599 — 1621 DUR, MDX, NTH
**Femine:** 1537 — 1540 LDN, SCO
**Fennell:** 1963 YKS
**Fenner:** BKM, KEN, OXF
**Fensham:** 1720
**Fenwick:** 1592 — 1891 (int) DUR, NFK, SCO
**Fernie:** Wales
**Ferrari:** 1891 NFK
**Fewell:** 1881 ESS
**Finch:** 1542 — 1911 (int) KEN, LDN, LEI, SCO, SRY, WIL
**Findley:** 1891 DUR
**Finn:** KEN
**Finney:** 1829- present CHS, DBY, IRE, LAN, LDN, LEI, MDX, NIR, NTH, SAL, STF, Wales, WAR.WOR
**Fisher:** 1590 -n 1911 (int) SSX, YKS
**Fiske:** 1891 NFK
**Fitzgibbon:** 1881 KEN
**Flaherty:** IRE, LDN
**Flear:** 1774 — 1961

**Fleckie:** 1770 BOR, NBD, SCO
**Fleming:** 1748 YKS
**Fletcher:** 1620 — 1939 BKM, BRK, DBY, DOR, HUN, LDN, NTH, SAL, SRY, SSX, WAR, YKS
**Flight:** 1906 SSX
**Flinn/Flynn:** 1743 — 1904 DBY, KEN, SRY, YKS
**Flint:** LIN
**Flodder:** 1645
**Florence:** 1825 — present (int) ABE, BKM, BRE, CHS, DBY, FLN, HEF, LEI, MGY, OXF,SAL, STF, Wales (esp. S.), WAR, WOR
**Follows:** Present HEF
**Fopton:** 1891 DUR
**Ford/Foord:** 1673 — 1891 (int) DEN, DEV, GLA, HAM, HEF, IoW, MON, SOM, SSX, WOR, YKS
**Foreman:** 1906 — 1912 SSX
**Forrest/Forest:** 1891 DUR, KEN, LDN, NBD, NFK, SFK, YKS
**Foster/Forster:** 1891 BFD, BKM, DBY, KEN, LDN, NBL, NFK, NTH, SFK, SSX, YKS
**Foulkes/Fowkes:** 1825 — 1879 COR, DBY, PWY, SSX
**Foulston:** 1881 KEN
**Fowler:** 1881 BFD, IRE, LAN
**Fowling:** 1641 YKS
**Fox:** 1850 — present (int) CAE, DBY, FLN, KEN, LAN, LDN, SSX, YKS
**Foxall:** 1975 NTT
**Foxon:** 1881 NTT
**France:** 1727 NTH
**Francis:** 1891 — present DBY, LDN, NBL
**Frankham:** 1815 — present BKM, BRK, DBY, HAM, LEI, NTT, SRY, SSX, WIL
**Franklin/ Frankland:** 1807 — 1909 DBY, LAN, LDN, NFK, SFK
**Fraser:** 1745 SCO
**Freelove:** 1891 SSX
**Freeman:** 1865 DBY, HAM, HRT, KEN, LDN, SRY
**French:** 1910 KEN, LDN
**Frewen:** BKM, BRK
**Friend:** 1625 KEN, NTH
**Frizzell/Frizel:** 1748 YKS

**Frost:** 1851 DBY, YKS
**Fulcher:** HAM, LIN
**Fullen:** CUL, IRE
**Fuller:** 1891 — 1921 DUR, SSX,YKS
**Fulton:** HAM, SRY
**Funnel:** KEN
**Furniss:** 1700 YKS
**Fury/Feary:** 1891 — present BRE, CAR, DBY, IRE, SWA, Wales, YKS
**Furrans:** 1824 DBY
**Fussel:** 1610 YKS
**Gabb:** 1891 GLS
**Gabriel:** 1577 BRK
**Gagino:** See Gawino
**Gaines:** 1844 — 1888 KEN
**Gallagher:** IRE
**Gam:** 1765 NTH
**Gamble/Gamel:** 1738 — 1908 HRT, LDN, LIN, NIR, NTH
**Gamester/ Gamster:** BKM, BRK, CUL, DUR, GLS, HAM, HEF, IoW, NBD, SAL, WIL, WOR, YKS
**Gammon:** HAM
**Gannett/Garnett:** 1881 — 1891 HRT
**Gard(i)ner:** 1875 — 1932 ESS, KEN, LDN, SSX
**Garey:** 1891 MDX, SRY
**Garrett:** 1705 — 1909 (int) BFD, NFK, YKS
**Garvey:** 1851 ARM, YKS
**Garwood:** HAM
**Gaskin:** 1578 — present (int) CAM, DBY, ESS, LDN, LIN, NFK, NTH, SFK, YKS
**Gass/ Gaze:** 1891 ESS, GLS
**Gasser:** HAM, NFK
**Gatehouse:** 1912 — 1973 (Int) KEN, SSX
**Gaul:** 1613 YKS
**Gaven:** 1881 LAN
**Gawino/Gagino:** 1505 — 1623 (int) SCO, YKS
**Geddes:** 1800 SCO
**Geer:** 1881 KEN
**Gentle:** 1858 — 1955 (int) IRE, LAN
**Gent:** 1720 NTH

**George:** 1554 — 1891 (int) LDN, NBL
**Geraghty:** IRE, YKS
**Gerrard:** 1968 — 1971 KEN
**Gess/Guest:** 1891 DEV, ESS, GLS, HAM, LDN, MDX, NTH, SRY, SSX, USA
**Gibben:** 1851 IRE, YKS
**Gibbs:** 1605 — 1891 (int) BRK, SRY, STF, WOR, WRX
**Gibson:** 1579 — present (int) DBY, DUR, NBL, NFK, NTH, SCO, YKS
**Gilbert:** BKM, BRK, HRT, LDN, LIN
**Gilby:** 1891 LDN
**Giles:** 1832 — 1920 BRK, DOR, ESS, KEN, LAN, LDN, MDX, SSX, USA
**Gill:** 1891 KEN, SRY, YKS
**Gillam/Gillham:** 1798 HAM, NTH, SAL, SRY, SSX
**Gillard:** 1840 — 1916 DEV, LIN
**Gillies:** 1851 DFS, YKS
**Gillman:** 1852 — 1869
**Gilroy:** 1851 LAN, YKS
**Ginnett:** SSX
**Girling:** 1891 LDN
**Gladwell:** 1686
**Glaizier:** 1891 SSX
**Glaster:** YKS
**Glen:** 1755 KEN, YKS
**Glover:** 1891 — 1918 SSX
**Goble:** 1909 — 1918 SSX
**Godberry:** LIN
**Goddard:** 1881 HAM, KEN
**Godden:** 1968 — 1972 KEN
**Godfrey:** MDX
**Godsmark:** 1909 — 1914 SSX
**Godward:** 1918 SSX
**Golb(e)y:** AUS, HAM, SSX
**Golding:** 1891 KEN, SSX
**Goldman:** 1891 LDN
**Goldsmith:** 1881 ESS, KEN, LDN
**Gollather:** SRY, SSX
**Good:** 1881 WOR

**Goodman:** BKM
**Goodwill:** 1891 DUR
**Goodwin:** Midlands
**Goody/Gooday:** 1849 — 1851 ESS, SFK, YKS
**Gordon:** 1670 — 1933 (int) DUR, ROX, SAL, SCO, SSX, YKS
**Gorman:** 1866 — present DBY, LAN, SAL, Wales
**Gosler:** 1924 SSX
**Goss:** No information
**Gostelow:** OXF
**Gough:** 1902 SSX
**Gow:** 1881 KEN
**Grace:** OXF
**Graham:** 1662 — 1891 DOR, HAM, HRT, KEN, LAN, NBD, SCO, YKS
**Graig:** 1891 YKS
**Grainge:** 1664 SCO, YKS
**Grainger:** 1891 HAM
**Grant:** 1699 — 1865 (int) HRT, SCO, YKS
**Graves:** 1960 HEF
**Gray:** 1576 -present BFD, CAM, CHS, CUL, DBY, DOW, DUR, ESS, GLS, HAM, HRT, HUN, IRE, KEN, LAN, LDN, LEI, LIN, NBL, NFK, NTT, NTH, SFK, SX, YKS, Wales
**Grayland:** SRY
**Greedas:** LDN
**Green:** 1574 — present (int) BKM, BRK, CAM, DBY, GLS, HAM, KEN, LDN, NTH, OXF, SOM, SRY, SSX, Wales, WAR, WIL, YKS
**Greenstreet:** 1820 KEN
**Green(a)way:** 1891 — 1902 ESS, LDN
**Greenwood:** 1891 YKS
**Gregory:** 1815 — present BRK, DBY, HAM, HUN, LDN, MON, SFK, SRY
**Greig/Gregg:** 1792 — 1880 (int) NFK, SCO
**Grice:** BKM, BRK
**Griffin:** 1599 — 1705 (int) DBY, YKS
**Griffiths:** 1825 — 1925 DBY, DUR, FLN, KEN, OXF, Wales
**Griggs:** 1901 — 1908 GLS, HAM, SOM, SSX
**Grime:** 1881 LAN
**Grimwood:** No information

**Gritt/Grote:** 1905 — 1912 BRK, HAM, SRY, SSX
**Groom:** Wales
**Grounsel:** 1891 SRY
**Grunder:** 1851 KER, YKS
**Gubbins:** 1966 — 1968 KEN
**Gudgeon:** KEN
**Guest:** See Gess.
**Guiver:** HRT
**Gumble:** 18991 — 1906 E.Anglia, ESS, HRT, KEN, LDN, MDX, NFK, SFK, SSX
**Gupwell:** 1806 NTH
**Gurnit/Gurnye/Gurney:** 1741 NTH
**Gurr:** 1912 SRY
**Guthrie:** 1891 YKS
**Habard:** 1954 KEN
**Hackshaw:** KEN
**Hadfield:** 1712 DBY
**Hadley:** 1891 NBL
**Hadson:** 1891 NBL
**Haines/Haynes:** 1891 BFD, SSX
**Halden:** 1891 SRY
**Hale/Hail:** 1861-1891 BFD, GLS, MDX, Midlands, WRC, YKS
**Halford:** 1791 — 1860 LEI
**Hall:** 1622 — present (int) CHS, DBY, GLS, HRT, KEN, LDN, LIN, NFK, SAL, SCO, SRY, YKS
**Hallas:** 1963 CUL
**Hallett:** SSX
**Halliday:** 19th C SCO, YKS
**Hallier:** GLS
**Hamer:** 1891 YKS
**Hames/ Ames/ Aimes:** 1675 — present (int) DBY, NTT
**Hamilton:** 1865 — 1891 MDX, SCO
**Hammett:** DOR
**Hammond/Hamon:** 1592 — 1899 (int) SRY, WAR, YKS
**Hampton:** 1891 HAM, LDN, MDX
**Hancock:** KEN
**Hanson:** KEN
**Harber/Harby:** 1729 — 1923 KEN, SSX, YKS
**Hardcastle:** YKS

**Harding:** 1742 — 1891 (int) HUN, LDN, LIN, SRY
**Hardingham:** 1881 NFK
**Hardy:** 1709 — 1837 (Int) BRK, DBY, DEV, ESS, HAM, HRT, IoW, LAN, NFK, SFK, SOM, SRY, WIL, YKS
**Hares:** See Ayres
**Hargreaves:** 1653 YKS
**Harker:** 1950 — present CUL, YKS
**Harland:** SSX
**Harper:** 1774 — 1851 YKS
**Harrington/Arrington:** 1621 — 1881 ESS, LEI, MDX
**Harris:** 1556 — 1915 (int) BKM, BRK, CAM, DBY, DEV, DOR, DUR, ESS, HAM, HRT, KEN, LDN, MDX, NFK, OXF, SFK, SRY, SSX, STF, WOR, YKS
**Harrison:** 1574 — present (int) CHS, COR, CUL, DBY, DEV, KEN, LDN, LIN, NBL, SFK, SSX, USA, YKS
**Hart:** 1807 — 1936 IoM, KEN, SFK, WAR
**Hartley:** 1881 LAN
**Hartwell:** BRK
**Harvey:** KEN
**Harwood:** 1891 SSX
**Hastings:** 1891 YKS
**Hatfield:** 1712 — 1773 DBY. Cp Hadfield
**Hathaway:** 1880
**Hather:** 1528 DBY, LDN
**Hatherall:** WIL
**Hatseygaw:** 1640 — 1642 SCO
**Hatton:** 1766 — 1891 SRY, YKS
**Haw(s):** 1554 — 1792 KEN, SCO, YKS. Cp How
**Hawkes:** LDN
**Hawkins:** 1812 — 1891 AUS, SOM, SRY, SSX, STF
**Hayward:** 1841 — 1905 (int) GLS, LDN, OXF, SSX
**Hayes:** 1881 — 1891 KEN, LDN, STF, WAR
**Hayhre:** 1881 SFK
**Haynes:** See Haynes
**Hazard:** BKM, LDN, YKS
**Hazeldine:** 1881 SOM
**Hazelhurst:** DBY
**Head:** 1913 — 1920 SSX
**Headley:** SSX

**Heald:** 1806 AUS, NTT. Aka for Taylor
**Heap(s):** 1775 — 1850 DBY
**Heartless:** 1722 NTH
**Heath:** 1825 — 1930 BFD, BKM, BRK, DBY, GLS, KEN, LIN, NTH, OXF
**Heaton:** 1632 YKS
**Hebblewhite:** 1891 YKS
**Hebrard:** 1965 — 1967 WOR
**Heddon:** 1671 YKS
**Hedges:** 1675 — present (int) DBY, ESS, HAM, KEN, LIN, SSX
**Heeson:** YKS
**Heebef:** 1891 NBL
**Heffernan:** KEN
**Helden:** KEN
**Hemmitt:** 1912 SSX
**Hennesley:** 1851 NFK
**Herman:** 1891 NFK
**Heron/Hearne/Herring:** 1558 — present AUS, BFD, BKM, BRK, CAM, COR, DBY, DUR, FIF, GLS, HEF, HRT, HUN, KEN, LAN, LDN, LEI, LIN, MDX, NAM, NBD, NFK, NTT, NTH, OXF, SCO, SFK, SOM, SRY, STF, Wales,WAR, WIL,WRX, YKS
**Herrett:** 1919 BKM, BRK
**Herrick:** 1891 LDN
**Herrikings:** 1881 BFD
**Herring.** See Heron.
**Herrington:** DBY
**Herton:** 1881 KEN
**Heskey:** DBY 1696
**Heslop:** CUL
**Hewer:** NTH, WAR
**Hewitt/Hewett:** 1891 — 1910 KEN, NFK, SRY, SSX
**Hibberd:** 1909 BKM, BRK, HAM
**Hickman:** 1891 — 1940 LDN, Midlands, SSX, YKS
**Hickmot:** 1912 SSX
**Hicks/Higgs:** 1795 — 1909 BRK, DBY, HAM, KEN, MDX, SRY
**Higgin(s)/Eggins/Heggins:** 1595 — 1950 (int) DEV, LDN, SCO, SRY, SSX, YKS
**Higginbottom:** — present DBY

**Higgs:** See Hicks
**Hilden/Hildings:** 1638 — 1961 (int) CAM, ESS, KEN, LDN, SSX
**Hill(s):** 1638 — 1983 (int) HRT, KEN, LDN, SSX, YKS
**Hillier:** DOR
**Hillman:** 1911 SSX
**Hilton:** 1567 — 1891 (int) HAM, KEN, MDX, NFK, SCO, SRY, SSX
**Himess:** 1881 KEN
**Hinchiffe:** LAN
**Hind:** 1851 YKS
**Hines:** 1937 KEN
**Hinkley/Hinckley:** 1891 HRT, KEN, SSX
**Hinson:** 1836 — 1881 (int) LDN, SSX
**Hird:** 1720 — 188 (int)1 STF, YKS
**Hiscox:** STF, WAR
**Hislop:** 1708 — 1804 CUL
**Hitchcock:** 1891 KEN, MDX
**Hoadley:** See Oadley
**Hobbing:** BKM, BRK
**Hobday:** 1891 ESS
**Hodge(s):** 1739 — 1977 (int) KEN, LIN, NTH
**Hodgkiss:** 1803 — 1908 WOR
**Hodgson:** 1663 DUR, SCO, YKS
**Hodkin(s):** 1871 DBY, WOR
**Hogan:** KRS, PER
**Hogdon/Hogben:** 1891 KEN
**Hogg:** 1796 — 1873 BOR, SCO
**Holder:** 1744 YKS
**Holdsworth:** 1891 YKS
**Holford:** 1873 GLS
**Holland:** 1732 — present BKM, CAM, CON, DBY, DEV, KEN, LEI, NTH, NTT, OXF, SOM, SRY, STF, WAR, YKS
**Hollett:** SSX
**Hollingdale:** 1891 LDN
**Hollins/Hollinges:** 1619 — 1686 YKS
**Hollison:** Wales
**Hollister:** SRY
**Holloway:** 1891-1932 DEN, DUR, KEN
**Hollowes:** 1583 DBY

**Ho(l)mes:** 1638 — present (int) ESS, LDN, LIN, NIR, NFK, NTT, SAL, SFK, SSX, YKS
**Holt:** LAN
**Holyoake:** 1851 DEV
**Honour:** 1738
**Hood:** 1851 — 1950 LDN, MDX, SRY, YKS
**Hooker:** 1847 — 1907 HRT. MDX, SRY, SSX, USA
**Hooper:** 1908 HRT, NFK, SFK
**Hope:** E. Anglia, LDN, NFK
**Hopkins:** 1881 LAN
**Horar:** 1881 ESS, LDN
**Horlbey:** 1891 MDX
**Hornby:** 1891 KEN
**Horne:** KEN
**Horner:** 1594 YKS
**Hornik:** HRT, LDN
**Horton:** 1580 YKS
**Hoskins:** 1908 — 1940 HEF, KEN
**Houghton:** 1712 YKS
**How:** 1702 YKS. Cp Haw.
**Howard:** 1740 — 1954 (int) COR, CUL, DBY, KEN, LAN, MDX, STF, WAR, YKS
**Howden:** 1891 NFK
**Howen:** See Owen
**Howitt:** 1698
**Hoyle:** 1881 DEV
**Hubbard:** 1891 HRT
**Hubert:** 1891 SRY
**Hudson:** 1878 — 1881 CHS, DBY, ESS
**Huggins:** No information
**Hughes:** 1771 — 1875 (int) BRK, COR, DBY, DEV, DOR, GLS, HAM, KEN, LDN, NTH, NZ, OXF, PEM, SOM, SSX, WIL, YKS
**Hulbert:** GLS
**Humbles:** 1891 MDX
**Humm:** ESS
**Humphries/Humphrey:** 1770 — 1960 (int) DBY, KEN, LDN, OXF
**Hungate:** 1660 YKS
**Hunt:** 1791 — 1891 ESS, GLS, HAM, LDN, OXF

**Hunter:** 1891 YKS
**Huntingfield:** HAM
**Huntley:** KEN
**Hurley:** 1891 SSX
**Hurst:** 1881 DUR, SFK
**Husband:** 1616 YKS
**Hutchin(g)s:** 1863 -1874 BRK, GLS, MDX, SRY
**Hutchinson:** 1891 BOR, SSX, YKS
**Hutson:** 1881 NFK
**Hyland:** 1908 SSX
**Ibbetson:** 1851 YKS
**Illett:** 1881 CAM
**Illingworth:** 1891 DUR, YKS
**Ince:** 1891 ESS, HRT, LDN, MDX, SFK, SSX
**Indow:** 1891 NBL
**Ineson:** YKS
**Ing:** HAM
**Ingle:** BFD 1881
**Ingram:** 1621 — present BKM, BRK, CMN, GLS, HEF, HRT, KEN, LIN, PWS, SAL, SOM, SSX, WAR, YKS
**Inman:** 1632 YKS
**Inwood:** 1715 BKM, BRK, NTH
**Ironside:** ABD
**Irving:** 1819 GLS, SCO, SOM, WIL
**Isaac(s):** GLS, HAM, W.Country
**Isau:** 1900 DBY
**Isden:** LDN, SSX
**Izzard:** 1891 SSX
**Jackson:** 1527 — 1995 BKM, CHS, DBY, ESS, KEN, LAN, LDN,LEI, LIN, MDX, SCO, SRY, SSX, STF, WAR, WES, YKS
**Jacques/Jaggs:** LDN
**Jam(i)eson:** 1698 — 1978 SCO, YKS
**James:** 1750 — present ABE, CHS, CLW, COR, DBY, DEV, DOR, ESS, GLS, HAM, IRE, KEN, LAN, LDN, MDX, OXF, SRY.SSX, SWA, USA, Wales, YKS
**Jamphrey:** FIF
**Janes/Jaynes:** 1839 SOM
**Jarman:** 1891 NFK
**Jarlett:** LIN

**Jarvis/Jervis:** 1803 — 1858 Midlands, especially NTT
**Jaynes:** See Janes
**Jeeves:** KEN
**Jeffs/Jeffrey/Jeffers:** 1675 — present AUS, DOR, DUR, GLS, HAM, HRT, KEN, NTH, OXF, USA, YKS
**Jefferson:** 1891 DUR
**Jenkins:** 1794 — 1881 BRK, GLD, Wales, WIL
**Jennings:** 1891 HRT, KEN, YKS
**Jennison:** 1891 YKS
**Jermy:** 1851 NFK
**Jervis:** See Jarvis
**Jinks:** KEN
**John(s):** 1706 — 1913 BRK, GLS, HEF, WIL
**Johnson:** 1496 — present BFD, CAM, CHS, DBY, DUR, ESS, HAM, HRT, HUN, KEN, LDN, LIN, NFK, NTH, NTT, SCO, SRY, SSX, STF, WIL, YKS
**Joliffe:** SRY
**Joll(e)y:** HUN, LIN
**Jolser:** LIN
**Jones:** 1567 — present AUS, BKM, BRE, BRK, CAR, CHS, DBY, DEN, ESS, GLA, GLS, HAM, HEF, JSY, KEN, LAN, LDN, MDX, MGY, NTH, OXF, PWY, SAL, SRY, SSX, Wales, WOR, YKS
**Jordon:** 1674 GLS, HEF, KEN, YKS
**Jorisse:** 1635 SCO
**Joules/Jowles:** 1825 — 1942 (int) DBY, SFK, USA
**Jowett:** 1851 YKS
**Joyce:** IRE
**Judge:** SSX 1881
**Junnix:** 1909 LDN
**Jury:** 1881 KEN
**Just:** 1881 KEN
**Kairns:** See Cairns
**Kay(es):** 1881 — 1983 (int) KEN, LIN
**Keats:** KEN
**Keeler:** HAM
**Keenan:** 1891 DUR
**Keet/Skeet(s):** 1772-present. DOR, HAM, HEF, KEN, SCO, SRY, SSX

**Kefford:** LDN
**Keith:** See Keet
**Kelby, -ie:** 1970 AYR
**Kelly:** 1697 — 1891 (int) AUS, BKM, DUR, IoW, IRE, KEN, LDN
**Kemp:** AUS, SSX
**Kempster:** HAM, KEN
**Kendall:** 1599 YKS
**Kennedy:** 1439 -present (int) AUS, BEW, BOR, HUN, NTT, SCO
**Kent:** 1881 — 1913 DUR, LAN, LDN, SSX
**Kerr/Carr:** 1625 — 1869 (int) BOR, HUN, NBL, RFW, SCO, YKS
**Kerry:** HAM
**Kershaw:** 1891 YKS
**Ketts:** 1807 CAM, KEN
**Kidd:** 1891 DBY, NFK
**Killick/Keylock:** 1893 — 1932 KEN, SSX, STF
**Killthorpe:** See Chilcott
**Kinasson:** 1656 YKS
**Kindon:** YKS
**King:** 1615 (int) — present BFD, BRK, ESS, HAM, KEN, LDN, LIN, NTT, SSX, USA, WIL
**Kingston:** 1891 HRT
**Kirby:** 1888 LAN, SFK
**Kirk:** 1891 DUR, LIN
**Kirkwood:** 1891 CUL
**Kitcher:** SOM, WOR
**Kitch(e)man:** 1610 — 1851 (int) YKS
**Kitson:** 1891 MDX, YKS
**Kitt:** 1881 CON, ESS
**Kivell:** 1881 DEV
**Knell:** 1881 KEN
**Knight:** 1725 — present CAN, HAM, KEN, LAN, NBL, WKS
**Knighton:** 1891 LDN, WIL
**Knowles:** 1808 DBY, YKS
**Lacy:** SAL
**Ladds:** MDX
**Laidlaw:** 1787 — 1814 SCO
**Lakey:** KEN, LDN
**Laley:** 1851 YKS
**Lamb:** 1657 — present (int) BRK, HAM, LDN, NFK, NTH, SRY,

WAR, YKS
**Lambert:** 1685 — 1891 (int) SSX, YKS
**Lambourne:** 1782 — 1850 NTT, OXF, WAR
**Lamp:** — present KEN
**Lancaster:** 1592 DUR, LEI
**Lane:** 1812 — 1940 BFD, DBY, HAM, KEN, LDN, LAN, MDX
**Laney:** SRY
**Lang:** 1851 ESS, YKS
**Langlands:** 1908 SCO
**Langley:** 1802 STF
**Langridge:** 1905 KEN
**Lark:** HUN
**Larkson:** HUN
**Latham:** 1639 — 1794 (int) YKS
**Laurence/Lawrence:** 1609 — 1891 (int) GLS, LDN, MDX, Wales, WAR, YKS
**Law:** See Laws
**Lawford:** MDX
**Lawlor:** 1553 SCO
**Law(s):** 1881 — 1901 ESS, DBY, HAM, HRT, LDN, SSX
**Lawley:** 1841 YKS
**Lawson:** 1676 HAM, HRT, NTH, SRY, YKS
**Laycock:** 1671 YKS
**Lazenby:** 1767 YKS
**Lazone:** KEN
**Learoid:** 1724 YKS
**Leatherhead:** 1765 — 1877 (int) HRT
**Leatherland:** 1831 — 1914 KEN, SAL
**Leckenby:** 1721
**Lee:** 1625 — present AUS, BEW, BFD, BOR, BRE, BRK, CAE, CAM, CHS, CON, CUL, DBY, DEN, DEV, DOR, DUR, ESS, GLA, GLS, HAM, HEF, HRT, HUN, KEN, LAN, LDN, LEI, LIN, MDX, MGY, MON, NBD, NFK, NTH, NTT, OXF, RHO, SAL, SCO, SFK, SOM, SRY, SSX, STF, TOR, Wales, WES, WIL, WAR, WOR, YKS
**Leach:** 1918 SSX
**Leighton:** CAM
**Leleham/Leeming/Leeding/Leman:** 1612 — 1881 (int) DBY, HUN, YKS

**Lenark:** 1881 LEI
**Leonard:** 1881 LAN
**Leslie:** NBD
**Levi/Levy:** 1851 LDN, Poland, STF, WAR
**Lewis:** 1775 — present (int) GLS, HAM, WAR **Leyland:** 1891 YKS
**Light:** 1725 — present DBY, HAM, LDN, MDX, NTH, NTT, SSX
**Lightfoot:** BFD
**Lilley:** MDX
**Limson:** 1881 LDN
**Linch:** 1965 IRE
**Lindsey:** See Linsley
**Lineker:** LIN
**Lines:** 1891 HAM, Midlands, NBL
**Linsley/Lindsey:** 1714 LDN, MDX, SCO
**Linwood:** CAM, YKS
**Lister:** 1891 YKS
**Little:** 1684 — 1706 CUL, GLS
**Livermore:** 1891 — 1909 HAM, KEN, MDX
**Llewellin:** CAM, MDX, WAR, YKS
**Lloyd:** 1819 — 1881 DBY, HEF
**Lock:** 1725 — present ABE, AGY, CAE, CHS, DBY, DEN, FLN, GLA, GLS, HAM, HEF, KEN, LAN, LDN, LEI, LIN, MDX, MON, NTH, NTT, OXF, SAL, SFK, SOM, SSX, STF, USA, Wales, West Country, WIL, WOR, YKS
**Lockley:** STF
**Loder:** SRY
**Loft:** 1881 — 1891 BFD, KEN
**Loftus:** 1881 WRX
**Loil:** SAL
**Loker:** CAM
**Long:** 1850 — 1901 ARL, HAM, HRT, MDX
**Longworth:** 1881 LAN
**Lord:** BRK
**Lotherington:** 1891 LDN
**Louth:** YKS
**Love:** 1881 — present CHS, KEN
**Lovelage:** 1881 HUN
**Loveland:** LDN, MDX, SRY

**Lovell:** 1487 (claimed) — present AUS, BRK, CAE, CGN, CHS, CMN, CON, CUL, DBY, DEN, DEV, DOR, GLA, GLS, HAM, HEF, KEN, LAN, LDN, LIN, MDX, MER, MGY, MON, NTH, NTT, OXF, PEM, PWY, SAL, SCO, SOM, SRY, SSX, STF, USA, Wales(N), WAR, WIL, WOR, Wales, YKS
**Lovelock:** STF
**Loveridge:** 1792 — present (int) AUS, BFD, BKM, Black Country, BRK, CAM, CHS, DBY, DEV, DOR, ESS, GLS, HAM, HEF, HRT, HUN, KEN, LDN, MDX, NTH, NTT, OXF, RHO, RUT, SAL, STF, WAR, WIL, WOR, Wales
**Lovey:** CON, LDN, WIL
**Lowrie:** SCO
**Lowther:** 1775 — present CUL, DBY, LAN, NTT
**Luddington:** HUN
**Lundy/Lundie:** 1770 SCO
**Lyons:** NFK
**MacAlister:** 1891 — 1970 SCO
**McArthur:** 1919 — 1964 SCO
**MacBride:** 1827
**McCallum:** 1919 — 1974 (int) SCO
**McCann:** HUN
**McCarl:** 1881 KEN, LDN
**McCarthy:** 1881 — 1974 HAM, IRE, KEN, LDN, SOM, SSX
**McChesney:** IRE
**McCleaw:** 1881 BFD
**McCracken:** 1881 LAN
**McCready:** 1881 — present CHS, DBY, IRE, LEI, NTT, STF, YKS
**McCloskey:** 1840 NIR
**McCormick:** 1826-1834 IRE, YKS
**McCracken:** 1881 LAN
**McCreery:** KEN
**McCurdy:** 18440 NIR
**McDermott:** 1831 — 81 IRE, YKS
**McDonagh:** 1848 — present AUS, IRE
**McDonald:** 1714 — present (int) DBY, NBL, SCO, STF, USA, YKS
**MacFarlane:** 1750 — 1977 CUL, IRE, NIR, SCO, Wales, YKS
**McFee/McPhee:** 1856 — present NTH, SCO. Duffy is a common Aka for the family

**MacGilvron:** 1821 NIR
**McGrady:** 1881 LAN
**McGregor:** 1974 BEW, SCO
**McGuin:** LAN, YKS
**McGuire /Maguire:** 1840 — 1952 IRE, NIR, YKS
**McIlpherson:** 1671
**McIntyre:** 1881 LAN
**McKames:** IRE, LAN, SCO
**McKay:** 1840 — 1952 DUR, NIR, SCO
**MacKeig:** NFK
**MacKenzie:** 1932-1974 HRT, LDN, SCO
**McKie:** 1881 LAN
**McLaren:** 1891 — present NBL, SCO
**McLaughlin:** 1821 NIR, YKS
**M(a)cLean/Macklin:** 1618 — present (int) AUS, BFD, CAM, CHS, DBY, ESS, HAM, HUN, ISR, KEN, LAN, LIN, NFK, NTH, SCO, SFK, SRY, SSX, STF, WIL, YKS
**McLeod:** 1891 LDN
**Macmillan:** 1746 — 83 (int) DEV, LDN, SCO
**McMullen:** 1983 DEV
**MacNair:** LAN, NBL, SCO, YKS
**MacNee:** LAN, NBL, SCO, YKS
**MacNeill:** 1891 — 1962 (int) SCO
**McPherson:** 1700 NTT, SCO
**McQuillian:** 1891 DUR
**McShane:** LKS
**McVey, -Veigh:** 1851 DOW, YKS
**Mabbutt:** BRK
**Mace:** 1735 — 1921 DUR, LAN, LDN, NFK, NTH, SCO, USA
**Maddox/ -ocks:** 1778 YKS
**Madley:** 1881 KEN
**Magee:** 1891 LDN
**Maguire:** See McGuire
**Mahoney:** 1853 — 1906 KEN, SSX
**Maile:** 1949 LDN
**Mair:** See Meyer
**Maitby:** BRK
**Major:** 1855 LIN
**Makeham:** 1851 NFK

**Maley:** KEN
**Mallens:** 1891 MDX
**Mallett:** 1891 — 1907 HRT, SSX
**Mander/Maunder:** 1848 — 53 LIN
**Manes:** 1891 SSX
**Manklow:** 1881 — 1891 HEF, SSX
**Manley:** 1908
**Mann:** 1891 KEN, SRY
**Manning:** 1881 HRT, HUN, IRE, LDN, WAR
**Mannion:** 1906 Wales
**Manser:** 1853 KEN, LDN
**Mansfield:** 1891 YKS
**Mantel:** KEN
**Manton:** 1695 — 1881 (int) NTH, WOR
**Mapplebeck:** 1891 DUR
**Markland:** 1881 LAN
**Marks:** 1991 DEV, LDN
**Marles:** DEV
**Marlow:** 1789 CAM, YKS
**Marriott:** 1851 — 1881 COR, YKS
**Marsh:** 1933 KEN
**Marshall:** 1580 — present (int) AUS, DBY, DUR, LAN, NFK, NIR, NTH, PER, SCO, SRY, YKS
**Martin:** 1569 — 1891 BRK, LDN, LEI, NBL, NTT, SRY, WIL, YKS
**Marzelos:** 1977 — 81 CHS, LAN
**Maslin:** GLS, WOR
**Mason:** 1583 — 1881 (int) CUL, KEN, YKS
**Masters:** 1881 KEN
**Matchett:** LEI
**Matchwell:** Present
**MatHEF:** 1876 DBY
**Matskalla:** 1553 SCO
**Matthews:** 1709 — present BRK, ESS, GLS, HAM, KEN, LDN, MDX, NTH, SAL, SRY, SSX, Wales. (This name is also an aka for the Scamp family.)
**Matthis:** 1891 MDX, SSX
**Maud:** 1681 YKS
**Maughan:** See Mochan.

**Maunder:** See mander
**Mawbley:** OXF
**Maxwell:** 1613 — 1881 (int) OXF, SCO, YKS
**Mayne:** 1891 LDN, MDX
**Mears:** 1891 HAM, KEN, SSX
**Meath:** 1954 KEN
**Meche:** 1539 STF
**Meggett:** 1829 AUS, HEF
**Mellor:** 1820 — 1879 DBY
**Melrose:** GLS
**Menday:** BKM, BRK
**Mepham:** SSX
**Mercer:** 1789 — present (int) CAM, DBY
**Merchison:** 1970 SCO
**Meredith:** DUR
**Merrick:** 1891 NBL, SCO
**Merry:** 1870 OXF
**Metcalfe:** 1709 — 1875 (int) NFK, YKS
**Metherell:** 1881 DEV
**Meyer/Mair:** 1891 HUN, LDN
**Middleton:** 1528 — 1851 (int) HAM, LIN, SSX, YKS
**Midmore:** 1881- 1906 SSX
**Migild:** 1704 YKS
**Miles:** 1617 — 1891 DEV, KEN, OXF, SSX
**Miley:** 1891 SRY, SSX
**Mill(s):** 1743 — 1914 BRK, DBY, DEV, HAM, KEN, LDN, NFK, OXF, SRY, SSX, WOR
**Millem:** 1913 — 24 SSX
**Milleneaux:** 1673 YKS
**Miller:** 1725 — present (int) AGY, CHS, CUL, DEV, ESS, HAM, KEN, LAN, LDN, LIN, MDX, NBD, SCO, SOM, SRY, SSX, WES, WIL, WKS, WOR, YKS
**Mill(s):** 1825 — 1920 GLS, HAM, SRY
**Millward/ Millwood/ Millards:** 1789 — 1962 DBY, Midlands
**Miners:** COR
**Minny:** 1736 DBY, SCO
**Minta:** 1820 IRE, SFK
**Mitchell:** 1667 — 1930 (int) DBY, HAM, KEN, LDN, MDX, NBL, NFK, FK, SSX, YKS

**Mobbs:** 1923 LEI, NTH
**Mochan/ Maughan/ Morgan/ Mongan/ Mangan/ Mohan:** 1567 — present (int) AUS, DBY, DUR, HAM, IRE, MDX, NTT, SFK, SSX, Wales, WIL, WKS
**Moenseir:** NBL
**Moley:** 1907 SSX
**Molinadi:** 1886 DBY
**Mongan:** See Mochan
**Monk(s):** 1825 (int) LAN
**Montgomery:** 1865 SCO
**Moody:** KEN 1955
**Moon:** 1881 NTH
**Moore(s):** 1582 — 1913 (int) KEN, LDN, LIN, SSX, STF, YKS
**Mooright:** 1891 MDX
**Moortemoor:** See Mortimer
**Morgan:** See Mochan
**Morley:** 1891 MDX, SRY, YKS
**Morrell:** HRT
**Morris/Morrice:** 1705 BFD, LDN, NTH
**Morrison:** 1891 SCO, YKS
**Morrow:** NIR
**Mortimer/Morrtemoor:** 1851 DEV, NFK
**Morton:** 1676 — 1960 (int) DBY, LEI, NBL, SSX
**Mosby:** 1845 YKS
**Moscab:** 1766 DBY
**Moseley:** 1891 DUR
**Mosroessa:** Holland, SCO
**Moss:** 1891 GLS, KEN
**Moulson/ Moulton:** 1879 WAR
**Mowbray:** 1902 SSX
**Muffin:** BFD
**Muggleton:** 1881 BFD
**Mulisheo:** 1907 SSX
**Mulleyn:** See MacLean
**Mullinger:** 1870
**Mulrooney:** 1967 KEN
**Mulroy:** NBL
**Mulverdine:** HUN
**Mundey/ Monday:** 1591 — 1938 (int) BFD, IRE, KEN, LDN,

WIL, YKS
**Munro:** 1838 NSW
**Murphy:** 1825 — 1891 DUR, IRE, KEN, LAN, NBL, SRY
**Musgrave:** 1573 — 1711 LDN, SRY
**Musier:** 1907 SSX
**Musk:** LDN, NFK, SFK
**Musto/ Musty/ Musko:** 1831 — 1909 GLS
**Myalt:** 1725 STF
**Myers:** 1891 YKS
**Nail:** 1891 ESS, SSX
**Nany(e):** 1552 — 1596 NTH Cp Neyn
**Napolian:** 1881 SFK
**Nash:** 1912-13 SSX
**Naulls:** 1881 ESS, LDN
**Nautle:** SSX
**Naylor:** HAM
**Nazy:** 1821 NTH
**Neale/Niel/Neil:** 1675 — 1891 (int) CHS, ESS, LDN, NFK, WAR
**Nedby:** KEN
**Nelmes:** AUS 1840
**Nelson:** 1847 — 1891 LDN, LIN, NBL, YKS
**Newberry/ Newbury/ Newby:** 1684 — present (int) CAM, CUL, DBY, DUR, GLS, KEN, LEI, LIN, NFK, NTT, NTH, SAL, SCO, SSX, WAR, YKS
**Newell:** BRK
**Newham:** 1642 YKS
**Newland:** SRY, SSX
**Newley:** 1914 SSX
**Newman:** 1972 KEN, WIL
**Newport:** 1959 KEN
**Newsom(e):** 1891 Cul, NBL
**Newton:** 1612 — 1891 (int) DEV, MDX, YKS
**Neyn:** 1540 — 1553 SCO. Cp Nany
**Niaren:** 1704 SCO, YKS
**Nichols/Nicholson/ Nicholas:** 1554 — present (int) BFD, BRK, CAM, CON, CUL, DBY, DEV, ESS, GLA, GLS, HAM, HEF, HRT, KEN, LAN, LDN, LEI, LIN, MON, NBL, NFK, NTT, OXF, SAL, SCO, SOM, SFK, SSX, STF, Wales, WAR, WES, WIL, WOR, YKS

**Niel:** See Neale
**Nixon:** KEN
**Noble:** BKM, BRK
**Noakes:** 1879 — 1891 DBY, ESS, LDN
**Noble:** 1610 — 1792 NTH
**Nock:** STF, WOR
**Nodle:** 1729 YKS
**Norman:** 1891 — 1924 SSX
**Norris:** 1803 — 1918 ESS, SCO
**North:** 1752 DBY, LDN
**Northan:** LDN
**Norton:** LDN, SAL
**Notterwood:** 1677 YKS
**Novice:** No information
**Nox:** 1962 Midlands
**Noyes:** 1897 SSX
**Nunns:** 1946 — 1973 LDN, SRY
**Oadby:** 1891 SRY
**Oadley/Odell/Hoadley:** 1739 — present (int) BFD, CAM, LAN, MDX, NBL, NFK, SFK, SRY, SSX, STF
**Oakley:** 1891 SRY, SSX
**Oats:** 1913 SSX Cp Coates.
**O'Brien:** 1963 — present DBY, IRE, NTT
**O'Connor/ Connor:** 1834 — present DBY, ESS, IRE, SFK, SSX
**Odam:** 1891 MDX
**O'Dell:** See Oadley
**O'Dogerty:** BFD
**O'Donaghue:** 1963 — 1972 IRE
**O'Driscoll:** 1972 IRE
**Offley:** 1836
**Ogilvie:** 1768 — 1860 SCO
**Olden:** 1881 CHS
**Oliver:** 1830 — 1891 DBY, HAM, KEN, SSX
**O'Neill:** 1850 — present IRE, NIR, SCO, WES
**Onrded:** 1808
**Orchard:** 1825 — present BRK, COR, DEV, GLS, OXF, SOM, WIL, Black Country
**Ord:** No information
**Organ:** WAL

**O'Riley:** 1963 — 1972 IRE
**Orrer:** 1907 SSX
**Osborne:** LDN, NTH, Wales
**Osmund:** 1776-1774 HAM, SSX
**Othen:** HAM, MDX
**Overy:** 1920 SSX
**Owen(s)/Howen:** 1778 — 1881 CAM, CGN, CMN, DBY, GLA, NFK, NTH
**Oxley:** YKS
**Oxpring:** 1585 YKS
**Pablio:** 1891 YKS
**Page:** 1720 — present (int) DBY, GLS, HAM, KEN, NTH, SSX
**Pain:** HUN, KEN
**Painter:** 1615 NTH
**Paish:** 1832 — 1835
**Palchett:** 1891 NTH
**Pale:** 1827 HRT
**Pallenden:** 1891 SSX
**Palmer:** 1605 — 1968 (int) CAM, DBY, DUR, ESS, IRE, KEN, LDN, LIN, NTH, OXF, SAL, SFK, SOM, SRY, USA, WAR, WOR, YKS
**Pannell:** 1898 HAM, SRY, SSX
**Paramore:** 1891 SSX
**Pardoe:** GLS, OXF
**Park:** 1807 — 1891 NBL, YKS. Cp Parker
**Parker:** 1592 — 1909 BKM, ESS, HRT, LDN, LEI, MDX, NTH, OXF, SRY, SSX, YKS
**Parkin:** 1705 YKS
**Parkinson:** 1616 YKS
**Parry:** 1873 GLS, HAM, STF
**Parsons:** 1833 JSY
**Partington:** LAN
**Partland:** 1873 GLS
**Partridge:** DBY
**Pateman:** 1911 HAM, LEI, LDN
**Pathford:** 1891 SRY
**Paton:** 1691 YKS
**Patrick:** 1881 CUL
**Patterson/Pattinson/ Pattison:** 1765 — 1935 (int) NTT, YKS

**Payne:** 1891 GLS, MDX
**Peach:** 1835 DBY
**Peakman:** STF
**Pearce:** See Pierce
**Peck:** 1633 YKS
**Peal:** 1564 YKS
**Pearson:** 1721 — 1906 NTH, SSX
**Pebody:** 1848 NTH
**Peek:** 1881 KEN
**Peet/Peat:** 1844 — 1891 LDN, SRY
**Pegg:** 1891 NBL
**Pegler:** 1839
**Pegram:** HRT
**Pelham:** 1891 LDN
**Pellen:** KEN
**Pendleton:** ESS
**Penfold/Pinfold:** 1800 — present BRK, COR, DBY, DEV, DOR, ESS, HAM, KEN, LAN, LDN, MDX, NFK, OXF, SFK, SOM, SRY, SSX, USA, YKS
**Penn:** 1891 SRY
**Peover:** 1881 CHS
**Percago:** 1881 HUN
**Percival:** NTH
**Perfect:** KEN
**Perkins:** 1817 — 1913 NTH, SSX
**Perks:** 1939 KEN
**Perring:** 1912 SSX
**Perry:** 1690 — 1963 (int) BRK, ESS, GLS, HAM, KEN, OXF, SSX, WIL
**Petch:** 1671 YKS
**Peters:** 1564 — 1891 (int) DEV, LDN, MDX, SRY
**Petersen:** CMN, PEM
**Peto:** 1881 SSX
**Petronella:** Dubiously claimed, once, as a surname in HAM. See the forename Petronella in the companion section.
**Pettigrove:** 1891 — 1913 MDX, SSX
**Pettyt/Pettitt:** 1567 — 1881 (int) SFK, STF
**Pew:** 1773 YKS
**Philby:** 1881 HUN

**Philip(s):** 1605 — 1956 (int) ESS, KEN, LDN, SRY, SSX, STF, WAR, YKS
**Philpott:** 1881 KEN
**Phoenix:** 1820 NTH
**Pickering:** 1794 NTH
**Pickett:** IRE, KEN
**Pickles:** No information
**Pidgely/Pitchley:** 1881 — 1911 ESS, HAM, IOW, KEN, MDX, SRY, SSX
**Pidgeon:** 1912 — 1918 KEN
**Pierce/Pearce:** 1675 — present (int) BFD, BKM, DBY, DOR, HAM, KEN, LIN, SSX, USA, WIL
**Pike/Pikey:** 1891 — 1894 BRK, CUL, HAM, MDX, WIL
**Pilcher:** 1891 SSX
**Pilkington:** 1891 NBL
**Pinder:** 1720 — 1925 DBY, YKS
**Pinfold:** See Penfold
**Pink:** 1881 LIN
**Pinkerton:** 1724 SCO
**Pinkney:** 1627 DUR, YKS
**Pinniger:** 1891 DUR
**Piper:** 1891 SSX
**Pitcher:** KEN, NFK
**Pitchford:** KEN
**Pitchley:** See Pidgley
**Plant:** LDN
**Plumb:** DBY, NTT
**Plunket:** 1800
**Pocket:** 1942 SRY
**Pocock:** BRK
**Podalze:** MDX
**Pogue:** 1972 KEN
**Poll:** 1891 NFK
**Pollard:** MDX
**Pollensen:** 1881 ESS
**Popple(s):** LEI, NTH, RUT, E Anglia
**Poplett:** LDN
**Porter:** 1676 — 1900 (int) ESS, LDN, YKS
**Porteus:** 1717 YKS

**Portingall:** 1602 LAN
**Portington:** 1596 YKS
**Portsmouth:** BRK
**Potter:** 1846 — 1891 DBY, LDN
**Potts:** 1851 YKS
**Powell/Poole:** 1589 — 1950 BFD, ESS, KEN, LDN, NTH, SAL, SRY, WIL, YKS
**Powers:** 1960 MON
**Pratt:** HUN
**Prattley:** 1881 WOR
**Preece:** 1991 HEF
**Prentice:** HEF
**Prescott:** 1881 STF
**Prestage:** 1910 SSX
**Preston:** BFD
**Preeswell:** 1853 KEN
**Price:** 1587 — present (int) BRE, CHS, DBY, DEV, GLS, HEF, IRE, JSY, KEN, LAN, LDN, LIN, Midlands, MON, NFK, NIR, NTT, NTH, PEM, SAL, SFK, SSX, SWA, USA, WAL, YKS
**Pride:** IRE
**Priestley:** 1587 YKS
**Primley:** 1881 LIN
**Pring:** 1906 SSX
**Print:** 1891 LDN
**Printer:** 1909 SFK
**Pritchard:** 1891 SSX
**Procter:** 1650 — 1891 (int) MDX, MON, YKS
**Prosser:** 1881 MON
**Proudly:** 1820 — 1914 LDN, SRY, SSX
**Pullein/Pullen:** 1641 1891 (int) GLS, KEN, SSX, YKS
**Pullinger:** 1851 YKS
**Pullman:** 1891 SSX
**Purchas(e):** 1891 — 1902 DUR
**Purnell:** 1826 SOM
**Pyman:** 1891 HRT
**Quartermain:** No information
**Quentin/ Quinton:** 1920 — present DBY, LDN, SSX
**Quick:** COR, DEV, MON, STF, Wales
**Quilligan:** 1900 — present DBY, IRE

**Quinlan:** LDN
**Quinn:** 1851 — present DBY, KEN, NTT, WKS
**Quinnell:** 1967 — 1969 KEN
**Radford:** 1891 LIN
**Rafferty:** 1881-1930 BRE, CMN, GLA, IRE
**Rainbow:** BFD
**Rains:** 1975 KEN
**Rames:** 1753 YKS
**Ramp:** KEN
**Ramsay** 1760 SCO
**Randall:** 1610-1694 KEN, SRY, SSX, YKS
**Ransley/Ramsley:** 1861 — 1940 AUS, KEN, SSX
**Ransome:** 1926 CAM, KEN
**Raper:** 1891 DUR
**Raspberry:** 1880-1953 DBY, LDN, ` LEI
**Ratcliffe:** 1881 — 1891 NBL, NTH, SSX, WOR, YKS
**Rawlin(g)s/Rollings:** 1740 — 1909 BRK, BKM, DOR, HAM, MDX, YKS
**Rawson:** 1594 — 1891 (int) DBY, YKS
**Ray/Rye:** 1898 — present BFD, HAM, KEN, SOM, SRY, SSX
**Reader:** 1851 — 1891 NBL, WAR, YKS
**Reading:** OXF
**Redfe(a)rn:** 1891 YKS
**Redpath:** 1800 SCO
**Redworth:** 1891 — 1953 KEN, LDN
**Rees:** 1881 KEN, Wales
**Reeves:** SSX
**Reid/Reed/Read:** 1748 — 1970 (int) FIF, HAM, KEN, PER, SRY, SSX
**Renton:** 1881 ESS, LDN
**Restorick:** JSY
**Reuben/ Rewbrey:** 1700 — 1759 LDN
**Reynolds:** 1825 — present (int) ESS, KEN, LDN, SSX, YKS
**Rhodes:** 1678 — 95 (int) LIN, YKS
**Ribbern:** 1891 YKS
**Rice:** 1954 — 1963 KEN
**Richards(on):** 1644 — 1891 (int) CHS, DBY, HAM, LAN, LIN, NTT, NTH, SCO, SOM, SSX, WAR, YKS
**Richford:** LDN 1891

**Richmond:** 1866 GLS
**Rickman:** HAM
**Ridd:** 1996 STF
**Ridley:** 1891 — 1924 LDN(N), SSX
**Riley. See Ryles.**
**Rillett:** 1881 LIN
**Ringham:** KEN, LDN
**Ringrose:** 1891 NFK
**Ripley:** 1897 — present HAM, KEN, LDN, MDX, SRY, SSX, SE Counties
**Rippington:** OXF
**Roach:** 1853 KEN, LDN
**Roake:** 1676 CUL, LDN, YKS
**Roberts:** 1528 — 1925 (int) BKM, CAE, CHS, COR, DBY, DUR, ESS, GLS, HAM, KEN, LAN, LDN, LIN, MER, MON, NBD, NFK, OXF, PWY, SFK, SRY, SSX, YKS, Wales generally, W Country
**Robertson:** 1690 — 1972 (int) CAM, SCO, YKS
**Robinson:** 1602 — 1976 BFD, CAM, DUR, ESS, HAM, KEN, LAN, LDN, LIN, NFK, NTH, NTT, SAL, SCO, SSX, WAR, YKS
**Rochester:** 1754 DUR
**Rock:** 1841 — 1866 CHS, LAN
**Rodwell:** SSX 1912
**Roebuck:** 1730 YKS
**Rogers:** 1725 — 1841 (int) CHS, COR, DBY, HAM, HRT, LAN, LEI, MON, NTT, SAL, SRY, SSX, STF, YKS
**Rogerson:** 1933 MON, SAL
**Rolf/Rolph:** 1891 SRY, WIL
**Rollings:** See Rawlings
**Rollinson:** 1933 SAL
**Romana/ Romney:** 1567-1623 (int) SAL, SFK
**Rooney:** 1851-present DBY, IRE, LDN, NTT
**Rootham:** 1891 SRY
**Rose:** 1724 — 1930 (int) BRK, DOR, GLS, HAM, LDN, OXF, SFK, SSX
**Roseigh:** 1955 KEN
**Roselands:** 1881 MNT
**Roser/ Rosser:** See Rossiter
**Ross:** 1714 — 1960 (int) COR, KEN, SCO, YKS

**Rosser:** See Rossiter
**Rossi:** 1891 SSX
**Rossiter/Roster/ Rosser/ Roser:** 1830 — 1920 AUS, BFD, BRK, GLS, KEN, LDN, MNT, SFK, SRY, SSX, WIL
**Rostagina:** HAM
**Rostron:** 1891 YKS
**Row(e):** 1723 — 1906 (int) NTH, YKS
**Rowel(s)/ Rowles/ Rolls:** 1814 — 1898 HAM, OXF, YKS
**Rowland(s) /Rolland(s):** 1549 — 1912 (int) CAM, DUR, HAM, LDN, NTH, SSX, YKS
**Rowley:** 1891 — 1900 GLA, HAM, KEN, LDN, MDX, MON, NBD, NIR, NTH, NZ, STF, YKS
**Royle/ Royal:** 1891 LAN, YKS
**Rudd:** 1891 NFK
**Rumble:** 1905 SSX
**Rush:** NFK 1891
**Russell:** 1881 — 1908 DUR, ESS, KEN, MDX, SRY, SSX
**Rust:** 1891 LIN
**Rutherford:** 1884 — present KEN, SCO. Cp Ruthven
**Ruthven/Rivens:** 1772 — 1860 AYR, BOR, DFS, SEL. Cp Rutherford
**Rutter:** HAM
**Ryan:** 1807 — 1970 (int) BOR, DUR, IRE, KEN, NBD, SSX
**Rye:** See Ray
**Ryles/Riley:** 1582 — 1970 (int) CAR, CHS, GLA, GLS, HAM, IRE, KEN, LDN, SSX, WAL, YKS
**Sabey:** BFD
**Sadler:** YKS
**Salmon:** 1848 DBY, IRE
**Sandam:** 1671 WIL
**Sands/Sandys:** 1848 — 1851 NFK, SSX
**Sanger:** 1873 — 1950
**Saunders/Sanders:** 1625 -1925 BKM, COR, DBY, DEV, DOR, DUR, HAM, HEF, IoW, KEN, LAN, LDN, MDX, NBL, SOM, SRY, SSX
**Sanderson:** KEN
**Savage:** 1891 HAM, HUN
**Sawley:** 1649 YKS
**Saxby:** 1738 — 1750 YKS

**Sayers/Sawyer:** 1857 — 1881 KEN, SSX
**Scammell:** 1891 LDN
**Scamp:** 1599 — present (int) BFD, DBY, HAM, KEN, LDN, NBL, NFK, NOT, SAL, SFK, SRY, SSX, WAL, WIL, WOR
**Scarrett/Skarrett/SHEFrett/Scarlet/ Skerry:** 1775 — present AUS, BFD, BKM, BRK, CAM, CHS, DBY, DEV, ESS, GLS, HAM, HEF, KEN, LAN, LDN, LEI, LIN, MDX, NTH, NTT, OXF, POW, SAL, SOM, SRY, STF, WAL,WAR, WIL, WOR
**Schofield:** 1648 YKS
**Schooling:** 1891 ESS
**Scott:** 1583 — 1977 (int) CAM, DBY, DEV, GLS, HAM, IRE, KEN, LAN, LDN, NFK, NTH, RFW, SRY, YKS
**Seager:** 1881 KEN
**Seales:** 1891 YKS
**Searle:** WOR
**Sedgwick:** GLS, LAN
**Seed:** YKS
**Selby/Sealby:** 1673 — 1891 LDN, SCO, SSX, `YKS
**Seldon:** 1891 SSX
**Selmes:** 1914 SSX
**Sevil:** DOR
**Sevellth:** 1881 KEN
**Severn:** WOR
**Severs:** 1891 SSX
**Shadlock:** 1851 STF
**Shanks:** LDN
**Shanley:** 1891 DUR
**Shannard:** 1891 SRY
**Shapcott:** 1975 KEN
**Sharp(e):** 1766 — 1881 GLS, WIL, YKS
**Sharplin:** HRT, LDN
**Sharlot:** See Charlotte
**Shaw:** 1567 — present (int) BFD, CAM, CHS, DBY, ESS, HRT, HUN, IRE, KEN, LDN, LEI, NBD, NFK, NTH, NTT, SAL, SCO, SFK, STF, WAR, YKS
**Shawger:** 1899 SSX
**Shearing:** ESS, KEN
**Sheen:** 1796 — 1952 (int) CAR, WIL
**Sheepwash:** 1760 — 1891 KEN

**Sheffield:** DBY
**Shelleto:** LDN
**Shenton:** 1564 DBY
**Shepherd:** 1688 — 1912 (int) DOR, HEF, HRT, KEN, LDN, MDX, OXF, SAL, SSX, WIL, Midlands
**Sherrard/Sherred/Sherwood/ Sterrard:** 1822 — 1911 HAM, LDN, SRY, YKS
**Sherridan:** 1960 — present DBY, IRE, NTT, Midlands
**Sherriff/Sherrett:** 1706 — 1995 (int) AUS, BKM, CHD, CMN, DBY, LDN, LEI, LIN, NFK, NTT, NTH, OXF, SAL, STF, WAR, WAR, WOR
**Sherwin:** 1909 HAM
**Sherwood:** See Sherrard
**Shevlin:** 1933 — present WAL
**Shipley:** 1736 BKM
**Shipman:** 1790 — 1850 NFK, SFK
**Shipton:** No information, except that Mother Shipton of Knaresborough, YKS, with its petrified cave, was claimed as a Gypsy, though I do not know on what evidence
**Shires:** 1638 YKS
**Shirley:** 1891 NBL
**Shoesmith:** ESS, HAM
**Short:** 1919 SSX
**Showbridge:** 1891 SRY
**Shrubsall:** KEN
**Shuker:** 1786 DBY
**Sibley:** BFD, SRY
**Sillicott:** 1881 SSX
**Simms:** 1767 — 1807 DBY, YKS
**Simmons/Simons:** 1851 BKM, BRK, YKS
**Simpson:** 1592 — 1915 (int) CAM, DBY, DUR, KEN, LDN, OXF, SSX, YKS
**Sinclair:** LDN
**Sines:** See Synes
**Sinfield:** 1815 — 1881 (int) LDN
**Singleton:** 1600 YKS
**Sirr/ Skurr:** 1724 — 1729 YKS
**Sissons:** 1791 YKS
**Sivers/ Sivier:** 1891 — 1906 KEN, SSX

**Siviter:** MDX
**Sivon:** 1913 SSX
**Skeet(s):** See Keet
**Skelton:** 1940 KEN
**Skerry:** See Scarrett
**Skidmore:** LDN
**Skinner:** CAM
**Slack:** HUN
**Slater:** 1881-1884 DBY, **SSX**
**Sleddin:** 1676 YKS
**Slender:** 1851 — 1956 HUN, MON, NFK, SFK
**Slim/ Slinn:** 1881 DBY, LEI, STF
**Sloper:** OXF
**Small (s):** 1797-1881 COR, DBY, DEV, DOR, ESS, GLO, HAM, KEN, MON, NFK, SCO, SFK, SSX, SOM, WOR, USA, West Country, E Anglia. Cp Smallbones
**Smallbones:** 1729 — 1940 (int) South country. Cp Small
**Smalley:** 1572 — 1676
**Smallman:** HEF 1881
**Smallwood:** 1589 — 1851 STS, YKS
**Smart:** 1763 — present (int) BRK, DBY, NBL, NTT, SOM, WIL
**Smith:** 1625 — present AUS, BFD, BKM, BRK, CAM, CAN, CHS, CUL, DBY, DOR, ESS, GLS, HAM, HEF, HRT, HUN, KEN, LAN, LDN, LEI, LIN, MDX, MON, NBL, NFK, NTH, NTT, OXF, RUT, SAL, SCO, SFK, SOM, SRY, SSX, STF, WIL, WAR, WOR, YKS, E Anglia, Cape of Good Hope. (One or other of the various and extensive Smith families branches has probably travelled in every county in the British Isles and several other countries at one time or another.)
**Snelling:** BKM, BRK, SSX
**Snook:** COR
**Snow:** 1982 KEN
**Soder:** BKM, BRK
**Solomon:** 1851 BKM, Poland
**Sope:** KEN
**Sorrell:** KEN, LDN, SSX
**South:** CAM
**Southern/Southam:** 1834 — 1871 SRY
**Southwood:** 1891 LDN

**Sowden:** 1720 YKS
**Sowerby:** 1881 CUL
**Sparks:** 1891 — 1903 DEV, NFK, SSX
**Sparrow:** 1960 Midlands
**Spencer:** 1623 — present (int) DBY, DUR, KEN, LDN, LEI, NFK, OXF, SRY, YKS
**Spice:** 1914 SSX
**Spicer:** 1906 SSX
**Spiers:** 1881 SSX
**Spragg/ Sprague/ Sprigg:** 1843 DBY
**Springate:** 1881 SSX
**Spugnall:** 1881 KEN
**Spurrett:** OXF
**Squires:** 1659 — present (int) DBY, DOR, LDN, LEI, LIN, WOR, YKS
**Stacey:** 1891 — 1909 HAM
**Staff:** No information
**Stafford:** 1779 NTH
**Stagg:** SOM
**Stalk:** 1914 SSX
**Standing:** 1891 SSX
**Stanford/ Staniforth:** 1680 — 1921 (int) DBY, SSX
**Stanley/Stanlick:** 1594 — present BFD, DEV, DOR, ESS, GLS, HAM, Holland, HRT, KEN, LAN, LDN, LIN, MDX, NTH, NTT, SAL, SOM, SRY, SSX, STF, USA, WIL, YKS
**Stanton:** 1876 — 1891 YKS
**Stapells:** 1741 NTH
**Stapleton:** YKS
**Starsmore:** 1881 BFD
**Staveley:** KEN 1891
**Stead:** 1632 — 1743 (int) YKS
**Steadman/Steedman:** 1881 LIN, STF
**Steel(e):** 1743 — present (int) DBY, YKS
**Steggall**
**Stenning:** 1891 LDN, YKS
**Stentiford:** 1881 DEV
**Stephens/Stevens:** 1722 — present (int) BFD, BKM, BRK, DBY, DEV, DUR, ESS, GLS, HEF, HUN, KEN, LDN, MON, SAL, SFK, SSX, STF, WAL, WAR, WOR, WRX

**Stephenson:** 1744 — 1891 DUR, YKS
**Stephney:** OXF
**Sterling:** See Stirling
**Sterrard:** See Sherrard
**Stewart/Steward:** 1597 — present (int) ABD, CUL, DUR, KEN, LDN, LKS, PEM, PER, SAL, SCO, STI, USA, YKS
**Stickley/Stickels:** 1957 — 1968 KEN
**Stirling/Sterling:** 1714 — 1967 (int) CUL, KEN, SCO
**Stock(s):** 1851 — 1891 NFK, YKS
**Stockbridge:** 1891 SRY
**Stocker:** BRK, HAM
**Stoke(s):** 1872- 1971 HAM, IRE, LDN, USA, WIL
**Stone:** 1867 — 1914 ESS, HAM, KEN, LAN, LDN, MDX, SRY, SSX
**Storer:** 1881 DBY, LDN, MDX
**Storey:** 1832 — 1855 YKS
**Stork:** 1881 HUN
**Stow(es):** LDN
**Strand:** 1891 DUR
**Strange/ Strong:** 1623 — 1670 YKS
**Street**: 1881 ESS, HAM, LDN, SRY
**Streeter:** 1881 ESS
**Strong:** See Strange
**Stroud:** 1891 SRY
**Strudwick:** 1891 NFK
**Stubbs:** 1891 DUR
**Stubley:** DBY, LEI
**Sturgess:** 1891 HRT
**Suet:** LIN
**Sullivan:** 1834 — 1902 NBL, OXF, SSX
**Summerfield:** BKM, BRK
**Summers:** 1891 NFK
**Sutherland:** 1891 YKS
**Sutton:** 1677 — 1736 NTH
**Swain:** No information
**Swale(s):** 1679 — present (int) CUL, YKS
**Swallow:** 1881 — 1891 DUR, LIN, NBL
**Swan:** 1849 — 1891 ESS, LDN
**Swarbrick:** 1881 LAN

**Sweatman:** 1881 HRT
**Swift:** 1608 — 1866 (int) DBY, GLS, MON, NTH, SOM, SRY, WAR
**Swindon:** 1682 YKS
**Swiney:** 1881 DEV
**Switchback:** 1891 HRT
**Sword:** 1759 YKS
**Sykes:** 1891 HUN, YKS
**Sylvester:** 1580 YKS
**Synes/Symes/ Sines:** 1891 — 1972 BKM, BRK, HAM, LDN, SRY, SSX
**Tait:** 1762 — 1839 BOR, NBD, SCO, YKS
**Tamlin:** 1913 SSX
**Tams:** See Toms
**Tamsett:** 1881 KEN, LDN
**Tandy:** 1875
**Tann:** 1859 — 1983 NFK
**Tanner:** SRY. No further information
**Tanser:** LEI
**Tansey/Tanzy:** No information
**Taplin:** 1909. No further information
**Tapsell/ Topseel:** 1891 DUR, LDN, MON, WAR
**Tarling:** 1956 ESS
**Tasker:** 1891 SSX
**Taylor:** 1570 — present (int) ABE, AUS, BFD, CHS, COL, DBY, DEN, DEV, ESS, FLN, GLS, HAM, HEF, HRT, HUN, KEN, LAN, LDN, LEI, LIN, MDX, MON, NFK, NTH, NTT, SAL, SFK, SRY, SSX, STF, WAL, WAR, WIL, WOR, YKS
**Teeth/Tooth:** 1891 — 1908 DBY, SRY, SSX
**Telling:** SOM
**Temple:** 1953 CAM
**Templeman:** No information
**Tenny:** DBY, NOT, STF, WOR
**Terry:** 1889 — 1911 KEN, NFK
**Tetley:** 1891 YKS
**Thaniel:** 1791 YKS
**Thatcher:** 1891 — 1909 LDN, SSX
**Theakstone:** 1697
**Thomas:** 1567 — 1979 (int) BFD, BRK, CGN, DBY, DUR, KEN,

LDN, MDX, NTH, SOM, STF, YKS
**Thompsett:** SSX
**Thom(p)son:** 1588 — 1933 (int) AYR, BKM, BRK, CAM, CAR, CGN, DEV, DOR, DUR, GLA, HAM, HEF, HRT, KEN, LIN, NFK, NTH, SAL, SOM, SRY, SSX, WAL, YKS
**Thorley:** SAL
**Thorn(e):** 1891 ESS, HUN, LDN
**Thornham:** No information
**Thornton:** 1851 GAL, LAN, Midlands, YKS
**Thorpe:** 1951 CAM, HUN, NFK, SFK, YKS
**Thresall:** HUN
**Thurston:** 1881 HRT, NFK
**Tibbles:** HRT
**Tice:** LDN
**Tidy:** SSX
**Titmus:** MDX
**Tobin:** LAN
**Toby:** See Doby
**Todd:** DUR, KEN, WIL
**Tomkins:** 1891 MDX
**Tomlin:** 1891 NFK
**Tomlinson:** 1851 DEV, SOM, YKS
**Tompsett:** 1891 KEN, SSX
**Toms/Tams:** 1998 DBY, HUN, KEN, NBL, SAL
**Tonks:** CAN, LDN
**Toogood:** 1791 — present DBY, GLS, LEI, SAL, WAL, WRX
**Tooley:** No information
**Tooth:** See Teeth
**Toop:** DEV, GLS
**Topseel:** See Tapsell
**Torrie:** SCO
**Totten:** 1891 DUR
**Tow:** 1848 — 1861
**Towler:** 1817 — 1819 DBY
**Towner:** 1624 — 1891 (Int) DBY, SSX
**Townsend/Townend:** 1775 — present (int) AUS, BRK, DOR, DUR, HAM, LAN, LEI, OXF, SSX
**Townsley:** 1669 — present (int) SCO, YKS
**Trainer:** 1820 DBY

**Trayler:** 1891 LDN
**Treeby:** 1979 KEN
**Trees:** Aka for Wood
**Trelining:** 1881 NTH
**Treviller:** 1881 COR
**Tribe:** BKM, BRK
**Trickett:** No information
**Trimmins:** 1873 GLS
**Trotter:** 1623 SCO
**Troutt:** 1822 SOM
**Tuck:** BRK,. SRY, WIL
**Tugby:** HRT, LDN
**Tugg:** 1742 YKS
**Tune:** 1891 YKS
**Tunnycliffe:** 1729 DBY
**Turnbull:** 1886 BOR, DBY
**Turner:** 1891 — 1909 DOR, HAM, KEN, LAN, NFK, SFK, SRY, WES, YKS
**Turpin/ Tupen:** 1751 — 1914 (int) KEN, SSX
**Turton:** 1851 — 1891 YKS
**Turville:** 1850 HAM
**Tuttle:** ESS
**Twaddle:** 1741 SCO, YKS
**Tweedy:** 1676 SCO
**Twigdon:** LIN
**Twinley:** KEN
**Twinn:** HRT, LDN
**Tyler:** 1870 — 1968 CAM, HRT, KEN, LDN, SRY
**Tyrant:** 1891 NBL
**Tyrell:** 1891 SSX
**Tyres:** 1610 YKS
**Umbrella:** 1881 ESS
**Underwood:** 1964 Midlands
**Upton:** HRT, KEN, LDN
**Usser/Usher/Uzzle:** 1765 — 1883 LDN, MDX, YKS
**Valder:** KEN
**Valentine/Vallentyne:** 1577 — 1875 (int) CUL, KEN, LAN, MDX, NTH, SCO, SSX, YKS
**Vallis:** See Wallace

**Vanis:** SAL, STF, WAR. Aka for Heron. Cp Vines
**Vanner:** 1926 SSX
**Varey:** 1702 — present (INT) CHS, CUL, DBY, KEN, LAN, WES, YKS
**Varley:** 1788 YKS
**Vaughan:** 1734 — 1881 CAR, GLA, MON, NBD, NTH, PEM, RAD, SAL, SOM
**Vaus:** 1796 YKS
**Vellam:** LIN. No further information
**Venus:** 1912 — 1913 SSX
**Vernon:** 1891 LDN
**Veti:** 1891 YKS
**Vickers/Vigor(s):** 1909 — 1912 SSX
**Vinall:** LDN, OXF
**Vincent:** 1859 — 1909 KEN, NFK
**Vinden:** 1909 NFK, SFK, SRY
**Vines:** 1714 — 1800 LEI. Cp Vanis
**Vinson:** 1810 STF
**Virgo:** 1908 — 1909 HEF, STF, WOR. Cp Bergo
**Waddington:** 1891 KEN
**Wade:** BRK
**Wadham:** KEN. No further information
**Wagner:** 1851 RFW, YKS
**Wain:** OXF
**Wainwright:** 1891 LDN, NBD. Aka for Boswell
**Waite:** 1828 — 1949 (int) ESS, YKS
**Wakeley:** BKM, BRK
**Walker:** 1567 — 1965 (int) BRE, BRK, COR, DBY, DEV, GLA, HAM, KEN, LAN, LDN, NTH, NTT, OXF, SCO, SAL, SOM, SSX, STF, WOR, YKS
**Wall:** 1849 — 1861 SAL, STF, GLA, LAN, WOR, YKS
**Wallace/ Vallis/ Wallis:** 1791 — 1854 (int) DBY, HAM, HRT, KEN, SCO, WIL
**Wallen:** KEN. No further information
**Waller/Whaley:** 1571 — 1923 (int) LAN, NTT, YKS
**Wallett:** DUR, NBD, OXF, YKS
**Wallser:** BFD, DEV
**Walmsley:** 1809 — 1812. No further information
**Walpole:** 1891 NFK

**Walter:** 1881 KEN
**Walton.** See Whatton.
**Wann:** 1541 SCO
**Ward:** 1717 — present (int) AUS, CHS, DBY, ESS, FLN, GLS, HEF, IRE, LDN, NFK, NTH, SSX, YKS
**Warden:** BKM, BRK
**Wardle:** 1881 CHS
**Wardman:** 1743 YKS
**Ware:** 1906 SSX
**Wareham:** 1914 SSX
**Warn:** 1913 SSX
**Warner:** 1891 DUR, HEF, KEN, LDN
**Warren:** LDN
**Warrington:** 1891 DUR
**Warwick**: LIN
**Washington:** 1628 STF
**Washman:** 1881 SSX
**Wass:** 1881 LIN
**Waterfield:** 1902 — 1928 NFK, SSX
**Waterman:** 1891 SRY
**Waters:** 1881 BKM, BRK, CMN
**Waterton:** 1891 LDN
**Waterworth:** 1851 YKS
**Watford:** 1891 DBY
**Wathen:** See Wharton
**Watkins:** BOR
**Watkinson:** 1826 YKS
**Watland:** 1880 DUR
**Watney:** LDN
**Watson:** 1579 — 1920 (int) DBY, DUR, IRE, LDN, LIN, MDX, NTT, REW, SCO, YKS
**Watton:** See Wharton
**Watts:** 1891 KEN, SRY
**Waydon:** See Wharton
**Weald:** 1881 LIN
**Weatherhead:** KEN, LDN
**Weaver:** DBY
**Webb/Webster:** 1590 — present (int) AUS. BKM, CAV, DBY, ESS, GLS, HRT, KEN, LDN, MDX, NFK, SAL, SFK, SOM, SRY,

SSX, WIL, YKS
**Webber:** COR
**Webbman:** KEN
**Wedgewood:** 1881 STF
**Weeks:** 1594 — 1836 (int) HAM, MDX, SOM
**Welch/ Walsh/ Welsh:** 1751 — present (int) AUS, BKM, DBY, DUR, ESS, HAM, HEF, HRT, HUN, IRE, LAN, LDN, LIN, NTH, SAL, SFK, SSX, WAL, YKS
**Welling:** 1851 DEV
**Wells:** 1750 — 1935 BKM, DBY, DOR, HAM, KEN, LDN, LIN, SOM, SSX, STF, USA, WAR,WIL, YKS
**Wenham:** KEN, SSX
**Wenman:** 1909 BKM, BRK, GLS, KEN, SRY, SSX
**Wesseldine:** lin
**West:** 1751 — 1928 DBY, KEN, LAN, SSX, YKS
**Westrop:** 1891 ESS, LIN, NFK
**Westwood:** YKS
**Wharnell:** See Wharton
**Whatnell:** See Wharton
**Wharton/ Whatnell/ Wharnell/ Whatton/ Wathen/ Watton/ Waydon:** For a considerable period, perhaps always, Wharnells, Whatnells and Whartons have been the same family, the surnames being variations. 1554 — 1967 (int) BKM, DBY, DUR, ESS, GLS, HEF, HRT, LAN, LIN, Midlands(W), MON, NFK, OXF, SAL, SRY, STF, USA, WAL, WOR, YKS
**Wheatley:** 1891-1901 DBY, DUR, NFK
**Wheeler:** 1806 — 1915 (int) HAM, KEN, LDN, NBL, SSX, WIL
**Whiddington:** 1891 LDN
**Whitaker:** 1881 LAN, LDN
**White:** 1465 — 1970 AUS, BKM, BRK, COR, CUL, DBY, DOR, DUR, HAM, HRT, HUN, KEN, LDN, MDX, NBL, NFK, NTH, NTT, SAL, SCO, SFK, SOM, SRY, SSX, USA, WIL, YKS
**Whitehead:** 1891 YKS
**Whitham** 1840 DBY
**Whitlock:** BFD, BKM, KEN, WIL
**Whittendon/Whittington:** 1891 KEN, YKS
**Whittle:** 1772 DOR, YKS
**Wickenden:** 1891 ESS

**Wickham/ Wickram:** 1891 — 1913 SSX
**Wicks:** 1891 LDN, MDX, SRY
**Wiggens/ Wickens:** 1912 — 1915 BKM, BRK, SSX
**Wiggett:** 1782 NFK
**Wilcox:** 1900 GLS
**Wild(e):** 1726 — 1913 (int) BKM, SSX
**Wildash:** SRY
**Wilkie:** 1800 SCO
**Wilkins:** 1881 — 1913 SSX
**Wilkinson:** No information
**Wilks:** 1881 ESS, WOR
**Willenden:** 1891 SRY
**Willens:** See Williams
**Willett:** 1778 — 1923 (int) HAM, IoW, KEN, MDX, SRY, SSX, YKS
**Williams/Willens:** 1645 — 1979 (int) AGY, BRE, BRK, CAE, COR, CUL, DBG, DBY, DEV, DUR, ESS, GLA, GLS, HAM, KEN, LDN, LIN, MDX, Midlands, NBL, NFK, OXF, SSX, STF, SWA, USA, WAL(S), YKS
**Williamson:** 1651 — present (int) CHS, DBY, NIR, SCO, YKS
**Willis:** 1833 — 1921 AUS, SSX, WIL
**Willoughby:** 1891 — 1913 KEN, SSX
**Willoughton:** 1891 LDN
**Wills:** HAM
**Wilmott:** 1891 DOR, HAM, SRY, WIL
**Wilshaw/ Willshire/ Wiltshire:** 1801 — present. BRK, CAM, DBY, DUR, Midlands, NTH, OXF
**Wilson:** 1599 — 1990 AUS, CUL, DBY, DUR, HAM, IRE, KEN, Midlands, LAN, LIN, MLN, NBL, NFK, NOT, SAL, SCO, SFK, SRY, SSX, STF, USA, WAL, WES, YKS
**Wilton:** No information
**Wimpenny:** 1891 YKS
**Winder(s):** 1812 SSX
**Windmile:** 1881 GLS
**Winfield:** BFD
**Wingrove:** KEN
**Winman:** 1910 SRY
**Winson:** 1891 SSX
**Winter:** 1623 — present (int) CHS, DBY, LIN, LDN, SAL, SFK,

SSX
**Wiper:** 1780 SCO, YKS
**Witcher:** 1911 HAM
**Witts:** 1844 — 1871 GLS
**Wivermore:** ESS
**Wood:** 1581 — present AUS, BFD, CAE, CHS, CMN, DBY, DOR, GLS, HAM, HRT, IRE, KEN, LAN, LDN, MDX, MER, MGY, MON, NFK, OXF, SAL, SCO, SFK, SSX, STF, WAL, WIL, YKS
**Woodall:** 1801 — 1850 BFD, WOR
**Woodcock:** 1881 HUN, MON
**Woodward:** 1751 — 1886 DBY, NOT
**Woodyear:** 1891 LDN
**Woolford:** WIL
**Woolgar:** 1891 LDN
**Woolley:** 1828 — 1909 CHS, DBY
**Woolnough:** 1891 NFK
**Woolridge:** 1881 WOR
**Worley:** 1881 HRT
**Worrell:** 1711-present (int) BFD, DBY,
**Worthington:** 1724 BRK
**Wray:** 1891 LDN
**Wrenn:** LDN
**Wright:** 1610 — 1901 (int) DBY, ESS, HAM, KEN, LIN, NFK, SFK, SSX, YKS
**Wyatt/ Wyeth:** 1891 BRK, MDX
**Wyles:** 1912 SSX
**Wyn(ne):** 1843 — 1983 KEN, NFK, SFK
**Yalden:** See Yelding
**Yarnell/ Yarnold:** 1832 AUS, WOR
**Yates/ Yeates:** 1796 — 1914 SAL, SSX, YKS
**Yelding/ Yeldan/ Yalden:** 1891 — 1912 KEN, LDN, SSX
**York(e):** LDN
**Yorkston:** 1714 — 1770 SCO
**Young:** 1543 — 1900 (int) AUS, Barbados, BEW, BKM, BOR, CAN, DBY, DOR, DUR, E. Anglia, ESS, IRE, KEN, LAN, LDN, LEI. MDX, NBL, NFK, OXF, RUT, SCO, SFK, SOM, SRY, SSX, STF, WOR, YKS

# Chapter 3
# Romany and Traveller Forenames

Researching Gypsy forbears is notoriously difficult for a variety of reasons. One of the very few benefits, however, is the range of unusual forenames found amongst Gypsies. As with all families, these names tend to remain in particular families, and therefore the appearance of such a name can provide valuable clues for the researcher. It highlights new areas of research and gives pointers to families likely to be connected.

The following list does not claim to be complete. The 40 commonest names have all been non-family attributed, and the remainder are taken only from my own notes on well over 200,000 records of Gypsies, from the mid 16thC, which I hold. Someone researching their own family will be aware of other unusual names either not listed here at all, or not listed as belonging to their family. No listing like this can *ever* claim to be complete because new knowledge is forever being added. I am conscious that Scottish and Irish Traveller names are not well represented here.

Rather, the listing should be used as a sign post for future genealogical probing.

As to the names themselves, some are distinctively Gypsy and rare — if they occur at all — amongst non-Gypsies. These are always very valuable for identifying Gypsy families. Other forenames are common amongst Gypsies and amongst the remainder of the population, but even these names, in conjunction with others, can indicate Gypsies.

Occasionally, names are deliberate falsehoods by Gypsies. Sometimes they are obscenities in the Romany language (and I have omitted these because they could mislead the unwary family genealogist), others are made-up on the spur of the moment. Only experience can be used to identify these.

Usually, I have linked together variations on a name, but not always — for instance, Emilia, Emila and Emelieh are listed under Emilia, but Emily is regarded as a separate name, though clearly connected. My reasons for so doing are, frankly, sometimes based only on my perception or experience of hearing the name personally. If, for instance, I have heard two distinct variations on a name *within the same family*, I have tended to see them as separate names, though other Gypsy genealogists may not agree. With a name like Trannetta, I have found 13 variations, all clearly originating from Trinity, but the latter is listed separately as within families I have only ever experienced the name as a clearly different one from Tranetta/Trianti/Trainti etc.

Finally, some names fall into the category of complete misunderstandings, either on the part of the Gypsies, or that of the clerk in holy orders or census official. A splendid example of this is Countelater for a baby: *Count her later*, of course.

It should be noted that just because a name has not been recorded here with a particular family, it does not mean that the name might not be associated with other families — it indicates only that I have not yet found evidence for it.

Naturally, names reflect history and certain names are associated with certain periods in the past. However, whilst British gorjers often change names with current fashions, Romany people have relied much more on traditional names within their family.

## Types of Forename

Gypsy forenames can be divided into the following categories, each of which can be sub-divided:

1. Standard and common gorjer names such as John, Mary etc.
2. Biblical names — Aaron, Judith etc.
3. Names deriving from places — Bohemia, Mayfield etc
4. Foreign names — Heinrich, Ludwig etc
5. Names of famous people — Nelson, Byron etc
6. Names from famous events — Trafalgar, Crimea etc
7. Nicknames — Corky, Shotgun, Tibby etc
8. Names of flowers and other plants — Daisy, Gerania etc
9. Names that sound nice — Comfort, Bobbum, Dinkie
10. Names caused by mispronunciation — Harroly (for Riley), Pawni (for Penny)
11. Names made from phrases and concepts — Godbehear, Snow-Ellen

12. Names from surnames — O'Connor, Newbury
13. Names derived from titles of people — Major, Rabbi
14. Names from observations, especially of peoples' characters — Star, Happy, Mouse
15. Names derived from jokes against Gorjers — the commonest of these is Minch/Minj which appears in several parish registers, but these are not included as being clearly bogus.
16. Names which may be derived from Romany, or which sound like Romany — Daiki, Siminta.
17. Names of uncertain or unknown derivation

## Commonest Gorjer Names

I have surveyed the gorjer names as used by Gypsies from all 200,000 plus records which I hold and the following are the commonest, in rank order (most used first). Each of these names is used by at least 200 families or sub-families. For instance, almost every British Romany family appears to have at least one William/Bill.

1. William
2. John
3. Elizabeth
4. Thomas
5. Sarah*
6. Mary
7. Ann(e)/Annie
8. James
9. Robert
10. George
11. Mary Ann(e)
12. Jane
13. Joseph
14. Henry
15. Hannah
16. Samuel
17. Maria
18. Charles

19. Edward
20. Margaret
21. Harriet
22. Caroline
23. Phoebe
24. Louisa
25. Martha
26. Cornelius
27. Eliza
28. Arthur
29. Rebecca
30. Susanna
31. Catherine
32. Emma
33. Matilda
34. Richard
35. Rodney
36. Lucy
37. Susan
38. Benjamin
39. Frances
40. Walter

*The Gypsy version of this name, Saiera, is not included with this version.

# Gypsy Forenames and the Surnames Associated with them

**Aaron**: Arnold, Bland, Boswell, Cooper, Evans, Finney, Fletcher, Harris, Heron, Holland, Jackson/Jacques, Law, Lee, Lovell, Loveridge, Morgan, Oadley, Rogers, Shaw, Smith, Steward, Webb, Young. Cp Aron
**Abbey:** Smith, Wilson
**Abbury:** Webb
**Abdeel:** Lee. Cp Adbeel
**Abe:** Ashton, Lee, Orchard
**Abel:** Boswell, Green, Harris, Lee, Lock, Rogers, Smith
**Abendigo** (sic): Lee
**Aberilda**: Boswell
**Aberoine:** Smith
**Abi/Abbey (m):** Heron, Miller, Rossiter, Wilson
**Abia:** Taylor
**Abigail (f):** Boswell, Bowden, Boyling, Brown, Burton, Butler, Gray, Heron, Lambert, Lee, Mace, Newbury, Scott, Smith, Young
**Abimmelech, -eck:** Taylor
**Abitha:** Butler
**Abner:** Fuller
**Abraham/Abram (m):** Ayres, Booth, Boswell, Buckland, Cooper, Curtis, Delaway, Dimberline, Edmonds, Emmett, Golby, Gray, Green, Griffiths, Heron, Hughes, Johnson, Jolley, Jorisse, Joules, Keet, Kemp, Lee, Levy, Lovell, Marshall, Musto, Orchard, Othen, Reynolds, Ridley, Ripley, Roberts, Rogers, Scott, Shaw, Sherriff, Smith, Stanley, Swallow, Taylor, Thatcher, Waddington, Wilson, Wood.
**Abraham** (f): Boswell
**Absolom/Absalom:** Bean/Beany, Boswell, Collison, Cooper, Danner, Jones, Lee, Lock, Smith, Tooth
**Abuy (m):** Gray
**Achsah:** Lee
**Ackford:** Boswell
**Acorn (f):** Andrews, Heron, Shaw.
**Acquilla:** See Aquilla.
**Acquittina:** Baillie
**Ada:** Baker, Barrick, Boswell, Bradford, Brown, Buckley, Carter,

Collins, Coate(s), Cooper, Dixey, Draper, Duck, Finney, Gamble, Gass, Gray, Gregory, Headley, Heron, Howard, Johnson, Lee, Lock, Lovell, Loveridge, Mace, Matthews. Mooright, Nichols(on), Oadley, Parker, Penfold, Pitchley, Porter, Robinson, Rogers, Rose, Rowley, Ryles, Scamp, Scarrett, Sloper, Smith, Stanley, Stephens, Tapsall, Taylor, Tetley, Turner, Welsh, West, Wallett, Whatnell, Whitney, White, Williams

**Adam**: Boswell, Brown, Lee, Lock, Stephens, Tait, Wood, Yorkston
**Adbeel:** Lee. Cp Abdeel
**Addie:** Lee
**Addlarania:** Brown
**Adelaide**: Boswell, Garrett, Gregory, Lee, Mace, Nail, Scamp, Smith, Vaughan, Whatnell
**Adele/Adel:** Smith
**Adelina/Adeline**: Boswell, Finn, Smith
**Adiah:** Lock
**Adma (m):** Lee
**Adolphina:** Boswell
**AdolphusAlphus**: Boswell, Buckland, Buckley, Gray, Lock, Lovell, Loveridge, Ripley, Smith, Wood
**Adora:** Lee
**Adorn**: Boswell
**Adrian:** Chapman, Gray, Scamp
**Aeneas (m):** Rogers
**Affiance:** Orchard
**Agata:** Boswell
**Aggi (m):** Boswell
**Aggie (f):** Boswell, Florence, Shaw, Taylor.
**Agnes**: Blyth, Boswell, Brown, Buckley, Carter, Chelenor, Clarke, Cooper, Cox, Dellerye, Early, Faw, Florence, French, Gamester, Gardner, Gray, Green, Gregory, Heron, Hicks, Hogg, Howard, Hunter, Jackson, Johnson, Kempster, Lee, Little, Lock, Lovelage, Lovell, Loveridge, Martin, McDonald, McKenzie, Morley, Nichols(on), Noakes, O'Neil, Potter, Price, Ripley, Rogers, Rolf, Scamp, Scarrett, Scott, Shaw, Smallwood, Smith, Stanley, Tait, Taylor, Waterfield, Whatnell, Wilks, Wilson, Wood
**Agnesi:** Price
**Agruilla:** Smith
**Aguilla/Guilly**: Boswell, Small

**Agustus:** See Augustus
**Aira/Aior:** Burton, Wood
**Airant (m):** Heron
**Airus:** Wood, Young
**Aiza:** Boswell, Lee
**Alabaina/Alobobun/Albinia/Albina/Alobubinen (f):** Fowkes, Glover, Jones, Lee, Rogers, Scamp, Wood.
**Alabon:** Smith
**Alam(e)ena/Alamaania:** Boswell, Lee, Robinson, Small, Wharton
**Alan:** Eaton, Lovell, Scamp, Scarrett, Smith, Summerhill
**Alana:** Hilton
**Alathea:** Boswell
**Albany:** Smith
**Alberdine:** Smith
**Albert:** Ayres, Baker, Boswell, Brough, Brown, Bryant, Buckland, Butler, Camfield, Carter, Cheneler, Clouffle, Clowes, Cole, Collins, Colli(n)son, Colman, Cook, Cooper, Crighton, Deighton, Doe, Durrant, Eley, French, Garey, Giles, Golding, Gray, Griffiths, Harris, Heron, Horton, James, Johnson, Jones, Kempster, Kent, Leach, Lee, Lock, Livermore, Lovell, Loveridge, Mason, Matthews, Miller, Mitchell, Nail, Nelson, Newbury, Northan, Odam, Palmrt, Penfold, Pike, Porter, Powell, Rawlings, Rhodes, Roberts, Rose, Sa(u)nders, Scamp, Scarrett, Sedgwick, Shawyer, Sheen, Sloper, Smith, Stephens, Sterling, Stokes, Stone, Swales, Synes, Tapsell, Taylor, Thatcher, Townsend, Virgo, Walker, Wallett, Wood, Wyles, Young
**Alberta:** Small
**Albin:** Boswell
**Albina/Albinia:** See Alabaina
**Alby (m):**
**Aldeane:** Lovell
**Aldenby (m):** Lee
**Aldie:** Colbert
**Aldous:** Lee
**Aleaf:** Boswell
**Alec:** Stewart
**Alenia:** Smith
**Alesimar:** Gray
**Aletha/Alethea:** Gray, Nicholson

**Alex:** Laidlaw, Stephenson
**Alexander:** Boswell, Brown, Cleghorn, Cochrane, Crole, Faw, Gamel, Gordon, Harrison, Heron, Hogg, Jackson, Johnson, Kennedy, MacDonald, Laidlaw, Lee, Lovell, McLean, Miller, Morrell, Munro, Nelson, Richards, Ridd, Ripley, Scamp, Shaw, Smith, Stewart, Stubbs, Todd, Townsley, Valentine, Wagner, Wilson, Wood
**Alexina:** Rostron
**Aley:** Boswell
**Alfred/Alf/Alfie:** Adams, Arnold, Ayres, Baker, Bond, Booth, Boswell, Bowers, Brown, Buckland, Burgess, Burton, Butt, Campbell, Carter, Collins, Colman, Cooper, Davies, Dixon, Dolan, Duck, Duvall, Eastwood, Edmonds, Edwards, Efemia, Finney, Fletcher, Ford, Foster, Fuller, Gannett, Gaskin, Gess, Gilby, Giles, Godsmark, Gray, Gregory, Hammond, Harris, Harvey, Haws, Head, Heron, Hicks, Hillman, Hinkley, Holmes, Huggins, James, Jones, Kent, Lee, Light, Lovelock, Loveridge, Mace, Manning, Miller, Mills, Mitchell, Morley, Moss, Orchard, Palmer, Penfold, Phillips, Reynolds, Ripley, Robinson, Rose, Scamp, Scarrott, Scott, Sheen, Sherriff, Small, Smith, Stephens, Stewart, Stock, Swales, Taylor, Thomas, Thorpe, Todd, Tugby, Walker, Waller, Walsh, Webber, Welsh, Wilkins, Williams, Wood, Worley, Young
**Algar:** Boswell, Frankham, Franklin, Johnson, Lee, Smith, Taylor
**Algernon:** Smith, Stanley
**Ali:** Ayres, Evans, Heron, Jones, Smith
**Alice:** Ayres, Beldorn, Black, Booth, Boswell, Bowers, Britton, Broomhead, Brown, Buckland, Buckley, Burton, Butler, Clarke, Clarkson, Collison, Cooper, Cox, Critchley, Crumpton, Culline, Day, Dixon, Douglas, Eastwood, Edmonds, Eggins, Elliott, Faa, Finney, Ford, Fowkes, Frankham, Garey, Gatehouse, Gray, Gregory, Gritt, Guthrie, Hardingham, Harland, Harris, Hedges, Heron, Himess, Holland, Holmes, Hunter, Hurst, Jackson, Johnson, Jones, Keet, Kent, Kirby, Lee, Leleham/ Leeming/ Leading, Leatherland, Light, Lightfoot, Lovell, Loveridge, Mace, Matthews, McLean, Mitchell, Musto, Newbury, Nichols(on), Noble, Oadley, Parker, Payne, Peat, Penfold, Peters, Pharo, Pitcher, Powell, Price, Print, Ray, Reid, Richardson, Ripley, Roberts, Robinson, Rogers, Rose, Roser, Rostron, Rowley, Sanger, Scamp, Scarrett, Scott, Shaw, Shepherd, Sherriff, Shevlin,

Simpson, Sleddin, Small, Smith, Snelling, Stead, Stephens, Stewart, Stock, Swales, Synes, Tapsall, Tarling, Taylor, Thatcher, Thomas, Vaughan, Walker, Waterfield, Welsh, Wenan, Whatnell, Williams, Wilshire, Wilson, Winter, Woolnough, Wood, Woolley
**Alicia:** Gray, Sherriff
**Aligal:** Ayres
**Alisa:** Topseel
**Alisha:** Heron
**Alison:** Brown
**Alistair:** Jamieson, McCarthy
**Alith(e)a:** Butler, Holland, Scarrett.Cp Allisia
**Allamina**: Boswell
**Allen/Allan (m):** Boswell, Buckley, Dixie, Hyland, Lee
**Allen (f):** Boswell
**Alley:** See Ali.
**Allisia:** Green, Smith. Cp Alithea
**Allison (m):** Flear
**Alma** (m): Boswell, Bruce, Deckins, Lee, Smith
**Almia:** Harris. (In this family, the name Almia appears to be interchangeable with Eli)
**Alobubun:** See Alabaina
**Alog (f):** Chilcott
**Alona**: Boswell
**Alonza**: Boswell
**Alphonzo:** Tann
**Alts (f):** Lee
**Alva:** Biddle, Scarrett
**Alverdine (m):** Smith
**Alvie/Alvey:** Buckley, Eastwood, Hedges
**Alvina:** Lee
**Alwyn:** Finney
**Aly:** Gray
**Amadine/Ammadine:** Booth, Brown
**Amaletta:** Davies, White
**Amalia:** Cooper
**Amanda:** McCarthy, Scamp
**Amane:** Barnes
**Amar:** Hilton
**Amaria**: Boswell

**Amaritta:** Gupwell
**Amarylis:** Draper, Smith
**Amaziah (m):** Holland, Inwood
**Amberline:** Ayres, Sheen
**Ambi:** Lovell
**Ambolina**: Boswell
**Ambretty:** Sherriff
**Ambrose**: Barton, Batty, Blakey, Booth, Boswell, Buckland, Buckley, Coomb(e)s, Cooper, Draper, Finney, Gray, Lee, Lovell, Marshall, Mill, Newbury, Reynolds, Roberts, Sherriff, Smith, Stephens, Thorpe.
**Ambrosia:** Boswell
**Amelia**: Bailey, Berriman, Boswell, Burton, Calverley, Cooper, Draper, Elliott, Evans, Gray, Gritt, Heron, Hughes, Johnson, Lee, Lovell, Loveridge, Mace, Martin, Nichols(on), Penfold, Pidgley, Procter, Rock, Rogers, Scamp, Scarrett, Sherriff, Smith, Stephens, Taylor, Thompson, Vanis, Willett
**Amelus:** Smith
**Amerdine:** Biddle, Scarrett
**Amereta:** Lee
**Amerus:** Smith
**Amica:** Oadley
**Amilina:** Smith
**Ammadine:** See Amadine
**Amoret(t)a**: Boswell
**Amos**: Barber, Barton, Black, Bloomfield, Booth, Boswell, Braddock, Burton, Cooper, Faw, Foreman, Heron, Hill, Killick, Lee, Lovell, Loveridge, Mosby, Pilcher, Price, Scott, Shepherd, Smith, Swales, Thompson, Wells, Welsh, Young
**Amroos:** Taylor
**Amy/Amey**: Anderson, Beckett, Bond, Boswell, Brown, Buckland, Buckley, Burton, Calverley, Camfield, Carter, Chapman, Cooper, Cox, Davies, Eastwood, Faw, Frankham, Fuller, Gess, Gray, Green, Harris, Heron, Hughes, Knight, Lee, Light, Lock, Macklin, Mann, Marshall, Martin, Matthews, Mills, Nichols(on), Oadley, Osmond, Penfold, Pickett, Procter, Ripley, Roberts, Sa(u)nders, Showbridge, Smith, Stone, Tapsell, Taylor, Thompson, Topseel, Wells, White, Wilson
**Amyas:** Heron

**Anceline:** See Anselina
**Anchorn:** Smith
**Andanias:** Smith
**Anderson:** Johnson
**Andio:** George
**Andrew**: Blythe, Boswell, Brown, Buckland, Davies, Deighton, Faw, Fisher, Gorman, Gray, Heron, Hogg, Kerr, Law, Lee, Lock, McMillan, Mitchell, Morgan, Nichols(on), Purchase, Ryles, Scamp, Selby, Smith, Taylor, Tugby, West, White, Williams, Winter, Young
**Angel:** Heron
**Angela:** Gray, Scamp
**Angelica:** Scamp
**Angelina**: Boswell, Butler, Collins, Cooper, Emmett, Finney, Gatehouse, Giles, Gray, Gregory, Heron, Lee, Lewis, Lock, Lovell, Loveridge, Rogers, Scamp, Scarrett, Sheen, Small, Smith, Sutton, Thompson, Wharton, Whatnell, Wilks
**Angelo:** Percago
**Angie:** Booth
**Angus (m):** Boswell, Scott
**Angus (f):** Blythe, Lees
**Anice/Anis:** See Annys
**Aniletta:** Camfield, Isaacs
**Anita:** Ball, Lee
**Anjorina:** Taylor
**Anmal:** Taylor
**Ann(e)/Anna:** Many families.
**Annabella/-lle:** Heron, Lee, Lock, Musto, Penfold, Swales
**Annanias**: Boswell, Faw
**Annaron:** Florence
**Annas (f):** Lee, Lock
**Annel (f):** Rogers
**Annementey**: Boswell
**Anniadine:** Booth
**Annie:** Many families.
**Annis**. See Annys
**Annoria**: Boswell
**Annys/Anis/Anice:** Boswell, Finney, Gray, Heron, Lee, Lock, McLean, Shaw, Smith

**Anorettie:** Lee
**Anro:** Kennedy
**Anscomb:** Smith
**Anselina/Anceline:** Boswell, Buckland, Cooper, Draper, Green, James, Knight, Lee, Lovell, Loveridge, Smith, Stephens
**Anselo/Anslow:** Ayres, Boswell, Cooper, Draper, Reuben, Smith
**Ansey:** Lock, Price
**Anslow:** Cooper
**Anteane:** Donea
**Anthea:** Smith
**Anthony**: Boswell, Faw, Ford, Gawino, Gray, Lee, Hammond, Heron, Higgin, James, Johnson, Mills, Musgrave, Nicholls, Robinson, Scamp, Scarrett, Smalley, Smith, Stead. Vallentine, Wheeler, Wilson
**Antonia:** Godfrey
**Antonio:** Molinadi, Nichols(on), Sa(u)nders(on)
**Apollis (m):** Heron
**Appy**: Boswell. (Var. on Absalom.)
**Aquil(l)a/Gulley:** Boswell, Brinkley, Buckland, Draper, Newbury, Oadley, Small, Smith, Tapsell, Wood. Cp Equally
**Arabella/Arbella**: Boswell, Florence, Gess, Lee
**Arabella-Protesia:** Boswell
**Araine**: Boswell
**Aram:** Draper
**Aramena:** Cordery, Jones, Lock, Taylor
**Arbella:** See Arabella
**Arcalah/Archelah (f):** Draper
**Archer**: Boswell, Price, Wood
**Archibald**: Boswell, Douglas, Gray, Lee
**Archie:** Booth, Boswell, Finney, Huggins, Lee. MacAlister, Scamp, Taylor, Webber
**Archilaus:** Smith**Arecom (m):** Heron
**Arenoth:** Todd
**Arimal:** Taylor
**Aris (m):** Reynolds, Stephens
**Arkless/ Archelaus/ Arti/ Ark/ Arty:** Boswell, Buckley, Holland, Lee, Lock, Lovell, Reynolds, Smith, Stephens, Williams, Wood, Young (This name was probably originally a variant on Hercules, and cp Harkless and Artless.)

**Army (m)**: Boswell, Burton, Taylor.(This is not the same name as Arny.)
**Army (f)**: Lock, Taylor
**Arno**: Boswell, Brown, Loveridge
**Arnold**: Smith
**Arny**: Taylor
**Ar(r)on**: Booth, Light, Smith. Cp Aaron
**Arran (m)**: Lee
**Arsary**: Gray
**Arthena**: Lee
**Arthur**: Many families.
**Art**: Smith
**Arti**. See Arkless.
**Artless**: Boswell. Cp Arkless and Hercules.
**Artuly**: Draper, Stanley
**Artur**: Smith
**Asa**: Lee, Twin
**Ascony**: Loveridge
**Asena**: Cooper, Smith
**Ashby**: Boswell
**Ashela (f)**: Burton, Florence, Price, Taylor
**Ashena**: Boswell
**Asher**: Boswell
**Ashford**: Boswell
**Asho (m)**: Lee
**Ashriel**: Smith
**Ashton**: Boswell
**Asker**: Redworth
**Aslog (f)**: Heron
**Asme**: Lee
**Athalia(h) (f)**: Ayres, Boswell, Gray, Lee, Lovell, Nichols(on), Smith, Whatnell
**Athamon**: Mace
**Athelastan**: Lamb, Scamp
**Ather (f)**: Lee
**Athera (m)**: Lee
**Athliar (f)**: Boswell
**Athol**: Heron, Huggins
**Atkins (m)**: Brines

**Attaliah:** Ayres
**Audrey:** Brown, Butler, Miller, Price, Smith, Thorpe, White
**Augusta**: Boswell, Green, Sherriff, Showbridge, Snook
**Augustin:** Smith
**Augustus/Agustus/Gus**: Boswell, Giles, Gray, Head, Heron, Mace, Stanley
**Aurelia (f):** Oadley
**Auther (m):** Lee
**Ava:** Glover
**Averell:** Marshall, Price
**Avernina:** Baker
**Avery:** Heron
**Avis:** Scamp
**Avlah:** Smith
**Awlwin:** Heron, Thomas
**Aylwin:** Heron
**Ayrton:** Young
**Azariah:** See Oseri
**Azgad**: Boswell
**Aznah:** Lee
**Azuhbah/Azuba**: Blyth, Boswell, Loker
**Baby:** Collins, Dinson. Cp Biabai.
**Badelia (f):** Gray
**Baden:** Scamp
**Badger:** Gray, Kilsby, Lakey
**Baggy:** Taylor. Cp Baugus
**Baias** See Bias
**Baina (f):** Lovell, Loveridge, Stephens
**Bairam/Bouram/Byram** Lock, Young. Cp Byron
**Bairance:** Lee
**Baker (m):** Davies
**Bala (f):** Lee, Penfold
**Ball (f):** Boswell
**Ballam (f)** Davies
**Baptist:** Faw
**Barach (m):** Wood
**Barant:** Young
**Barbara**: Boswell, Corbett, Heron, Hird, Hislop, Lee, Lovell, Marshall, Martin, Newbury, Noble, Price, Rogers, Scamp,

Scarrett, Smith, Winter, Yorkston
**Barclay**: Boswell
**Barendon:** Buckland
**Barley:** Lee, Smith, Synes
**Barlow:** Waite
**Barnabus:** Mace
**Barnaby:** Gibson, Smith
**Barnard:** Lee
**Barnes (m):** Brown, Lee
**Barnet:** Carter, Lee, Scamp
**Barney**: Boswell, Mace, Scamp
**Baron:** Deighton
**Barraclough (f):** Brown
**Barry:** Lee, Scarrett
**Bart:** Smith
**Bartholomew**: Baptist, Boswell, Finney, Gray, Lee, Pinfold, Smith
**Barthy:** Smith
**Bartley**: Boswell, Gorman, Smith
**Basil:** Smith, Welsh
**Bassett:** Light
**Bathia:** Lee, Orchard
**Bathsheba**: Bilton, Boswell
**Baugus:** Lee. Cp Baggy
**Baynet (m):** Lee
**Bazena:** Clayton
**Bealy:** Draper
**Beany:** Lee
**Beati/Beata/ Beat:** Boswell, Draper, Othen, Smith. Cp Beedi.
**Beatrice**: Armitage, Boswell, Buckley, Colbert, Cramp, Ford, Freeman, Hedges, Johnson, Lawrence, Lee, Noakes, Noble, Ripley, Rogers, Scamp, Scarrett, Small, Smith, Stephens, Tann, Taplin, Taylor, Tyrant, Young
**Beatrix:** Lee
**Beauchamp:** Small
**Becca:** Finney. See Becky.
**Beck**: Boswell
**Becky:** Amer, Carey, Clayton, Cooper, Heron, Lee, Lock, Skerry, Smith, Taylor, Wiltshire. (This name is probably a variation on Rebecca.)

**Beda:** Lock
**Bedahn:** Boswell
**Beecham:** Coate(s)
**Beedy:** Lovelock. Cp Beaty
**Beeston:** Cooper
**Bejaney**: Boswell
**Belethian**: Boswell
**Belfegum:** Thomas
**Belina:** Penfold
**Belinda:** Scamp, Trickett
**Bell (f):** Hunter
**Bella:** Blyth, Brown, Buckland, Burton, Cooper, Dawson, Elliott, Emmett, Finney, Florence, Gray, Halden, Heron, Hilton, Jinks, Jones, Lee, Lock, Palmer, Pettigrove, Powell, Scamp, Scarrett, Smith, Spurrett, Stephens, Toogood, Walmsley
**Bellamarina/ Bellamarinia:** Loveridge
**Belle:** Stewart
**Bellman:** Harris
**Bellwood (m):** Giles
**Belsah:** Taylor
**Belsher/Belcher:** Beam/Beamy, Buckland, Lee, Synes
**Belshosa:** Ford
**Belsibub:** Gray
**Belta:** Lewis
**Ben/Benjamin/Benny:** Many families.
**Bendigo:** Lee, Palmer, Smith, Thorpe
**Bengemen:** Taylor
**Benjamin:** Smith, White
**Benah:** Taylor
**Benn:** Lee
**Bennett (m):** Scamp
**Bennitha/Benetta**: Boswell, Taylor
**Bentley (m):** Lock
**Benturin (m):** Heron
**Berkely:** Ryles
**Berki:** Smith
**Bernard:** Beige, Boswell, Furniss, Heron, Hilton, Lee, Lovell, Mace, Smith, Young
**Bernice:** Lee

**Bernick:** Blyth
**Bernie:** O'Connor, Shaw
**Berrington:** Lewis
**Berryman**: Boswell
**Bert:** Hughes, Loveridge, Venus
**Bertha:** Boswell, Buckley, Burton, Finney, Gregory, Hitchcock, Howden, Lee, Lock, Lovell, Orchard, Sherriff, Smith, Taylor, Whatnell, Wilks, Wood
**Bertheni:** Smith
**Berther**: Boswell
**Bertie/Bert:** Evans, Glover, Heron, Loveridge, Reynolds, Scarrett, Smith, Wood
**Bertram:** Lee, Lovell, Shepherd, Smith
**Beryl/Berylena:** Price, Scamp
**Bessy/Bessie:** Butler, Davies, Ellis, Glover, Gray, Jones, Loveridge, Pike, Sa(u)nders, Scamp. Scarrett, Stanley, Wood, Woodward
**Bet**: Boswell, Collins, Ingram
**Bethany/ Bethania/ Bethena/ Bethornia**: Boswell, Gray, Lee, Mobbs, Smith
**Bethiah**: Boswell
**Bethsheby:** Lee
**Bethula:** Anchorn
**Beti:** Smith
**Betsy**: Ayres, Baker, Berry, Boswell, Buckland, Buckley, Collison, Cook, Collinson, Cooper, Dickinson, Draper, Edgerton, Emmett, Fowkes, Gatehouse, Green, Harris, Hedges, Heron, James, Johnson, Jones, Kerry, Lee, Lovell, Loveridge, Midmore, Miller, Murphy, Newbury, Nicholson, Orchard, Osborn, Pannell, Penfold, Proudley, Redfearn, Ripley, Rogers, Sa(u)nders, Scamp, Scarrett, Shaw, Sherriff, Smith, Stanley, Stokes, Swallow, Taylor, Todd, Webb, Wells, White, Williams, Winter, Wood
**Bettridy:** Sherriff
**Bettris:** Wilson
**Betty/Bettie**: Ayres, Boswell, Buckland, Buckley, Heron, Holland, Lee, Lock, Marshall, Newbury, Newland, Penfold, Pierce, Price, Scarrett, Shaw, Sherriff, Smith, Stone, Swales, Ward
**Betts (m):** Price
**Bevan:** Smith
**Beverley:** Shepherd

**Biabai:** Heron. Cp Baby
**Biari**: Boswell
**Bias**: Boswell, Heron, Smith, Taylor
**Bidi:** Burton, Gray, Heron, Lovelock, Mace, Mochan, Reynolds, Smith
**Bielby (m):** Lee
**Bietta:** Smith**Bill/ Billy:** Most families
**Bishton:** Burton
**Biti:** Heron, Mochan
**Bivanfordelme:** Lock
**Bizilia:** Biddle, Scarrett
**Black** (nickname): Found in most families before another name, eg Black Jack, Black Ben, Black Becky, Black Barbara, Black Billy etc.
**Blackberry:** Ayres
**Blackett (m):** Lee
**Blackbird (m):** Price
**Blacklock (m):** Lee
**Blakiston (f):** Lee
**Blanch(e):** Hamilton, Heron, McLean, Nelson, Scamp, Scarrett, Smith, Wass
**Blanco:** White. (Presumably as nickname)
**Blodwin:** Lovell
**Blucher:** Lee, Scamp
**Blyth:** Hurst
**Boaz**: Boswell, Lock
**Bob:** See Robert
**Bobbum**: Boswell, Smith
**Bobby:** See Robert
**Boggi:** Price
**Bohemia**: Boswell, Wood
**Boinia:** Scamp, Smith
**Bonas**: Boswell
**Booi**: See Bui
**Bolle**: Boswell
**Bondy:** Smith
**Bonner:** Brinkley
**Bonn(e)y (f):** Booth, Gray, Heron, Young
**Booth:** Gray

**Bosephannah:** Boswell
**Bosha:** Coode
**Bosko/Boska**: Boswell, Gray, Tann
**Boss:** Gilby
**Bostock (m):** Boswell
**Boswell (m and f):** Ward
**Bouram**: See Bairam
**Bowden (m):** Scamp
**Boyella:** Welsh
**Bozzy**: Boswell
**Brace (m):** Scamp
**Braintree:** Gray
**Bramwell (m):** Evens
**Brand (m):** Newbury
**Bredaraynor (m):** Lee
**Brenda:** Lee, Penfold, Smith
**Brian/Bryan:** Boswell, Clifton, Hail, O'Neill, Scamp, Smith
**Bridger:** Nelson
**Bridget**: Boswell, Brett, Finney, Florence, Flynn, Heron, Hislop, Kitcheman, Lee, Lovell, O'Neill, Rafferty, Riley, Scott, Shepherd, Smith, Thompson, Whatnell
**Bridgetta**: Boswell
**Bridgey:** Boswell
**Bridie:** McCready, Page
**Brierney:** Rafferty
**Brighton:** Clayton
**Brillness:** Pike
**Briton:** Smith
**Brittainy**: Boswell, Lee
**Brittania**: Ayres, Ball, Barney, Boswell, Buckland, Buckley, Cole, Cooper, Crocker, Eastwood, Frankham, Giles, Greenstreet, Gregory, Head, Heron, Hicks, Holland, Honour, Hughes, Keet, Lee, Lovell, Manley, Neale, Oadley, Orchard, Palmer, Penfold, Rawlings, Sa(u)nders/on, Scamp, Scott, Smith, Stanley, Stephens, Traylen
**Britty:** Bowers, Hilden, Lee, Mochan, Ord, Price. Also see Brittania
**Brown (m)**: Lee
**Bruce**: Boswell

**Brugman:** Hall
**Brui:** Lee
**Bryan:** See Brian
**Bucheman:** Taylor
**Bud:** Brown, Gray, Stapleton
**Budi:** Florence, Lee
**Buggi**: Boswell
**Buggins:** Boswell
**Bui**: Boswell, Brown, Heron
**Buller:** Boswell, Sherriff
**Bun:** Gray
**Bunch of May:** Taylor
**Bundle:** Cooper
**Bunter:** Eaves
**Bunting (m):** Scamp
**Bunty:** Gray
**Bunzy**: Boswell
**Burli/ Burley:** Lee, Price
**Burrell (m):** Giles
**Burridge:** Penfold
**Burston** (f): Boswell
**Burton:** Smith
**Bute**: Boswell
**Butlin:** Boswell
**Butty:** Smith
**Buzzy**: Boswell, Jones, Lock, Smith
**Byram:** See Bairam
**Byron**: Cp Bairam. Boswell, Buckley, Heron, Lock, Scamp, Young
**Byther:** Butler
**Bythwell:** Smith
**Cable:** Smith
**Cadalia:** Cooper
**Caelia (m):** Lee
**Caep (m):** Ripley
**Cail** (m): Adams
**Cain:** Baxter, Smith
**Caiter**: Boswell
**Caleb:** Beldam, Clayton, Gray, Heron, Lee, Smith, Wenman
**Caleato**: Boswell

**Calico:** Taylor
**Callarberry:** Fenner
**Callow:** Small
**Cally:** Thompson
**Cameron(m and f):** Gibson (m), MacDonald (f), Mclean (f)
**Camilla/Camelia/ Comelia:** Lee, Scamp, Sherriff, Turnbull
**Campin/Campion**: Boswell
**Camuthas:** Lee
**Carehappy:** Smith
**Carew:** Brewer
**Carl:** Scamp, Synes
**Carla:** Lee
**Carl Ludwig**: Boswell
**Carmalione**: Boswell
**Carmine:** Rossi
**Carnation** (f): Boswell, Butler, Florence, Frankham, Lee, Lock, Lovell, Smith
**Carol(e):** Price, Scamp
**Carolin (m):** Ripley
**Carolina:** Bond, Douglas, Loveridge
**Caroline/Carolyn:** Many families.
**Carolus**: Boswell
**Carr:** English
**Carrie/Carry (f):** Flear, Jones, Lee, Rossiter, Whatnell, Wilson
**Cashmere**: Boswell, Lovell
**Cashi:** Lovell
**Caslaletti:** Petrrs. Cp Consalletti.
**Casper:** Smith
**Cassandra:** Clarke
**Cassello:** Chilcott
**Cassi:** Mochan
**Cathalina**: Boswell
**Catherina**: Boswell, Lee
**Catherine/Cathren/Catharine:** Most families
**Catron:** Smith. (Probably a variant on Catherine)
**Cecil:** Appleton, Florence, Lee**, Lovell**
**Cecilia/Cecelia/Secelia:** Boswell, Cooper, Gentle, Heron, Lee, Lock, Mason, Oadley, Ransley, Roberts, Sherriff, Smith, Stanley, Stone, Thorley, West

**Cecily**: Boswell
**Ceilvancer (f)**: Lee
**Celentia**: Cooper. Cp Celina.
**Celia/Selia**: Ayres, Boswell, Chilcott, Cooper, Deighton, Eastwood, Emmett, Hedges, Helden, Heron, Izzard, James, Lee, Lovell, Moss, Ram(n)sley, Ripley, Roberts, Scamp, Sherrard, Stanley, Stone, Turner, Vaughan, Welsh, Williams
**Celicia**: Heron
**Celina**: See Selina
**Cendinia**: Smith
**Cenimenti/Cenometty**: Cooper, Lee. Cp Sinimenti etc
**Centa**: Smith
**Centine**: Heron
**Cephry**: Scamp
**Chaelwa**: Wildash
**Challotte/ Chalotte**: Smith
**Chance (m)**: Marshall
**Charity**: Bassett, Bean/Beany, Buck, Collins, Cooper, Fletcher, Harris, Johnson, Jones, Lane, Lee, Light, Loveridge, Penfold, Richardson, Ripley, Roberts, Ryles, Sa(u)nders, Scamp, Scott, Smith, Stanley, Taylor, Wilson
**Charlene**: O'Neil
**Charles/Charlie (m)** Most families
**Charles** (f): Boswell
**Charlotte/ Charlott**: Allen, Arnold, Ayres, Beckett, Bibbury, Birch, Booth, Boss, Bowers, Boyce, Boswell, Bowers, Braddock, Bridges, Britton, Brown, Buckland, Burton, Cattermole, Clayton, Collison, Cooper, Davies, Dawson, Elliott, Emmett, Fenner, Fletcher, Ford, Frankham, Gess, Gilham, Gray, Green, Gregory, Hammond, Harding, Harris, Hedges, Heron, Hilden, Hughes, James, Johnson, Jones, Kemp, Leatherland, Lee, Lovell, Loveridge, Mackenzie, Matthews, Miller, Mochan, Neale, Newbury, Nicholls, Noble, Orchard, Parker, Penfold, Powell, Price, Roberts, Rossiter, Rowland, Sand(y)s, Scarrett, Shaw, Sherriff, Smith, Stephens, Stewart, Taylor, Towler, Ward, Welch, Welling, West, Wheeler, White, Williams, Wood, Young
**Charmaine**: Finney, Scamp
**Chart**: Golby
**Chasey/ Chesi/Chacey**: Boswell, Burton, Heron, Price, Smith,

Taylor
**Cheryl:** Scarrett, Shaw
**Chesaia:** See Josiah
**Chewbacca:** Matthews. (In my opinion, a nickname)
**Chisletina/ Chisletina/ Chesledine:** Lovell
**Chiti:** Smith
**Chlar:** Smith
**Cho:** Gray
**Chorise:** Scamp
**Chorley:** Feltham
**Chrare:** Egubo
**Chris:** Smith
**Chrissany:** McLean
**Chrissie:** Carter
**Christian** (f): Blackie, Blyth, Boswell, Smith, Wilson
**Christian** (m): Boswell, Carr/ Kerr, Robinson
**Christiana (f)**: Boswell, Heron, Hunt, Lee, McLean, Orchard, Scamp, Smith, Swales, Walker, Ward
**Christie:** Clayton
**Christina/Kristina**: Atkinson, Boswell, Coats, Corkhill, Gray, Hunt, Odam, Orchard, Pidgley, Scamp, Scarrett, Stephenson, Swales, Tait
**Christine**: Boswell, Frankham, Graves, Lee, Scamp, Smith, Taylor
**Christmas (f):** Lee, Thomas
**Christobel:** Hicks
**Christopher**: Booth, Boswell, Brown, Curtis, Deighton, Emmett, Gibson, Gray, Hail, Harris, Heron, Herrick, Jackson, Jeffs/Jeffrey, Jones, Jordon, Jowett, Leckenby, Lee, Lovell, Marshall, Metcalfe, Musgrave, Newbury, Odam, Orchard, Penfold, Peters, Rose, Scarrett, Shaw, Simson, Smith, Stanley, Summers, Swales, Taylor, Thompson, Todd, Wilson, Wood, Young
**Christy/Christo**: Boswell, Young
**Chvaney:** Scamp
**Cicily**: Boswell
**Ciliande**: Boswell
**Cilvina:** Scamp
**Cinderella**: Ayres, Boswell, Cooper, Davies, Doe, Harris, Heron, Hillier, Lee, Loveridge, Ryles, Smith, Winter, Wood
**Cinerella:** Lovell

**Cinetta/ Cynetta:** Lambourne, Lee
**Cinnamenti/Sinamenti/Sinementia/Cintamenta:** Baker, Booth, Boswell, Frankham, Gardener, Gray, Heap, Heath, Heron, Johnson, Lee, Lovell, Scamp, Scarrett, Small, Smith, Synes, Taylor, Webb
**Cinterbury:** Scott
**Ciparania**: Boswell
**Cissy**: Boswell, James, Lee, Price, Ripley
**Claara:** See Clara
**Cladie:** Spurrett
**Clara/ Claara**: Boswell, Brown, Charles, Cooper, Cordes, Downes, Duck, Fick, Finney, Ford, Gardiner, Giles, Gray, Green, Harris, Heron, Hopewell, Hopkins, Jones, Lee, Lovell, Loveridge, Oadley, Scamp, Shaw, Smith, South, Squires, Stephens, Totten, Vanis, Walker, Young
**Clare/Clair:** Heron, Lee, Scamp, Shaw, Smith, Strand, Worrall
**Clarence**: Barron, Boswell, Harris, Smith
**Clarice:** Lovell
**Clarinda/Clarandry/Clarenda:** Baker, Scamp, Stanley
**Clarissa**: Boswell
**Clark**(e): Boswell, Lovell
**Clarman:** Boswell
**Claudie:** Ford, Gray
**Clemens:** Boswell
**Clement**: Boswell, Smith
**Clementia:** Loveridge, Stevens
**Clementina/-ne:** Aldridge, Ayres, Biddle, Blackman, Draper, Loveridge, McArthur, McCallum, Popples, Smith, Stephens
**Clevancea/Clevancy:** Lee, Boswell, Smith
**Clifford:** Culkine, Gray, Lee
**Climentia:** Stephens
**Cliver (f):** Rowel
**Cloden**: Boswell
**Clonus:** Shaw
**Closentine**: Boswell
**Clough (f):** Lee
**Clust:** Carter
**Coates (m):** Boswell, Scamp
**Coc(c)erelli:** Boswell

**Cocertelle:** Boswell
**Cock/Cocky:** Livermore, Lovell. Almost certainly a nickname.
**Cocker:** Smith
**Cockpot:** Gray
**Cocky:** Ball
**Cokey (m):** Smith
**Cole:** Walter
**Coley:** Smith
**Colin:** Boswell, Campbell, Scamp
**Colleen:** Shepherd
**Collette:** Scamp
**Collier (m):** Gray, Heron
**Coll(e)y (f):** Boswell, Stone
**Colston:** Lee
**Colt (f):** Lee
**Coly:** Smith
**Comelia:** See Camelia
**Comford**: Boswell
**Comfort/ Comphart**: Arnold, Boswell, Botton, Chater, Davies, Draper, Ellis, Gregory, Leatherland, Lovell, Smith, Stephens, Woodall
**Comla:** Smith
**Commersilla:** Boswell
**Con (f): Shevlin**
**Connab:** Finney
**Connah/-er:** Boswell, Finney, Scamp
**Connaught:** Ayres
**Conrad:** Heron
**Conselletti/ Conselliette/ Concilletta/ Kunsalletti/ Counselletti/ Counsellette/ Countelater/ Counseil:** Boswell, Brinkley, Cooper, Lee, Lewis, Cooper, Derrick, Herrick, Ripley, Scarrett, Shaw, Smith. Cp Caslelletti.
**Constance:** Barker, Boswell, Gray, Heron, Pierce, Smith, Wadham, Whitlock
**Constant:** Smith
**Constantine:** Parker, Smith
**Conyers:** Lee
**Cooper (m):** Gaskin, Sherriff
**Coralina/-ne/Koralina/Coraleana**: Ball, Boswell, Butler, Gray,

Lee, Macfarlane, Penfold, Scarrett, Sherriff, Smith, Synes, Taylor
**Coralinda:** Boswell
**Cordelia:** Ball, Jones
**Corey:** Dynes, Palchett
**Corin(n)e:** Finney, Ripley
**Corky:** Booth
**Corleander/ Coriliander (f):** Heron
**Corlinea:** Ball
**Cornation:** Boswell
**Cornelia/Cornalia:** Buckton, Butler, Davies, Loveridge, Smith
**Cornelius**: Many families
**Cornish (m):** Scamp
**Corolenia/Corallina:** Boswell, Smith
**Corrie (m):** Lovell, Smith
**Costelow:** Boswell
**Counselletti/tte:** See Conselletti
**Countelater:** See Conselletti
**Courtland:** Smith
**Cox (f):** Boswell, Brown
**Cox (m)** Stapleton
**Cox (f):** Gray
**Cradoc:** See Kradok
**Crafton/ Crapton:** Deighton
**Craig:** Gray, Scamp
**CrazyAnn:** Smith. Not actually a nickname but a variant on Trezian.
**Credi/Credder:** Price
**Credit:** Price
**Credoc.** Price. Cp Kradok.
**Crevaney:** Boswell
**Crime/Crimea:** Heron, Kindon, Price, Smith
**Criss (m):** Ripley
**Cristo.** See Christy
**Critty:** Smith
**Cross (m):** Heron
**Crowland:** Smith
**Crows:** Rippington
**Crowy:** Buckland, Heron
**Cruiser**: Boswell

**Cuddy:** Smith
**Cull, Cully (f):** Heron, Williams
**Cullimer (m):** Lamborne
**Culvator.** See Ovator
**Cunningham (m):** Sivers
**Curlinda:** Lee
**Currier:** Faw
**Curtis (m and f):** Sherriff
**Cushi:** Manning
**Cuthbert**: Boswell, Buckton, Elliott, Faa, Lee, Smith, Strange
**Cyana**: Boswell, Smith
**Cyasa:** Smith
**Cygnet/Signet:** Heron, Loveridge, Smith
**Cylia:** Lee
**Cynthia:** Lovell, Smith
**Cyphraelia**: Boswell
**Cyril:** Gray, Heron, Lovell, Scamp, Taylor
**Cyrus:** Rogers, Smith
**Dadi (m):** Gray
**Dafydd:** Wood
**Dagma(r):** Jackson, Sanger
**Dai**: Boswell
**Daiena/Daiona:** Boswell, Heron
**Daiki:** Gray
**Daisy (m)**: Boswell, Brazil, Childs, Gatehouse, Lee, Smith
**Daisy (f):** Buckland, Davies, Evans, Gray, Heron, Hunter, Lee, Mitchell, Scamp, Shepherd
**Daiverus:** See Diverus
**Dakota (f):** Marshall
**Dale:** Scamp
**Dalitha/ Delathy/ D'Leafy:** Loveridge
**Daliza:** Holland
**Damal:** Smith
**Damaris (f)**: Boswell, Ingram, Lee, Smith, Wood
**Dambros**: Boswell
**Damon:** Lee
**Dan**: Boswell, Cooper, Nicols(on), Ripley, Roselands
**Danbritty**: Boswell
**Danch (m):** Lee

**Dando:** Lee
**Dane:** Matthews
**Dangeful/Dangerfield/Dangerfill (m):** Ayres, Barney, Lee. Cp Dentiful
**Daniel/Danny:** Booth, Boswell, Butler, Clarke, Collins, Cooper, Crew, Crook, Davies, Day, De Marnes, Devitt, Dolan, Drew, Evans, Fletcher, Giles, Gilroy, Gray, Gumble, Hall, Ham, Harrison, Heron, Hickman, Kelly, Lee, Lock, Lovell, McCarthy, Morgan, Moulson, O'Neil, Osmond, Pullinger, Roberts, Scamp, Shepherd, Smith, Stephens, Synes, Taylor, Teeth, Thomas, Washington, Watney, Webb, Wilson
**Daphne:** Lee, Pidgley, Scamp, Stanley
**Darby:** Crowley
**Darcas:** Boswell, John. A variant of Darklis and Darker.
**Darcy:** Draper
**Dare:** Walker
**Darkest (f):** Arnold
**Darklis/ Darkless/ Darkus/Darcus/ Darkis (f):** Boswell, Buckland, Burton, Lee, Lewis, Price, Quenton, Smith
**Darnity/Darnaly:** Draper, Smith
**Dary:** Welsh
**Data:** Burton, Price. Cp Deta
**Dathina:** Boswell
**David/Dave/Davy:** Blyth, Boswell, Burton, Butler, Carter, Chapman, Colbert, Colley, Coster, Cox, Critchley, Eley, Evans, Faw, Finney, Gatehouse, Giles, Gray, Harris, Heron, Hogan, Hooker, Jackson, James, Johns, Johnson, Jones, Learoid, Lee, Levy, Loker, Matthews, Maxwell, McLean, Miller, Newland, Penfold, Pinkerton, Porter, Price, Pullman, Purnell, Rawlings, Reader, Richards, Rogers, Scamp, Sherrard, Sherriff, Slender, Smith, Stanley, Stephens, Stewart, Taylor, Teat, Turner, Vaughan, Walker, Webb, Williams, Wilson, Wood, Woodward, Young
**Davies:** Boswell
**Davock:** Marshall
**Dawn:** Lee, Scamp, Shepherd, Webb
**Dawson (f):** Marshall
**Deacon (f):** Boswell
**Deadle:** Smith

**Dean:** Scarrett
**Dearmont:** Smallbones
**Dearus:** Lovell
**Deavus:** Boswell
**Debawra/Debbarah/ Debery:** Lee
**Debbie:** Cameron, Gibson, McDonald, McLean, Scamp
**Deborah:** Ayres, Boswell, Lee, Morris, Palmer, Pidgley, Porter, Scamp, Scarrett, Todd
**Defiance/Defrance (f):** Orchard, Penfold, Roberts
**Dekamoh:** Lee
**Deladdus:** Lovell
**Delaia(h)/Delia/Deliah/ Dilaia/Dela/De La Railee:** Boswell, Florence, Gray, Heron, Jones, Lee, Lock, Lovell, Mace, Orchard, Parker, Penfold, Reynolds, Smith, Taylor
**Delana/Delenda/Dilana/Dillinder:** Boswell, Evans, Lee, Smith, Williams
**Delata/Delater:** Heron
**Delepha:** Smith**Delephis:** Smith. Cp Dalitha
**Delerana:** Boswell
**Deleta:** Boswell
**Delevi/ Delaifi:** Boswell, Lovell
**Delfi:** Smith**Deliah:** See Delaia
**Delilah:** Boswell, Deighton, Florence, Heron, Johnson, Lee, Scarrott, Shepherd, Sherriff, Smith, Stephens, Taylor
**Delilas/ Delias:** Lovell
**Delina:** See Delana
**Deliverance:** Gregory
**Delizah/Delizanna**: Boswell, Smith
**Delizanna**: Boswell, Smith
**Delmore (m):** Lock
**Delorei:** Heron
**Deloraifi/ Diloraifi/ De La Rifey:** Boswell, Lee, Lovell, Smith
**Deloreni/Delorayni:** Boss, Boswell, Heron
**Demaris:** Boswell, Wood
**Demembrah:** Lock
**Demer:** Matskalla
**Demiti:** See Dimiti
**Demon:** Lee
**Denine (f):** Gerrard, Scamp

**Denis** (f): Boswell, Scamp
**Denise:** Lee, Smith
**Dennis/Denny:** Booth, Donovan, Evans, Hanson, Heron, Loveridge, Scamp, Smith, Stephens, Taylor, Wheeler, Whitham
**Dennor:** Lock
**Dentiful:** Stanley. Cp Dangerful
**Denzillus**: Boswell
**Deogerous/ Deogernes (f):** Boswell, Lee
**Deogily:** Lee
**Derek/ Dereck:** Scamp, Stanley
**Dermot Lavis:** Boswell
**Desibera**: Boswell
**Desmond:** Lovell
**Deta:** Heron. Cp Data
**Devetta/Devit (f):** Boswell, Heron,. Young
**Dewhurst (m):** Harrison
**Deziah:** Gray, Orchard
**Diamond (f):** Price
**Diamond (m):** Lee
**Diana (h)/ Dianna:** Arnold, Bell, Boswell, Buckland, Deighton, Gregory, Lee, Lovell, Loveridge, Roser, Scamp, Scarrett
**Diane:** Boswell, Finney, Gordon, Gray, Holland, Hughes, Lee, Rawlings, Shaw, Steele, Webb
**Dick(y):** See Richard.
**Diddles:** Smith
**Didi:** Ayres, Taylor
**Digger:** Stanley
**Dilanda:** Boswell
**Dilarana:** Boswell
**Dill:** Gray
**Dillinder:** Boswell
**Dillis:** Finney
**Dilly/Dilli:** Coate(s), Green, Lee
**Diloraifi:** See Deloraifi
**Dimiti:** Buckland, Smith
**Dinah**: Boswell, Draper, Gray, Heron, Lee, Noble, Shaw, Smith, Swales
**Dinkie (f):** Taylor
**Dinniah:** Loveridge

**Diodatus**: Boswell
**Diogenes:** Lee
**Dion**: Boswell
**Dionisia:** Oxpring, Smith, Wood
**Ditfield (f):** Smith, Whatnell
**Diverus:** Lee, Smith
**Diverus/Divus/Dives:** Lee, Loveridge, Smith
**Dixie**: Boswell, Brown
**Dob:** Lee
**Docia:** See Dosia
**Doctor**: Boswell, Buckland, Gregory, Ingram
**Dodi:** Loveridge
**Doi:** Burton
**Dolas (f):** Lovell
**Dolly:** Boswell, Lee, Price, Sherriff, Taylor
**Dolores:** Evans
**Dolphin (m):** Harris
**Dolphus/ Dolfus/ Dolpherus**: Boswell, Finney, Heron, Lovell, Thorpe, Varey. Almost certainly derived from Adolphus/Rudolphus
**Dolphy**: Boswell
**Dominic:** Illingworth, Shadlock
**Domone:** Lee
**Dona**: (Note that this name is pron. with a long 'o' as in 'coal') Boswell, Buckland, Burton, Camp, Gray, Heron, Holland, Lee, Lovell, Mace, Middleton, Scamp, Smith
**Donald**: Boswell, Brown, Caird, Campbell, Faa, McDonald, Ransley, Stewart
**Donkey** (nickname): Boswell
**Donnert:** Faa
**Doodi (f):** Lee, Scamp
**Dookey/Dookie:** Cooper
**Dooriah:** Lovell
**Doovel:** See Doval
**Doovelkanesto:** Lock
**Dora:** Butler, Finney, Ford, Lock, Lovell, Penfold, Pierce, Scamp, Smith, Stanley, Taylor, Varey, Young
**Dorathia:** Lee
**Dorcas/ Dorcus**: Boswell, Heron, Lee, Nichols(on), Nodle, Rogers,

Shaw, Smith. This name is found amongst both men and women.
**Doreen:** Howard, Scamp
**Dorelia/Dorilia/Dorila**: Boswell, Cooper, Cordery, Heron, Jones, Lock, Scamp, Taylor
**Dorenia:** Deighton
**Dorinda:** Roberts
**Doris:** Herrett, Lovell, Scamp, Scarrott, Sloper
**Dorothea**: Boswell
**Dorothy**: Adams, Booth, Boswell, Buckley, Cameron, Douglas, Elliott, Lee, Lovell, Miles, Newman, Nichols(on), Noble, Parker, Penfold, Rawson, Rogers, Scamp, Scarrott, Skinner, Smith, Stewart, Swales, Thompson, Wilson, Wood
**Dorrie:** Lee
**Dosha:** Wells
**Dosia/Docia**: Boswell, Harris, Sawyer
**Dotia:** Ayres
**Dougie:** Taylor
**Douglas (m):** Ayres, Boswell, Finney, Gray, Heron, Jones, McLean, Price, Scamp, Smith
**Douglas (f):** Smith
**Dove:** Burton
**Dovel/Doovel/Duvel (m):** Boswell, Lock, Lovell, Taylor
**Dover (m):** Heron, Nelson
**Dovie:** Roberts
**Downi/Downey (f):** Heron, Stanton, Walker
**Downing:** Rowley
**Dozey:** Gaskin
**Draki:** Cooper, Jummix
**Draper:** Boswell
**Drewsella.** See Drusilla.
**Driscilla:** See Drusilla
**Drooi:** Lee
**Duanne:** Gray
**Druce:** Boswell
**Drus(c)illa/ Drewsella/ Drucelia:** Boswell, Campbell, Dalton, Elliott, Gray, Green, Heron, Johns, Joules, Lee, Rogers, Sherriff, Smith, Wood
**Dud:** Buckley
**Dudley:** Portman

**Dui:** Cooper
**Dummy:** Lock
**Duncan:** Crumley, Faa, Williamson
**Dunwell:** Brown, Johnson
**Duranda:** Smith
**Durant:** Lovell
**Duriah:** Lovell
**Duvel:** See Dovel
**Dya:** Baptista
**Dyonisia:** Boswell
**Eany:** Brown, Stapleton
**Earnest (sic):** Boswell, Merry, Wood. (In this case, Merry may well here be an aka for Wood. It is found as a forename in the Wood family.)
**Earthelba:** Boswell
**Easbell:** Light. Cp Isabel
**Easter (f):** Booth, Boswell, Jones, Lee, Mosby
**Easy:** Smith
**Eb:** Smith
**Ebenezer:** Boswell, Gray, Gregory, Lovell
**Ebony:** Booth, Smith
**Ed:** Fuller
**Eddard:** Brinkley
**Eddie:** See Edward
**Eden:** Boswell
**Edenham (m):** Heron
**Eder (f):** Heron
**Edgar:** Baker, Lee, Lovell, Smith
**Edginall:** Cater
**Edic:** Burton, Lovell
**Edingale/Edengull (f):** Boswell, Lee, Lovell, Smith
**Edith:** Barringer, Bothwell, Buckland, Burton, Canham, Cheeseman, Childs, Collins, Cox, Efemey, Elliott, Evans, Gray, Green, Gregory, Hawes, Heron, Hollinges, Lee, Lovell, Moseley, Nichols(on), Payne, Roberts, Savage, Scamp, Scarrett, Shepherd, Sherriff, Smith, Stanley, Waterton, Wood, Wright, Yates
**Edmund:** Boswell, Coleman, Fearne, Gray, Heron, King, Kitson, Lee, Lovell, Moss, Sa(u)nders(on), Smith, Spencer, Tullett, Wilson, Wood

**Edna:** Booth, Heron, Scarrett, Smith, Wood
**Edom:** Reuben
**Edrus:** Ayres
**Edward:** Many families
**Edwin:** Boswell, Buckland, Cooper, Doe, Evans, Fletcher, Ford, Goodman, Greenstreet, Heron, Johnson, Jones, Lee, Lovell, Loveridge, Mills, Orchard, Penfold, Ripley, Scarrett, Stanley, Smith, Taylor, Wenman, Wilson, Witney, Wood, Young
**Efusa:** Loveridge
**Eglentine:** Boswell
**Ehelia:** Boswell
**Eileen:** Finney, Herrett, Scarrett, Slender, Stone
**Eiram:** Oadby
**Eken:** Jackson/Jacques
**Elaine:** Lovell, Scamp
**Elamule:** Lee, Small
**Elanglass:** Mills
**Elaphen:** Williams
**Elby:** Buckley
**Elderia:** Boswell
**Elderifer/fee/fa:** See Eldoraifi
**Eldery:** Boswell
**Eldi:** Boswell
**Eldorai:** Boswell, Burton, Gregory, Heron, Jones, Joules, Lee, Lovell, Sherriff, Smith, Wood
**Eldoraifi/Elderifa:** Boswell, Buckland, Lee
**Eldorai-Jane:** Boswell
**Eldra:** Roberts
**Eldred:** Pierce, Winter
**Eleanor/Ellinor/Eleanore/ Ellenor**: Boswell, Braddock, Clarke, Connor, Davies, Douglas, Evans, Golby, Gtay, Greig, Heron, Huntley, Hurst, James, Jones, Lane, Lee, Lovell, Masters, Mitchell, Nelson, Nichols(on), Pattinson, Pidgley, Rainbow, Roberts, Robinson, Rogers, Ryan, Scamp, Scott, Shaw, Smith, Stephens, Storey, Townend, Webb, Wilson, Wood
**Eleen:** Shepherd
**Elegigor:** Smith
**Elena:** Heron, Holdsworth, Ratcliffe
**Elesheba:** Smith

**Elfer (m):** Heron

**Elgana:** Scamp

**Eli:** Boswell, Bull, Butler, Cooper, Frankham, Gregory, Harris, Head, Heron, Hughes, Lee, Lovell, Loveridge, Ray, Roberts, Scarrett, Shaw, Smith, Stanley, Whatnell, White. (Note that one of the Eli Harrises used the name as a variant on Almia.)

**Eliandra:** Boswell

**Elianor:** Lee

**Elias (m):** Ayres, Boswell, Bowers, Brown, Draper, Giles, Gray, Harris, Hedges, Heron, Lock, Loveridge, Robinson, Shaw, Smith, Spencer, Stephens, Stephney, Stokes, Stone, Swallow, Tood, Waterfield

**Elias (f):** Heron

**Eliastra:** Scarrett

**Elica:** Smith

**Elick:** Kennedy

**Elieza:** Jones

**Elifa/Elife:** Lee

**Eligh (f):** Gray

**Elijab** (sic): Boswell

**Elijah/Elija:** Ayres, Boswell, Buckley, Carey, Clout, Gray, Elliott, Gray, Heron, James, Johnson, Lee, Lock, Lovell, Mills, Odell, Pierce, Rogers, Sa(u)nders, Scamp, Scarrett, Shaw, Smith, Stone, Vaughan, Wharton, Wood, Young

**Elijahnseus:** Boswell

**Elik:** Boswell

**Elino:** Boswell

**Elinor:** Boswell, Martin

**Elise:** Boswell

**Elisha:** Boswell, Cooper, Heron, Smith, Taylor

**Eliza.** See Elizabeth.

**Elizabeth/Eliza:** Most families

**Elkennah:** Johnson

**Ella:** Burton, Butler, Gray, Scamp, Tetley, White

**Ellen/Ellin:** Adams, Bailey, Barrett, Beasley, Besford, Boswell, Boyling, Brazil, Buckley, Buff, Bugg, Burton, Butler, Camfield, Chaplin, Chapman, Charlot, Clarke, Collins, Cook, Connor, Cooper, Crittenden, Danner, Davies, Day, Devine, Draper, Eastwood, Edley, Edwards, Eland, Elliott, Evans, Finney. Ford,

Freeman, Gannett, Gatehouse, Gibson, Gorman, Gray, Gregory, Hall, Hallier, Harris, Harrison, Heron, Higgin, Hiscox, Holland, Holmes, Hughes, Hulbert, Indow, Isau, Jackson, James, Jamieson, Johnson, Jones, Lamb, Lane, Lee, Leyland, Light, Lovell, Loveridge, Mace, Martin, Matthews, McFarlane, Meredith, Miller, Mitchell, Morley, Moss, Murphy, Musto, Myers, Nichols(on), Pallenden, Parker, Parry, Penfold, Pettitt, Pierce, Pike, Pinfold, Price, Ratcliffe, Ray, Reader, Rhodes, Ripley, Roberts, Robinson, Rootham, Roser, Rowley, Ryan, Sadler, Savage, Scamp, Scarrett, Scott, Shaw, Sherriff, Shevlin, Shirley, Simms, Slender, Small, Smith, Spencer, Stephens, Tapsall, Taylor, Terry, Thompson, Todd, Tomlinson, Tooth, Varey, Varley, Vaughan, Walker, Wallett, Walsh, Ward, Weald, Westrop, White, Whatnell, Willett, Williams, Wilson, Wood

**Ellenwada:** Lee
**Ellerada:** Lee
**Ellice**: Boswell
**Ellick**: Kennedy
**Ellie:** Finney, Redworth, Smith
**Ellin(e)**: Boswell, Johnson
**Elliott:** Baker
**Ellis/Elus:** Boswell, Claydon/Clayton, Cook, Miller, Robinson
**Ellison:** Gibben
**Elnor (f):** Rogers
**Elsa:** Murphy
**Elsie**: Boswell, Collinson, Jones, Lovell, Mace, Ripley, Scamp, Scarrett, Taylor
**Elspeth:** Faw, Lindsay, Maxwell
**Elva:** Robinson
**Elvaina:** Emmett, Heron, Lee
**Elvaira**: Boswell, Gray, Heron, Lee
**Elvey/Elvie/Elvia:** Buckley, Giles, Green, Lee, Ripley, Rogers, Stone
**Elvina:** Boswell, Brown, Emmett, Reynolds, Scamp, Stone
**Elvira:** Buckley, Burton, Lee
**Elvirus:** Boswell
**Ely:** Mitchell. Possibly a variant on Eli.
**Emacena:** Lee
**Emancia**: Boswell

**Emanaia/Emmanaia:** Boswell, Heron, Smith
**Emarind:** Smith
**Emeni:** Smith
**Emeot:** Scarrott
**Emerus:** Lee
**Emery:** Lovell
**Emilia/Emila/Emelieh**: Boswell, Humphrey, Newbury, Scarrett
**Emily**: Ayres, Baker, Barton, Blackman, Bond, Boswell, Bowers, Boyling, Brooks, Buckley, Butler, Canner, Carter, Chamberlain, Cleghorn, Clouffle, Collins, Colman, Cooper, Crumpton, Daily, Davies, Eley, Elliott, Evans, Finney, Fletcher, Foster, Gray, Green, Greenway, Gregory, Grice, Griffiths, Hadley, Halden, Harding, Harris, Harrison, Heron, Hughes, Jennings, Johnson, Lee, Lovell, Loveridge, Miles, Miller, Moyne, Murphy, Neale, Nelson, Nixon, Oadley, Orchard, Pannell, Penfold, Pidgley, Price, Redworth, Richardson, Riley, Ripley, Robinson, Rose, Rossiter, Sa(u)nders, Scamp, Scarrett, Scott, Shaw, Shepherd, Sherrard, Slender, Smith, Stanley, Swales, Taylor, Thurston, Tyler, Veti, Ward, Webb, Welsh, White, Whitehead, Willenden, Wood, Wright
**Emlah:** Scarrett
**Emlyn**: Boswell
**Emma:** Many families
**Emmadine:** Booth, Brown
**Emmanuel/Emanewell/ Immanuel**: Baker, Bassett, Boswell, Buckland, Burton, Connell, Ford, Giles, Harris, Heap, Heath, Heron, Hicks, Lee, Loveridge, Mace, Price, Scarrett, Smith, Stephens, Taylor, Valentine. Probably the same name as Mannabel.
**Emme/Emmie/ Emmy**: Boswell, Cook, Green, Johnson, Ray, Smith, Willett
**Emmeline/Emmalina:** Dixon, Duffield, Lee, Young
**Emmett/Emot/ Emert:** Roberts, Wilson
**Emperor:** Boss, Boswell, Heron, Thorpe
**England (m):** Heron, Roberts
**Enjelina:** Gray
**Ena:** Mitchell
**Enid:** Buckley
**Ennin:** Gray
**Enoch/Enock/Enok**: Boswell, Gaskin, Harris, Heron, Lock,

Lovell, Loveridge, Shaw, Smith, Vaughan
**Enos:** Boswell
**Ephraim:** Booth, Boswell, Flear, Heron, Holland, Taylor, Walker, Wilson
**Eppy/ Eppie:** Lovell, McDonald, Varey
**Epson:** Jones
**Erbert:** See Herbert
**Erchie:** O'Neill
**Erelius:** Evans
**Eric:** Buckley, Heron, Scamp, Swales
**Erica/Erika (m):** Heron, Smith
**Ernest/Ernie:** Boswell, Cox, Draper, Eggins/ Huggins, Giles, Gordon, Gray, Heron, Lee, Leeson, Light, Lovell, Marshall, Mason, Matchett, Nixon, Penfold, Rawlings, Ripley, Roberts, Scamp, Scarrett, Shearing, Small, Smith, Tann, Taylor, Varey, Viney, Waite, White, Williams, Wood
**Ernestine:** Matthews
**Eros:** Heron, Robinson, Smith, Taylor, Cp Haros
**Erosabella:** Chilcott
**Erusha:** Boswell
**Erydina:** Smith
**Esaabella:** Hollowes
**Esau/Easaw:** Cartwright, Gray, Heron, Scarrett, Smith, Thorpe, Young
**Eser (m):** Heron
**Eshelender:** Heron
**Esho:** Smith
**Esme:** Johnson, Sherriff
**Esmeralda/Ismeralda:** Amer, Green, Hamer, Lee, Lock, Lovell
**Eso:** Smith
**Essa:** Smith
**Esther/Ester/Estha:** Ayres, Barton, Blyth, Boswell, Boyce, Boyling, Braddock, Brinkley, Brown, Buckland, Carter, Claydon/ Clayton, Clune, Cooper, Dennard, Dimberline, Eastwood, Faw, Ford, Gamester, Garrett, Gaskin, Grant, Gray, Harbour, Harris, Heron, Hicks, Hiscox, Hughes, Hunt, Lee, Loveridge, Marshall, Newley, Nichols(on), Osborne, Pierce, Randall, Rawlings, Ripley, Robinson, Rogers, Scamp, Scarrett, Sherriff, Smith, Spencer, Tann, Taylor, Theakstone, Thorne, Todd, Welsh, Wheeler,

Whitlock, Wilson, Winter, Wood, Young
**Ethel:** Boswell, Canner, Cater, Cooper, Fletcher, Gray, Gilby, Griffiths, Hall, Heron, James, Lee, Loveridge, Menday, Rawlins, Ripley, Rowley, Scott, Shepherd, Stanley, Stone, Wood, Young
**Ethela:** Synes
**Ethelbert:** Lovell
**Ethelenda:** Heron, Ryles
**Ethelreda:** Scamp
**Ethelward (m):** Scamp
**Etty/Ettie/Hetty:** Blyth, Boswell, Boyling, Jones, Sherriff, Smith
**Eunace:** Buckley, Claydon/Clayton, Lee, Smith
**Euphemia**: Boswell
**Eurosabella:** Chilcott
**Euryalus:** Florence
**Eusebius:** Boswell
**Eustace:** Gray
**Eva/Eve:** Boswell, Brinkley, Cooper, Frankham, Gray, Green, Lee, Lock, Lovell, Mitchell, Shaw, Smith, Snook, Varey
**Evan:** Lovelage
**Evelidia:** Smith
**Evelina/Eveline:** Boswell, Clarke, Palmer, Scamp
**Evelyn:** Batty, Boswell, MacDonald, Marshall, Ripley, Scamp, Sloper
**Evenilda:** Smith
**Evergreen (m and f):** Boswell (m and f), Heron (m), Price (f)
**Everilda:** Heron, Smith
**Everitt, -ett:** Elliott, Lee
**Evetti/Evetta:** Booth, Jones, Traylen
**Evrydina**: Boswell
**Evyrippe:** Boswell
**Ewin:** Mclean
**Ewing (m):** Stephens
**Exemphary:** Lee
**Exerify (f):** Boswell
**Exeriphgas**: Boswell
**Experience**: Boswell
**Ezabel:** Young
**Ezekiah:** Emmitt, Lock (Said to be a variant on Ezekiel, but more likely on Hezekiah)

**Ezekiel**: Baxter, Boswell, Braddock, Buckley, Jones, Lock, Roberts, Sherwood, Smith, Taylor
**Ezi/Ezzy:** Boswell, Evans, Heron, Roberts, Taylor
**Ezra:** Gray, Price, Scott, Wood
**Ezrie**: Boswell
**Ezzhau/Ezhaw:** Smith
**Faa:** Blyth
**Fabridge:** Smith
**Faden/Fardinand/Ferdinand:** Brown, Lee, Smith
**Fainena/Faiena:** Cooper, Penfold
**Faimi:** Smith
**Fainivel**: Boswell
**Fairnetti.** See Farnetty
**Faith**: Boswell, Finch, Gaines, Scamp, Smith
**Faithful:** Lee
**Faithina (m):** Lovell
**Faithenough:** Smith
**Falcon (m):** Walker
**Falhitt:** Baugh
**Fallerisa**: Boswell
**Fallowfield:** Anchorn, Lovell, Smith
**Famie:** See Faymie
**Familo (f):** Matthews
**Fan:** Deighton, Shaw
**Fandloe:** Loveridge
**Fani/Fany**: Boswell, Florence, Gray
**Fanny**: Arnold, Baker, Bell, Boswell, Campbell, Chapman, Cooper, Cox, Davies, Deighton, Draper, Emily, Finney, Ford, French, Fuller, Giles, Gollather, Gray, Greenway, Heron, Hinson, Holloway, James, Johnson, Jones, Kent, Knight, Leatherlund, Lee, Lovell, Loveridge, Matthews, McLean, Newbury, Newland, O'Dell, Pannell, Pettigrove, Price, Reader, Robinson, Roser, Scamp, Scarrott, Seager, Shaw, Sherrard, Smith, Stanley, Swallow, Todd, Tyler, Vernon, Walker, Watford, Wedgewood, Welsh, Winter, Wood, Young
**Fanny-Mant**: Boswell
**Farana**: Boswell
**Fardinand:** See Faden
**Farey:** Perkins

**Farmer:** Boswell
**Farnetty/Fairnetti/Farnetta/Fernetta/Franette/Fainette/Fernetti:** Ayres, Boswell, Buckland, Gray, Green, Heron, Lee, Scamp, Scott. Also see Fraynett
**Farrance (f):** Chilcott
**Fasche:** Cooper
**Faustina:** Boswell
**Faverel:** Heron
**Fay/Fe (m):** Wood. Probably an abbreviation of Feofilus.
**Faymi/Femi/Famie (f):** Boswell, Colman, Gray, Heron, Mochan, Robinson, Shaw, Smith, Taylor
**Fazenti:** Boswell
**Fazzi:** Boswell
**Fe:** See Fay
**Fee:** Price
**Feinise:** Lee
**Felere:** Boswell
**Feli (m):** Heron
**Felice:** Cooper
**Felicia:** Boswell
**Felix:** Boswell, Doran, Gray, Heron, Jordan, Lee, Shaw, Sherriff
**Femi:** See Faymi
**Fenella:** Wood
**Fenez(i)a:** Boswell
**Fenieman:** See Fenniman
**Fenloe:** Boswell
**Fennik/Fenwick:** Boswell, Heron, Lovell, Smith. Cp Phoenix
**Fennimore:** See Finnamore.
**Fennix:** See Fennik
**Feofilus:** Griffiths, Wood
**Ferdinand/Ferdinado:** See Faden
**Fergus:** Boswell, Scott
**Feriel (f): Heron**
**Fernetta:** See Farnetty.
**Fero (m):** Heron, Lovell. Cp Pharaoh
**Fezanti/Fezandi:** Buckland, Fenner, Smith. Cp Pheasant
**Fiancé/ Fiancy:** Green, Orchard, Richards, **Smith**
**Fiarice:** Smith
**Field (f):** Jackson, Rogers

**Filda:** Stanley
**Fili:** Gray, Green
**Filisia:** French
**Filliday:** Gray
**Finette:** Smith
**Finial:** Smith
**Finiman/Fenieman:** James, Jones, Lock
**Finnamore/Fennimore:** Boswell, Lee, Shaw. Cp Phinnymore
**Finney:** Shaw, Smith
**Fiona:** Scamp
**Flashun:** Lee
**Fleet (f):** Gray
**Fletcher (m):** Mansfield
**Fleur:** Chilcott
**Flewlin (m):** Shaw
**Flo(e(:** Brinkley, Scamp
**Floie:** Scamp, Townsend
**Flora:** Bennett, Boswell, Lee, Scamp, Smith, Stephens, Stork, Swales, Templeman
**Flore:** Lovell
**Florence:** Anthill, Boswell, Buckley, Butler, Chilcott, Crane, Drawbridge, Duck, Gorman, Gray, Heron, Hooper, Jones, Lee, Lovell, Loveridge, Lucas, Mace, Mears, Mills, Moss, Nelson, Osborne, Potter, Price, Putteich, Redfearn, Rogers, Savage, Scamp, Sloper, Smith, Stephens, Turner, Veti, Walker, Wheeler, Wood,
**Florentia:** Heron, Nelson, Smith
**Florina:** Cooper
**Florrie/Florae/Florie:** Booth, Boswell, Florence, Flynn, Ford, Griffiths, Hale, Hill, Johnson, Lee, Livermore, Nelson, Reynolds, Smith, Swallow, Taylor, Thomas
**Flossie:** Curl
**Flowery:** Scamp
**Floyd:** Wood
**Fountain:** Page
**Fowk (m):** Gray, Heron, Rogers
**Fox (f):** Douglas
**Foxton:** McKenzie
**Frampton (m)**: Baildon, Boswell, Buckland, Heron, Lee, Pickles,

Scarrett

**Fran:** Clayton/Claydon

**France:** Roberts

**Frances:** Arnold, Bailey, Boswell, Brown, Butler, Charlotte, Crocker, Davies, Eastwood, Elliott, Finney, Gaskin, Glaizier, Gollather, Gray, Hammond, Heron, Jones, Lee, Lovell, Mace, Martin, Metcalf, Mills, Pullen, Redworth, Richards, Robinson, Rogers, Rowland, Scamp, Shaw, Sherriff, Sivers, Smith, Strand, Swales, Swallow, Tetley, Thomas, Todd, Varey, Walker, Wallace, Wass, Wood, Young

**Francesca:** Boswell, Porter

**Francie/Francy:** Faw, Mitchell

**Francis:** Beckett, Boswell, Bowers, Bronger, Brown, Buckland, Carrick, Chilcott, Faw, Flynn, Garrett, Gaskin, Gray, Green, Hamer, Hardy, Harris, Heap, Heron, Hogg, Holmes, Holt, Hughes, Kelbie, Kitt, Lee, Light, Lovell, Lowe, Marshall, Miller, Noble, Parker, Penfold, Rawlins, Robinson, Rogers, Rostron, Rowland, Scamp, Shaw, Sherriff, Smallwood, Smith, Squires, Stephens, Stephenson, Sutherland, Swales, Thompson, Townsend, Traylen, Walker, Wallace, Ward, Welsh, Wheatley, Wharton, Wiltshire, Wood

**Francisca:** Porter

**Francisco:** Bankley

**Franette:** See Farnetty

**Frank:** Baker, Boswell, Bowers, Buckley, Carter, Collins, Cook, Cooper, Davies, Dinson, Dixon, Doe, Dolan, Elliott, Gurneye, Harber, Hardy, Hedges, Heron, Johnson, Jones, Kelly, Knight, Lee, Lovell, Mapplebeck, Miller, Mitchell, Nail, Page, Parker, Payne, Penfold, Ripley, Russell, Scamp, Sharp, Small, Smith, Stanford Stanley, Taylor, Todd, Vincent, Warner, Waterfield, Wharnell, Wharton, Wilson, Wood

**Frankie:** Scamp

**Franny (f):** Gray

**Fraser:** Boswell

**Fratlow:** Boswell

**Fraynett:** Boswell. And see Farnetty

**Fred/Freddy:** Adams, Alford, Booth, Boswell, Bowers, Brinkley, Buckland, Buckle, Bull, Cartidge, Cole, Finney, Florence, Ford, Frankham, Franklin, Gentle, Goldman, Goodwill, Gray, Harris,

Heron, Lee, Light, Lock, Loveridge, Miller, Orchard, Parker, Price, Ray, Reddfearn, Roberts, Robinson, Rust, Sands. Scarrett, Shaw, Sherriff, Smith, Swallow, Taylor, Turner, Venus, Walker, Webb, Whitlock, Wickens, Willett, Williams, Young
**Freda:** Black, Lee, Lovell, Parry, Smith
**Freddie:** Brinkley, Gray, Ray, Shaw
**Frederic(k):** Archer, Baker, Ball, Beckett, Bond, Booth, Boswell, Boyce, Bugg, Bull, Burton, Campbell, Carter, Chapman, Charles, Cooper, Day, Davies, Deakin, Dixon, Draper, Duck, Dye, Florence, Ford, Frankham, Fuller, Gamester, Gow, Gray, Green, Hale, Harrington, Harris, Heap, Heron, Hill, Hughes, James, Johnson, Jones, Lee, Linwood, Lock, Lovell, Loveridge, Matthews, McLean, Mochan, Moseley, Newbury, Parker, Penfold, Poll, Price, Ratcliffe, Ripley, Roberts, Rogers, Rowley, Sanger, Scamp, Scarrett, Scott, Shaw, Sivier, Small, Smith, Stanley, Stephens, Stork, Swales, Synes, Taylor, Todd, Twinn, Tyrant, Ward, Watford, Wenman, Weston, Westrop, Willett, Williams, Wood
**Freedom (m):** Boswell, Buckland, Cole, Gentle, Lane, Matthews, Randle, Rawlings
**Freedom (f):** Gentle
**Freeman:** Lane
**Frenny:** Scarrett
**Freya:** Scamp
**Friday (f):** Wilson
**Friederike (f):** Boswell
**Fright Fue:** See Fue
**Frind:** Lee
**Fronega:** Boswell, Johnson
**Fronya:** Young
**Fucsia:** Smith
**Fue:** Brown, Stapleton
**Funary:** Lovell
**Funny:** Barton
**Future:** Rogers
**Gabrail:** Redfern
**Gabriel:** Mercer, Price, Scarrott
**Gabriella:** Scamp
**Gad:** Taylor
**Gager (f):** Wood

**Gail:** Price
**Gainus (m):** Taylor. Cp Genus
**Gaius:** Lee
**Galick:** Smith
**Gamater/ Gamester:** Grace, Smith
**Gamfront: (m)** Boswell
**Ganation:** Buckley
**Garanor:** Smith
**Gardener:** Boswell
**Garforth:** Brook
**Garnation:** Smith
**Garrett (m):** Heron
**Garthorita:** Wood
**Gartrude:** Taylor
**Gary:** Cooper, Scamp
**Gaskell (f):** Grice
**Gateus:** Harris
**Gawin:** Trotter
**Gaye:** Scarrott
**Ged:** Lee
**Gehazi:** Quenton/Quinton
**Gelaias:** Price. Cp Golias
**Geleyr:** Baillie
**Gemma/ Grame:** Graeme, Scamp
**General:** See Gineral.
**Generina**: Boswell
**Genila/Genillia:** Bean/Beaney, Ripley. Cp Gentila
**Gennat:** Deighton
**Genobye**: Boswell
**Genti/Gentee (f):** Boswell, Boyling, Brazil, Buckley, Burton, Cooper, Deighton, Gray, Gudgeon, Heron, Jones, Joules, Leatherland, Lee, Livermore, Orchard, Palmer, Printer, Scamp, Shaw, Sherriff, Smith, Stone, Tompsatt. Var. on Gentila. Also see Genintea and Jenti.
**Gentil(l)a/ Gentilier:** Ayres, Cooper, Lee, Scarrett, Small, Smith. Cp Genila
**Gentinea:** Scamp. Also see Genti.
**Gentle (f):** Deighton, Small
**Genus:** Lee, Taylor. Cp Gainus

**Geo:** Douglas
**Geoffrey:** Lee, Scamp, Sherriff
**Geordie:** Faw
**George:** Most families.
**Georgie:** Boswell
**Georgina/Georgiano, /-a (f):** Allen, Boswell, Bowers, Buckland, Burton, Buttersmith, Chapman, Cooper, Draper, Florence, Holland, Jones,. Lee, Light, Lovell, Loveridge, Mitchell, Oadby, Palmer, Peat, Price, Primley, Sanger, Scamp, Small, Smith, Stephens, Taylor
**Georgina (m):** Boswell
**Gerald:** Johnson, Scamp, Smith
**Geraldine/Geraline:** Booth, Gaskin, Price
**Gerania:** Barney
**Geranimus:** Boswell
**Geranium:** Draper, Taylor
**Gerona (f):** Lock. Cp Gevena
**Gerry:** Foxall
**Gertrude**: Ayres, Boswell, Bothwell, Culline, Farnfield, Finney, George, Harbor, Heron, Hollister, Lee, Lovell, Ripley, Scamp, Scarrett, Shepherd, Smith, Taylor, Waite, Wood, Wright
**Gervas/Gervaise**: Boswell, Lee, Smith
**Gevena/Gevona (f):** Lock. Cp Gerona
**Gilbert**: Boswell, Cox, Finney, Ford, Johnson, Lovell, Scamp, Smith
**Gilderoy**: Boswell, Buckland, Clayton, Finney, Heron, Holland, Lee, Scamp, Smith
**Giles:** Boswell, Bowers, Green, Hather, McLean, Wallett
**Gillard (m):** Scamp
**Gillian:** Frankham, Lovell
**Gilly:** Finney
**Gillyam:** Boswell
**Gilroy:** Lee, Smith, Othen
**Gina:** Biddle, Scarrett
**Gineral/Gonerel:** Blyth, Buckland, Cooper
**Ginger:** Lee
**Gipsy:** Petulengro
**Gladys**: Ayres, Bacon, Boswell, Dale, Hough, Lee, Linwood, Lovell, Pike, Ripley, Scamp, Sherriff, Webber, Wilshaw

**Glenda:** Lee
**Gloreni/Glorina:** Evans, Heron, Lovell
**Gloria:** Lee
**Glorinda:** Scamp
**Glory:** Loveridge
**Glossop (f):** Watson
**Glover (f):** Boswell
**Glympton:** Clayton
**Godbehear:** Boswell
**Godfrey:** Boswell, Heron, Lovell, Wood
**Golden:** Hope
**Golia/Golier/Golias/Goley (m):** Beldom, Boswell, Coats, Doe, Gray, Heron, Price, Smith
**Goliath:** Boswell, Bowers, Cole, Heron, Shaw, Synes. Note that the names Golias and Goliath may be identical.
**Gonerel:** See Gineral
**Goney:** Robinson
**Gonrelatter:** Smith
**Gonzaletta:** Smith. Cp Kunsaletta
**Gooditer:** Richardson
**Goody:** Musgrave
**Goosie/Goosey:** Allen, Chilcott, Young
**Gorde:** Penfold
**Gordon (m):** Boswell, Cooke, Heron, Scamp, Scarrett, Stanley
**Gordon (f):** Price
**Gorgino:** Smith
**Gormy:** Gray
**Gotobed:** Flear (This name is almost certainly a joke at a census official's expense.)
**Grabham (f):** Davies
**Grace (f):** Boswell, Buckley, Couldon, Dye, Finney, Golding, Harbor, Heron, Johnson, Jones, Lee, Lovell, Mannion, Mosby, Scamp, Shiress, Sibley, Smith, Stewart, Swales, Taylor, Walker, Wilkinson
**Grace (m):** Boswell
**Graeme/Graham:** Lee, Scamp
**Grainzi:** Lee
**Graipi:** Anchorn, Lovell, Smith
**Grallina:** Smith

**Graner/Granor:** Eames, Evans
**Granny Mistress:** Stapleton
**Grasta:** Neyn
**Gravelini/Graveli/ Gravellene:** Bates, Boswell, Buckland, Heron, Lee, McFarlane, Robinson, Scamp, Sherriff, Smith
**Green:** Boswell
**Greengown:** Gray
**Greenleaf (f):** Boswell, Buckland, Heron, Lock
**Greenleaf (m):** Lock
**Greenshirt:** Carey. Presumably a nickname
**Gregory:** Webb, Wilson
**Grenton:** Boswell
**Greta:** Lee
**Griffith:** Edwards, Lee
**Grosabella:** Chilcott
**Grosvenor (f):** Scamp
**Gui:** Heron
**Guilly:** Smith. Cp Aquila
**Guliana**: Boswell
**Gully:** See Aquilla
**Gulvado**: Boswell
**Gulvater.** See Gulvado
**Gus:** Gray, Mace, Middleton. Probably deriving from Augustus. Cp Gustus
**Gussie:** Gray
**Gusta:** Palmer
**Gustarus:** Boswell
**Guster:** Heron
**Gustus/Gustun:** Smith. Variant on Augustus, cp Gus
**Gwen: Wood**
**Gwendoline:** Lovell, Taylor
**Gwyn:** Taylor
**Haddy:** Loveridge
**Hagar:** Burton, Heron, Stanley
**Haggi**: Boswell, Smith
**Hailwood:** Smith
**Hairam:** Boswell, Buckley
**Hairy:** Prestage. Nickname
**Haldenby:** Lee

**Hales (f):** Bridges, Fletcher
**Hambro:** Smith
**Hamilton:** Forest
**Hamlet:** Rogers
**Hammer:** See Hammerlane
**Hammerlane/Hameline/Hammer/ Hemelen/ Hamelen (m):** Boswell, Lee, Palmer, Sibly, Smith, Whatnell
**Hamutal:** Loker
**Hanara:** Smith
**Handrus:** Lee
**Hanibal:** Boswell
**Haniel:** Boswell
**Hann**: Boswell
**Hannah:** Most families
**Hanniel/Hannibel** (and variations): Boswell, Forest, Swales
**Hannis (f):** Miller
**Hanson:** Barnes
**Happy**: Boswell
**Hapsy:** Barton, Scamp
**Harce:** Brown
**Harcourt:** Taylor
**Harding (f):** McLean,
**Harding (m):** Odell
**Hardmaid**: Boswell
**Hardwick (m):** Lee
**Hardy (m):** Lee
**Harelip:** Matthews. Presumably only as a nickname
**Haremania:** Scott
**Hargreaves (m):** Lee
**Harker (m):** Lee
**Harkless:** Bluett, Smith, cp Arkless and Hercules
**Harold:** Boswell, Finney, Heron, Lovell, Miller, Mochan, Roberts, Smith, Welsh
**Haros:** Robinson, Smith. Cp Eros.
**Harriet/Harriott/Harriote:** Most families
**Harris:** Lovell
**Harrodine:** Gray
**Harroly/ Harilah/ Herilah**: Boswell. Cp Riley
**Harry:** Ashington, Baker, Ball, Boswell, Brazier, Burton, Butler,

Carter, Cater, Chilcott, Coate(s), Collins, Collison, Colman, Cooper, Draper, Farnfield, Fenwick, Finney, Freelove, French, Fuller, Godsmark, Graham, Gray, Gumble, Hall, Hamelen, Hedges, Heron, Holland, Jackson, James, Jones, Joules, Killick, Lee, Little, Lovell, Matthews, Middleton, Miller, Mitchell, Morgan, Myers, Nichols/Nicholson, Newbury, Orchard, Palmer, Percago, Phillips, Philpott, Price, Quinton, Rose, Ross, Rumble, Ryles, Scarrett, Selmes, Sevellth, Smith, Stephens, Sweatman, Sykes, Taylor, Thompson, Walker, Webb, Wells, Wenan, Wilson, Wood

**Hartley:** Boswell, Smith
**Harty:** Keet
**Harvey:** Boswell, Scamp, Smith
**Havant:** Scamp
**Hawel:** See Howell
**Hawen (m):** Lee (Possibly a variation on Hawniel, hence Hannibal.
**Hawker (m):** Scamp
**Hawksley (f):**
**Hawni:** See Horny
**Hawniel.** See Hanniel
**Hayar:** Burton
**Haydn:** Boswell
**Hayfield:** Buckland
**Hayward (m):** Scamp
**Hayse:** Boswe Scamp
**Hazel/Hazael:** Clarke, Lee, Scamp
**Heathcliff:** Boswell
**Hebekah:** Heron
**Hector:** Buckland, Fenner
**Hedji (m):** Heron, Sherriff
**Heidi (f):** Scamp
**Heinrich:** Boswell
**Helen:** Blyth, Boswell, Brown, Clarke, Collins, Cooper, Dawson, Douglas, Faa, Gilbert, Gray, Grice, Heron, Hodgson, Hogg, Humphries, Ingram, Lee, Lovell, McChesney, Noble, Oliver, Pendleton, Price, Redpath, Rogers, Scamp, Shaw, Sherriff, Smith, Spencer, Stephens, Taylor, Terry, Toogood, Wilson, Yorkston
**Helena (f):** Charlott, Greedas, Laurence, Quinlan, Scamp

**Hellewell:** Swales
**Hemerlon:** See Hammerlane
**Hemery:** Philip(es)
**Hemlock:** Smith
**Hendray:** Price, Reed
**Hennessey:** Griffiths
**Hennetta:** Lee. Probably a var. on Henrietta.
**Henny:** Loveridge
**Henrietta**: Baillie, Boswell, Buckley, Carter, Cheeseman, Cooper, Copeland, Fletcher, Florence, Giles, Hamer, Hasrings, Hobbing, Lee, Lock, Loveridge, Parker, Scamp, Smith, Taylor, Watson, Wilson
**Henrimaretta:** Lovell
**Henry:** Most families
**Hensley:** Davies
**Henty (f):** Boswell, Boyling, Sherriff, Smith
**Hepzibah/Hepsabel**: Booth, Boswell, Heron, Lee, Oadley
**Heraney:** Smith
**Herbert/Herbie/ Erbert:** Baker, Baxter, Blackman, Boswell, Buckland, Burton, Carter, Closs, Elphick, Gumble, Harris, Heron, Holland, Johnson, Jones, King, Lee, Lock, Lovell, Mace, Madley, McFarlane, McLean, Morris, Procter, Rickman, Ripley, Rogers, Sanger, Scamp, Scarrett, Sherriff, Small, Smith, Stanley, Tann, Townsend, Weller, Whatnell, Wood, Wyn, Young
**Hercules/ Herculis**: Boswell, Buckley, Clay, Gray, Smith, Young. Cp Arkless
**Herilah**: See Harroly and cp Riley
**Heron:** Smith
**Heshaw:** Smith
**Hesicam:** Alford
**Hesketh:** Lee
**Hesod**: Boswell
**Hester/ Hesther:** Boswell, Colley, Gamester, Hobbs, James, Lee, Lock, Rawlings, Roberts, Scamp, Shaw, Smith
**Hetty (f):** See Etty.
**Heturah (f):** Lee
**Heyward (m):** Scamp
**Hezekiah/Hezzy:** Boswell, Brown, Frankham, Griggs, Heron, Lee, Lock, Loveridge, Mellor, Penfold, Quentin, Roberts, Smith,

Stanley, Synes, Taylor
**Hezzy:** See Hezekiah.
**Hibernia:** Cook
**Hickings (m):** Scamp
**Hicks (m):** Scamp
**Hida:** Lovell
**Hiddy:** ` Smith
**Higgs:** Smith
**High:** Williams. Possibly a misunderstanding for Hugh.
**Hilarie:** Brown
**Hilda:** Finney, Harris, Lovell, Pike, Ripley, Scamp, Stone, Taylor
**Hiela:** Lovell
**Hilton:** Heron
**Hiram/Hyram:** Boswell, Buckley, Gray, Hopewell, Pidgley, Price, Rogers
**Hirrins:** Robinson
**Hiwel:** See Howel
**Hobey:** Smith
**Hogg:** Swales
**Holland (m):** Lee, Quick
**Hollidays (m):** Taylor
**Holly:** Hope
**Holmes:** Boswell
**Holt Hothea**: Boswell
**Homey/ Homei/ Homer:** Emmett, Harris, Heath, Lee, Lock, Scamp
**Honor(i)a (f):** Booth, Boswell, Heron, Lovell, Scamp
**Hono(u)r:** Boswell, Buckland, Hazard, `Smith
**Hookey:** Smith
**Hope (f):** Boswell, Johnson, Sherriff
**Hope (m):** Booth, Boswell, Finch, French, Lee, Price, Sherriff
**Hopeful:** Lee
**Hop-Pole:** Scamp
**Hopsalina (f):** Lovell, Loveridge
**Hopter (f):** Shaw. Nickname deriving from Helicopter as Kelly-Hopter
**Hora (f):** Boswell
**Horace**: Ayres, Boswell, Bowers, Coate(s), Colman, Finney, Hannah, Lee, Oadley, Scamp, Smith, Stanley, Tann, Taylor,

White, Willett, Winson
**Horatio/Oratio:** Brockless, Buckley, Lee
**Horny:** Lee (Not a nickname, but a var. on Hawen)
**Hosea/Hosey:** Boswell, Lee
**Hosanna/Hoshanna**: Boswell, Loveridge, Shales
**Hothe(a)miah:** Boswell
**Houge:** Ingram, Marshall. Prob. A variant on Hugh.
**Howard:** Critchley, Lovell
**Howell/Hawel/ Hiwel:** Boswell, Lovell, Wood
**Hubert:** Boswell, Lee, Osborne, Smith
**Hudson (m):** Lee
**Huestar (f):** Sherriff
**Hugh/Hughie**: Boswell, Burton, Connor, Cooper, Evans, Finney, Fury, Graham, Gray, Grice, Jackson, James, Jones, Lovell, Macfee, Maguire, Martin, McLaughlin, McLean, Mochan, Roberts, Robinson, Shaw, Simms, Smith, Steele, Swales, Wells, Williams,Williamson
**Hughes:** Boswell
**Hugo**: Boswell, Gibbs
**Humfriddi:** Taylor
**Humphrey:** Gray, Heron, Shaw, Smith, Taylor
**Hutson (m):** Mace
**Hutty:** Townsend
**Hyram:** See Hiram
**Iadire:** Frankham
**Ian:** Lee, Pattinson, Scarrett
**Ianvia:** Boswell
**Ida:** Boswell, Cole, Harrison, Hathaway, Mace, Sanger
**Iddaday/Idade:** Heron, Nelson
**Idris:** Lee, Lovell
**Idjun:** Cooper
**Iher:** Toogood
**Ike:** Smith
**Iles (m):** Scamp
**Ilona:** Lee
**Immanuel.** See Emmanuel
**Immyna:** Wood
**Ina:** Scamp
**Inan (m):** Gray, Heron, King, Young

**Indiana:** Lee
**Inez:** Lee
**Inji:** Heron
**Inverto:** Boswell
**Invicta:** Scamp
**Iram:** Oadley
**Irene:** Cooper, Finney, Gray, Lovell, Ripley, Robinson, Scamp, Scarrett
**Ireza:** Smith
**Iris:** Gaskin, Gray, Lovell, Scamp, Shepherd, Smith
**Isa:** Lock
**Isaac:** Bailey, Benton, Berry, Booth, Boswell, Brewer, Buckland,.Cash, Chadwick, Cook, Draper, Evans, Gray, Heron, Hobbing, Hollins, Hubert, Johnson, Joules, Laney, Lee, Light, Lovell, Macfee, Mapplebeck, Miller, Newbury, Newlands, Nichols/Nicholson, Odell, Penfold, Phillips, Price, Proudley, Roberts, Robinson, Rogers, Scarrett, Shaw, Shepherd, Sherriff, Simms, Sinfield, Smith, Stanley, Stewart, Swales, Taylor, Thompson, Todd, Welsh, Winter, Wood
**Isaba:** Boswell
**Isabel(l)(e)/Isobel:** Baine(s), Booth, Brown, Boswell, Denton, Duncan, Faw, Gordon, Harrison, Hatton, Heron, Hungate, Johnson, Lancaster, Lee, Pattinson, Penfold, Peters, Price, Redpath, Richardson, Scamp, Scarrett, Shaw, Smith, Swales, Taylor, Thompson, Valentine, Wilson
**Isabella/Esabella/ Isbella:** Booth, Boswell, Burton, Cartidge, Chilcott, Claydon/ Clayton, Collins, Davison, Deighton, Elliott, Fletcher, Florence, Foster, Gaskin, Graham, Gray, Harris, Hollowes, Johnson, Kennedy, Lee, Lock, Lovell, Marshall, Miller, Morgan, Palmer, Price, Rawlins, Roberts, Robinson, Rose, Scamp, Smith, Stenning, Stewart, Stubbs, Swales, Tait, Thompson, Todd, Turner, Walmsley, Wass, Watson, Williamson
**Isaiah:** Boswell, Butler, Heron, Holland, Lock, Lovell, Pierce, Smith, Winter
**Ishmael/Ismail:** Heron, James, Scarrett, Sherriff, Steele
**Ismeralda:** See Esmeralda
**Isot**: Boswell
**Isra:** Lee
**Israel**: Booth, Boswell, Draper, Evans, Gray, Lee, Lovell, Parker,

Sherrard, Smith
**Ithal:** Lee
**Ivan:** Lovell
**Ives (m):** Heron
**Ivory:** Taylor
**Ivy:** Hall, Hedges, Heron, Lee, Lovell, Pharo, Ripley, Scamp, Scarrett, Sloper, Taylor, Webber, Whittle
**Iyott:** Loveridge
**Iza:** Boswell, Heron, Lee, Young
**Izare:** Jackson
**Izeea/Iza:** Finney, Lock, Sherriff, Smith. Variant on Isaiah
**Izek:** Crosby
**Jabez:** Boswell, Buckland, Heron, Lee, Smith
**Jabita:** Lawson
**Jack**: Boswell, Botton, Brazil, Buckland, Burnside, Butler, Campbell, Chapman, Clarke, Cooper, Davies, Dawson, Dixon, Eastwood, Eaves, Elliott, Finney, Fuller, Gibson, Gray, Green, Gregory, Harnson, Harris, Heron, Higgins, Hiscox, How, Hughes, Jack, Jones, Killick, Kilrain, King, Lee, Lewis, Lock, Lovell, Loveridge, Mace, Mason, Matchett, Miles, Musto, Parry, Penfold, Powell, Porter, Price, Renals, Ripley, Roberts, Scamp, Scarrett, Shaw, Small, Smith, Stacey, Taylor, Todd, Townsend, Varey, Weaver, Webb, White, Williams, Wilson
**Jackie:** Taylor
**Jackson (m):** Lee
**Jacob**: Belcher, Biddle, Boswell, Buckland, Cooper, Eptall, Forest, Lee, Lowther, Marshall, Middleton, Miller, Ratcliffe, Rewbrey, Rossiter, Scarrett, Smith, Tait, Todd, Varey
**Jacqueline:** Finney, Gray, Scamp, Shepherd, Thomas
**Jade:** Gray
**Jago:** Boswell
**Jaina:** Buckley
**James:** Most families
**Jamie:** See Jamesa
**Jan:** Northan
**Jane/Janie:** Most families
**Janesa:** Strand, Young
**Janet/Janette:** Bassett, Beaney, Blythe, Boswell, Heron, Hilton, Jamieson, Kelbie, Killick, Lee, Lovell, Maxwell, Nicols/ Nicholson,

Parker, Price, Scarrett, Smith, Scamp, Stewart, Tait, Taylor, White, Wilson, Wood, Young
**Janetta:** Beaney
**Janice:** Lee
**Janie:** See Jane
**Janine:** Scamp
**Janne:** Kerr
**Janus:** Heron
**Jarrett:** Vaughan
**Jarv:** Calladine, Lee
**Jarvis**: Boswell, Heron
**Jason:** Gray, Webb
**Jasper**: Boswell, Cooper, Lee, Lovell, Scarrett, Shaw, Smith, Toogood, Wood
**Jay (m):** Marshall
**Jaynie:** See Jane
**Jean**: Boswell, Brown, Faw, Finney, Gordon, Heron, Hutchinson, Ingram, Kerr, Lee, Lowrie, Mackenzie, Ransley, Ross, Ruthven, Scamp, Shaw, Stone, Wilson, Yorkston
**Jeanette:** Cooper, Lee, Stone
**Jefferson:** Blyth
**Jeffery:** Lee, Smith
**Jellery:** Smith
**Jem/Jemmy:** Claydon/Clayton, Driscoll, Lee, Lovell, Mace, Smith
**Jemima**: Aldridge, Ayres, Black, Boswell, Brazil, Brown, Cox, Doe, Elliott, Fletcher, Frankham, Harris, Heron, James, Mitchell, Nichols, Nicholson, Pike, Porter, Rogers, Ryles, Scott, Shaw, Small, Smith, Vaughan, Walker, Yelding
**Jemys:** Gray
**Jenkin:** Cowdiddle
**Jennamintie:** Scamp
**Jen(n)ett(a):** Clarke, Dooley, Lovell, Marshall, Taylor, Walker, Wood, Young
**Jennifer: Lovell,** Scarrett, Scott, Smith
**Jenny**: Boswell, Collins, Cooper, Graham, Price, Wharnell
**Jentela/Jentilia/Jenteeler/Jentille:** Brines, Clarke, Harrison, Lee, Smith, Williams
**Jenty (f):** Colley, Gray, Lee, Smith. Var. on Genti.
**Jeppy:** Smith

**Jeptha:** Boswell, Varey
**Jeremiah:** Boswell, Buckley, Burton, Clayton, Griffiths, Hedges, Jones, Lee, Lock, Murphy, Penfold, Scott, Shaw, Sleddin, Smith, Swales, Swann, Taylor, Williams, Wood
**Jeremy:** Sowden
**Jerry:** Burton, Connor(s)
**Jerusalem:** Lovell, Smith
**Jesiah:** Smith
**Jesse/Jessie**: Ayres, Barnes, Booth, Boswell, Bray, Brown, Burton, Butler, Cooper, Crampton, Finney, Frankham, Gray, Griffiths, Hatton, Heron, James, Jones, Lee, Lovell, Loveridge, Odell, Penfold, Price, Ripley, Robinson, Shaw, Shepherd, Small, Smith, Taylor, Templeman, Wells, Wiggins, Woodyear
**Jesse (m):** Griffiths, Ripley, Roberts
**Jestin:** Lee
**Jethel:** Lee
**Jethro:** Shaw
**Jetta:** Lovell
**Jigero/Jigo:** Gray
**Jim:** See James
**Jim-Boy:** Frankham. The note under John-Boy also applies.
**Jiminez:** Malla
**Jin:** Smith
**Jineral.** See Gineral
**Jini/ Jinny:** Brown, Heron
**Jo (m):** Howard
**Joab:** Oadley, Smith
**Joah:** Lee
**Joan:** Boswell, Cole, Cowper, Finney, Heron, Inwood, Mochan, Noble, Scamp, Scarrett
**Jo(h)an(n)a (h):** Boswell, Evans, Heron, Holland, Johnson, Lock, Mochan, Murphy, Sherriff, Smith, Warner
**Joani**: Boswell, Jackson
**Joanna/Johanna:** Gray, Lovey, Scamp, Shentan, Sherriff
**Joanne:** Price, Stanley
**Joathan:** Lee
**Job:** Biddle, Boswell, Brazil, Buckland, Camfield, Carey, Castle, Clayton, Cole, Cooper, Davies, Gregory, Hares, Heron, James, Johnson, Jones, Lamb, Lee, Loveridge, Matthews, Nichols,

Nicholson, Orchard, Rawlings, Sa(u)nders, Sherrard, Sherriff, Smith, Stephens, Williams

**Joby/Jobi/Joeb:** Brinkley, Cooper, Gray, Johnson, Lee, Loveridge, Philip(s), Pidgley, Shaw, Smith, Stephens

**Jock:** Johnson, Marshall, McFarlane

**Jockey:** Webb

**Jodie:** Scamp

**Joe(y):** See Joseph

**Joel:** Baker, Boswell

**Joha:** Ingram

**Johann:** Cordes

**Joe:** See Joseph

**Joeb:** Ripley

**Joel:** Baker, Ward

**John:** Most families

**John-boy:** Though many Gypsies called John add '-boy' to it, as a kind of nickname, those listed here are individuals apparently specifically named John-boy: Butler, Connor(s), Marshall, Price, Taylor

**Johnny:** See John.

**Joiner:** Buckley

**Joleth:** Fowling

**Jonah:** Albon, Todd

**Jonas**: Boswell, Buckley, Dinson, Ellis, Gibson, Heron, Holdsworth, Heron, Holland, Huggins, Lee, Morton, Scarrett, Selby, Shaw, Sherriff, Small, Smith

**Jonathon**: Boswell, Brinkley, Burrow, Gamester, Heron, Herrett, Lee, Newbury, Odell, Orchard, Parker, Powell, Roberts, Scamp, Scarrett, Shepherd, Smith, Wharton, Wheeler, Wilson, Wood

**Jones:** Buckley

**Jonet**: Janet

**Joo:** Boswell

**Jorden (m):** Lee

**Jos**: Boswell

**Joscelin**: Boswell

**Joseph:** Adams, Anderson, Anthill, Archer, Arnold, Ashforth, Austin, Bailey, Baker, Ball, Barney, Barrkinger, Beckett, Berriman, Bibby, Billings, Birley, Booth, Boswell, Boyce, Bramwell, Breeds, Britton, Brooker, Brown, Buckland, Buckley,

Burgess, Burton, Caris(s), Carter, Cater, Chapman, Charlotte, Clarke, Clayton, Coats, Cooper, Crabtree, Cragg, Crutcher, Cundy, Davies, Dawson, Dean, Dixon, Doe, Dolan, Draper, Eastwood, Elvin, Emmett, Fenner, Ferrari, Finney, Fisher, Flint, Forster, Fox, Frankham, Gamester, Gilbert, Giles, Gillum, Goss, Gray, Green, Grunder, Guthrie, Hadson, Hall, Harrison, Harvey, Heron, Herrikings, Hicks, Hird, Hislop, Hogden, Holden, Holland, Howard, Hudson, Ironside, Iser, Jeffrey/ Jeffs, Johnson, Jones, Keith, Kitson, Kitto, Knowles, Leatherlund, Lee, Linwood, Little, Lock, Lovell, Loveridge, Lowther, Manton, Martin, Mason, Matthews, McCready, McLean, Miller, Mills, Mitchell, Mochan, Mosby, Munday, Newbury, Nichols(on), Noble, Northan, Oadley, Orchard, Palmer, Parry, Pebody, Penfold, Pew, Phillips, Powell, Price, Procter, Rawlings, Reader, Renton, Richardson, Ripley, Roberts, Rogers, Royles, Scammell, Scamp, Scarrett, Shaw, Shepherd, Sherriff, Shuker, Simons, Slimm, Small, Smith, Spragg, Squires, Stephens, Stokes, Swales, Swift, Tapsall, Taylor, Todd, Tomlinson, Vallis, Vanis, Varey, Vincent, Walker, Wallace, Waller, Wallett, Wathen, Watkinson, Wells, Welsh, Wesseldine, Whatnell, Whatton, White, Wilks, Williams, Willoughby, Wilson, Winders, Wood, Woolley, Young

**Josepha:** Berryman
**Josephine:** Lee, Roman. Scamp, Shepherd
**Josh:** Lovell
**Josho/Joshu:** Heron, Stanley
**Joshua:** Allen, Booth, Boswell, Carter, Cook, Cooper, Eley, Ford, Gray, Heron, James, Lee, Lovell, Loveridge, Nichols/ Nicholson, Scamp, Shaw, Smith, Stanley, Stephens,
**Josiah/ Josea/ Chesaia**: Baker, Boswell, Burton, Gregory, Heron, James, Johnson, Joules, Lee, Lovell, Price, Scamp, Sherriff, Small, Smart, Smith, Stacey, Vaughan, Waller, Wass, Wells, Willoughby
**Josias:** Baillie, Lee, Smith
**Joy:** Lee, Scamp
**Joyce:** Bridges, Cuthbert, Gamester, Gray, Heron, King, Lee, Lovell, Manito, Penfold, Scamp, Smith, Stone
**Jubilee:** Jeffs/Jeffrey, Young
**Jude:** Roberts
**Judith:** Boswell, Fleckie, Graeme, Heron, Park, Pierce, Smith

**Julia (f):** Boswell, Buckland, Buckley, Ford, Gray, Hall, Herrick, Irving, Lee, Lotherington, Lovell, Miller, Newbury, Northan, Robinson, Scamp, Scarrett, Smart, Smith, Stanley, Swales, Tanner, Taylor, Thompson, Walker, Westrop, Wood
**Julia (m):** Macfarlane
**Julian:** Clarke, Lee, Scamp, Smith
**Julie:** Booth, Buckley, Collins, Heron, Lee, McCready, McFarlane, Scamp, Walker
**Juliet:** Boswell
**Julietta:** Radford
**Julise:** Boswell
**July:** Heron, Stanley
**Jumbo:** Emmett, Heath
**June:** Gibson, McDonald, Scamp
**Juphmia:** Florence
**Jupiter:** Smith
**Justia (f)** Rogers
**Justin:** Green
**Justinia**: Boswell, Buckley, Redpath, Smith
**Justine:** Deighton
**Kadelia:** Brown
**Kai (f):** Scott
**Kaia**: Boswell
**Kahomi**: Boswell
**Kaki:** Boswell. I regard this as a nickname amongst Boswells and Locks, amongst whom it is used to denote a 'lazy' eye, or one eye brown and one blue.
**Kaladain:** Booth
**Kalvin:** Scamp
**Kane:** Boswell
**Karen:** Scamp
**Karl:** Gray, Shepherd
**Kashi:** Boswell
**Kate/Katie:** Anderson, Bell, Boswell, Buckland, Coleman, Cook, Cox, Dawson, Dixon, Drawbridge, Ellen, Ford, Frewen, Fuller, Giles, Gray, Griffiths, Hayes, Holmes, Laurence, Lee, Lovell, Miller, Payne, Ratcliffe, Redworth, Ripley, Royal, Rumble, Scamp, Scarrott, Smith, Stanley, Taylor, Webb, Willett, Wright
**Kath:** Davies

**Katherina/Katerina:** Ayres, Buckley, Clouffle, Scamp
**Katherine/Kathryn:** Boswell, Deago, Docuria, Faw, Heron, Hogan, Holloway, Kelbie, Lee, Little, Rogers, Ryles, Scamp, Taylor, Wood
**Kathleen:** Black, Buckley, Cole, Finney, Gilbert, Gomms, Green, Hawkins, Heron, Lee, O'Neil, Penfold, Ripley, Scamp, Scarrett, Smith, Stone, Taylor
**Kathleen (m):** Heron
**Katie/Katey:** Hames, Heron
**Katina:** Scarrett
**Katteran:** Wright
**Kay:** Scamp
**Kaylea/Kayley (f):** Gray, Shepherd
**Keith:** Scamp, Scarrett
**Kekka:** Green. Probably a nickname from the imperative negative of Romany KEK.
**Kelly:** Cameron, Gibson, Gray, McCready, McDonald, McLean, Scamp, Shaw
**Kendrick:** Lee
**Kenneth/Kenny/Ken:** Booth, Boswell, Brown, Gray, Lee, Lewis, Scamp, Smith, Summerhill, Taylor
**Kenred:** Smith
**Kenza:** Boswell, Green, Lee, Taylor
**Kenzie:** Boswell, Thorpe
**Kenzilia/-illa**: Boswell
**Keran Karen:** Boswell
**Kerenda:** See Kurlenda
**Kerenhapuch/-haprugh/ -lappuch (f)**: Boswell, Mace
**Keria:** Smith
**Kerlenda:** See Kurlenda
**Kerr (f):** Hurst
**Kerry (f):** Lee, Scamp
**Kesi:** Palmer
**Keson:** Loveridge
**Kestarton:** Boswell
**Ketty:** Lree
**Ketura-h (f):** Ayres, Buckley, Rogers, Smith, Stanley
**Kevin/Kevan:** Finney, Lee, Matchett, Scamp
**Keytumas:** See Kiomi

**Kezi/Kezia(h)/Keza/Kizzy/Kizie/ Kissi/ Kesi/ Keazer/ Kezzy/ Kesia:** Booth, Boswell, Buck, Buckland, Cole, Cooper, Ellis, Everett, Frankham, Fuller, Green, Gregory, Heron, Ingram, Jarvis, Junnix, Kilsbie, Kindon, Lee, Marney, McFarlane, Nichols, Nicholson, Palmer, Percago, Rawlings, Scamp, Scarrett, Scott, Shaw, Sherriff, Simms, Skerry, Smith, Woodward, Wright. Cp Kisby and Tizzy.
**Kezwell:** Griffiths
**Kezzy:** Scott, Smith
**Khulai/Kulai (m):** Gray, Heron
**Kiandra:** Lee
**Kidney (f):** Buckland, Heron
**Kim:** Scamp
**Kiomi/Keytumas/Keomi (f):** Bonnett, Boswell, Buckley, Gray, Lovell, Taylor (Keytumas is a census officer's interpretation of Kiomi.)
**Kiona:** Bennett
**Kisby:** Draper. Cp Kezi.
**Kit:** Booth, Calot, Lovell, Mochan
**Kitchin (f):** Lee
**Kitten:** Boswell
**Kitty:** Bacon, Boswell, Buckley, Dickinson, Evans, Jeffrey/Jeffs, Scamp, Weaver, Winders
**Kizzy:** See Kezi
**Knight (m):** Huxley, Lock
**Knightly:** Smith
**Knott (m):** Scamp
**Knowles:** Heron
**Kodi:** Jones, Taylor
**Koli:** Lee, Scamp
**Konki:** Boswell, Gray
**Koralina:** See Coralina
**Kradista:** Price
**Krado(c)k:** Price
**Kristina:** See Christina
**Kruger:** Kilsby
**Kruza:** Boswell, Sherriff
**Kuchi:** Smith
**Kudi:** Smith

**Kulai:** See Khulai
**Kunsaletti:** See Conselletti
**Kurlenda/Kerlenda/Kerenda:** Lee, Smith
**Labana:** Boswell
**Labinia (f):** Scamp
**Labon/Laban:** Boulter, Lee, Lovell, Taylor
**Laboriney:** Gray
**Lac(e)y:** Draper
**Lackey:** Donelly
**Ladin:** Lovell
**Laidlaw (f):** Hogg
**Laila:** Draper, Lee, Taylor
**Laini:** Cooper, Lee, Smith
**Laino:** Birch
**Laisia:** Lovell
**Lakey:** Smith
**Lalor:** Lovell
**Lamas:** Smith
**Lambert:** Moore
**Lamerok/Lamrok:** Lock, Lovell
**Lan:** Johnson, Smith
**Lancelot/Launcelot:** Brown, Collins, Lee, Smith
**Lancy:** Palmer
**Lander/Landra:** Boswell, Lee, Scamp, Scarrett, Sherriff, Smith. Cp Orlander, but note that this is not the same as Leander.
**Landra:** Hedges
**Laney:** Palmer
**Langdon (f):** Scamp
**Langdon (m):** Scamp
**Lanson (f):** Freeman
**Larby:** Golby
**Lardi (m):** Hedges
**Laresa/Larissa:** Gray, Lee
**Larkin:** Boswell
**Larry/Lary/Larrie:** Lee, Mannion, Percago, Shaw
**Lateshopper:** Lee (Nickname)
**Latimer:** Lee
**Latissia:** Boswell
**Latitia:** Rogers. Cp Letitia

**Launcelot:** See Lancelot
**Laura:** Ayres, Berry, Boswell, Carter, Ford, Gray, Heron, Lee, Lovell, Murphy, Norman, Scamp, Smith, Stround, Templeman, Toogood, Willoughby
**Laurel/Lorel (f):** Booth, Lovell, Smith, Taylor, Toogood
**Lauren:** Faw
**Laurence:** Boswell, Brown, Buck, Crosbiter, Cross, Deighton, Finney, Gray, Heron, Law, Lee, Marshall, McLean, Procter, Robinson, Shaw, Smith, Townsend, Wadham, Wood, Young
**Lauretta:** Matthews
**Laurina:** See Loriana
**Lavaithen/Levaithen (f):** Boswell, Buckley, Heron, Lee, Smith, Thorpe
**Lavender (f):** Heron
**Lavinia/Lavina/Lavaina/Livinia:** Bacon, Baker, Boswell, Buckland, Chilcott, Davis, Deacon, Frankham, Gray, Lee, Lock, Lovell, Matthews, Oadley, Procter, Rogers, Scamp, Scott, Sherriff, Small, Smith, Stokes, White, Williams, Wilson, Wood
**Lavanya:** Petulengro
**Laverne (f):** Marshall
**Lavoy:** Gray
**Lawler:** Scamp
**Lawrence:** See Laurence
**Layhe (f):** Boswell
**Layshi:** Boswell, Heron
**Lazarus:** Boswell, Buckley, Draper, Gray
**Lazzy:** Buckley, Lee, Palmer, Sibly, Smith. Probably an abbreviation of Lazarus
**Lea (f):** Shaw
**Leafy:** Loveridge, Smith. Cp Leathia.
**Leah:** Boswell, Davies, Evans, Heron, Johnson, Lovell, Munday, Penfold
**Lealie:** Scarrett
**Lean (f):** Scamp
**Leanabel/Leanable (f):** Butler, Gray, Smith
**Leandra/Leander/Leanda (f):** Boswell, Collinson, Green, Heron, Lee, Scamp, Smith, Williams. Note that this is not the same name as Lander.
**Leary:** Boswell

**Leathia (f):** Gray. Cp Leafy.
**Leberina:** Barron
**Ledie:** Light
**Lee (m):** Clarke, Fletcher, Foster, Rossiter, Scamp, Scarrett, Smith
**Lee (f):** Foster, Gray, Scamp
**Leena.** See Lena
**Lehanda (f):** Scamp
**Leila/ Lela:** Ayres, Scarrott
**Leki:** Wood
**Lelinda:** Chilcott, Loveridge
**Lementasia**: Boswell, Smith
**Lemen, -antina, -entina/ Lemmatany:** Boswell, Buckland, Clayton, Draper, Florence, Lee, Lovell, Loveridge, Mannion, Scamp, Sherriff, Smith, Stokes, Taylor
**Lemeril:** Mace
**Lemmy:** Cooper
**Len:** Watkins
**Lena/Leena:** Ayres, Ball, Boswell, Buckland, Camfield, Cooper, Cordes, Dear, Doe, Ellis, Gray, Johns, Jones, Lee, Murphy, Scamp, Smith, Spencer, Taylor, White, Woodward
**Lenda:** Baker, Boswell, Buckley, Fuller, Gray, Heron, Mitchell, Smith, Williams, Young
**Lenny/Lenni/Leni (m):** Buckley, Heron, Lovell
**Leo:** Buckland, Green, Smith
**Leon:** Boswell, Smith, Stephens
**Leonard**: Baker, Black, Boswell, Brinkley, Brown, Buckland, Buckley, Collins, Cooper, Coster, Farrow, Fletcher, Frankham, Fuller, Hamer, Hayhoe, Heron, Holland, Hughes, Johnson, Jones, Knight, Lee, Lock, Lovell, Loveridge, Mitchell, Parker, Pike, Ray, Ripley, Ross, Sayers, Scamp, Scarrett, Smith, Stanley, Stephens, Taylor, Wood
**Leondra:** Heron, Lee, Mace
**Leone:** Lovell
**Leonide**: Boswell
**Leonie:** Gannett
**Leonora**: Boswell, Fletcher, Heron, Gray, Mace, Matthews, Tann, Young
**Leopoli(n)us:** Mace
**Leopold:** Morton

**Lepeny:** Boswell
**Lepha:** Boswell
**Lepron(i)a:** Lee
**Leraina:** Harris
**Leri (m):** Gray
**Leshi:** Heron
**Lesley:** Scamp
**Leslie/Les:** Davies, Lewis, Lovell, Ripley, Roberts, Sanger, Scamp, Sloper, Taylor
**Lespanta:** Boswell
**Letitia/Leticia/Letitha/Liticia**: Adams, Beaney, Boswell, Carter, Emmett, Gentle, Heron, Lee, Lovell, Powell, Ripley, Rogers, Scamp, Shaw, Smith, Stephens, Valentine. Cp Latitia.
**Lettiaceneter:** Lee
**Lettice/Lettuce:** Boswell, Clayton, Gray, Lee, Nelson, Rogers, Smith
**Letty:** Cooper, Macfarlane, Ripley
**Levaithen:** See Lavaithen
**Levancy:** Boswell, Charlotte
**Levane:** Butler
**Leven:** Ward, Wood
**Levi:** Boswell, Buckley, Carey, Carter, Clayton, Cooper, Deighton, Draper, Finney, Gray, Harvey, Lee, Orchard, Mason, Ripley, Robinson, Rogers, Scarrett, Sherriff, Smith, Solomon, Stanley, Wiltshire
**Levina(h):** Boswell, Chapman, Lee, Smith. Cp Lovina.
**Levithen (f):** Smith
**Leweson:** Giles
**Lewis:** See Louis
**Lewisa:** Lee. Cp Louisa
**Leyler:** Williams
**Lias:** See Louis.
**Lib:** Pike
**Liban:** Smith
**Libby:** Boswell, Lee
**Liberina:** Barron, Gray
**Liberty (m and f):** Buckland, Camfield, Cole, Durrant, Hughes, Lovell, Loveridge, Smith, Stephens, **Vaughan**
**Libma:** Mills

**Licia:** Boswell
**Lidi:** Brown, Cooper, Deighton, Elliott, Oadley, Palmer, Smith. Cp Lydia.
**Lidia:** See Lydia.
**Life:** Stanley
**Lignairvitae:** Lovell
**Lil(l)a(h):** Buckley, Castle, Dixie, Lee, West
**Lil(li)b(o)urn:** Smith
**Lilian:** Boswell, Buckley, Duffy, Finney, Fuller, Lee, Linwood, Lovell, Mitchell, Penfold, Pike, Ripley, Scamp, Smith, Taylor
**Lillia:** Elliott
**Lilo/Lyla (f):** Loveridge, Miley
**Lily/Lillie/Lill(e)y/Lili (f):** Ayres, Barron, Boswell, Burton, Butler, Clarke, Dean, Eastwood, Finney, Fletcher, Frankham, Freeman, Fuller, Gray, Guthrie, Heron, Holland, Hope, Humphrey, Jones, Knight, Lane, Lawson, Lee, Lovell, Lowther, Mace, Macfarlane, Macklin, Menday, Morley, Moss, Oadley, Penfold, Ripley, Rose, Scamp, Sherriff, Small, Smith, Stephens, Sutherland, Swales, Taylor, Vinden, Walker, Waterfield, Wilson, Winson, Wray
**Lily (m):** Boswell, Butler
**Limi:** Florence, Jones, Lock, Taylor
**Limpedy/Limpetty:** Buckland, Draper, Lovell
**Limpson:** Buckland
**Lina/Lyna:** Boswell, Finney, Lock, Smith, Tompsett
**Lincham/Lingam:** Smith
**Linda/Lynda:** Buckley, Lee, Lock, Scamp, Scarrett, Smith
**Lindra:** Lee
**Lindsey/Lindsay (f):** Scamp, Todd
**Lindsey (m):** Scamp
**Linette/Lynette:** Heron, Scamp
**Liney:** Smith
**Lingam:** See Lincham
**Lingard:** Boswell
**Lingi:** Lee, Lovell, Scamp
**Linley:** Scamp
**Linyon:** Boswell
**Lionel**: Boswell, Davies, Lee, Lovell, Pablio, Smith
**Lipi (f):** Boswell, Lee

**Lisa:** Partridge, Scamp, Scarrott, Shepherd, Stephens
**Lisabell:** Scamp, Smith
**Lissie:** Shepherd
**Litha:** Buckley
**Liti:** See Lydia
**Liticia:** See Letitia
**Livinia:** See Lavinia.
**Liz/Lizzy/Liza:** Baker, Black, Boswell, Braham, Brown, Buckley, Cooper, Corbett, Crosse, Dawson, Day, Ellis, Gray, Griffiths, Hughes, Johnson, Jones, Kirkwood, Lambert, Lee, Light, Lewis, Lovell, Loveridge, Mantel, Mitchell, Morton, Oliver, Pettigrove, Ray, Shaw, Smith, Stokes, Varey, Webb, Wilson, Wood
**Llewellyn (f):** Lee, Lovell, Wood
**Lloyd (f):** Boswell
**Lloyd (m):** Boswell, Roberts, Wheeler, Wood
**Llyth (f):** Tuner
**Llywddan (f):** Wood
**Loany:** Boswell
**Lobb:** Loveridge
**Lockyer:** Boswell
**Lodger:** Lee
**Logan:** Heron, Lee
**Loia:** Luigi
**Lois:** Boswell, Izzard
**Loiza/Loisa (f):** Boswell, Lovell, Shaw
**Loli(f):** Buckland, Coleman, Finney, Heron, Lee, Lock, Penfold, Rossiter, Scamp, Smith, Wood
**Lomas (m):** Gray, Smith
**Lomba:** Lock
**Loomas:** Smith
**Loomi:** Boyling, James, Smith, Webb. (Var. on Salomi)
**Looie:** Smith
**Lora.** See Laura
**Lorel:** See Laurel
**Lorando:** Lee
**Lorancy/Lorenza:** Charlotte, Smith
**Loretta:** Rogers
**Lori:** Lovell, Powell
**Loriae:** Boswell

**Loriana/Lor(r)ina/Loreni/ Lorania/ Laurina:** Boswell, Lee, Mace, Matthews, Sherriff
**Lorna:** Scarrott
**Lorraine:** Barringer, Brazil, Buckley, Finney, Harris, Lee, Shepherd, Taylor
**Lot:** Lee
**Lottie/Lotty:** Elfes, Gamble, Holland, Lee, Scott, Smith, Young
**Lou:** Baker, Jones
**Louandra:** Boswell
**Louia:** Lovreridge
**Louie/Louee:** Camfield, Coates, Finney, Isaacs, Lock, Lovell, Loveridge, Orchard, Penfold, Randall, Roberts, Sanders, Smith, Turner, Varey, Whatnell
**Louis/ Lias/ Lewis:** Boswell, Buckley, Edwards, Heron, Ingram, Giles, Gray, Heron, Lee, Livermore, Lovell, Loveriedge, Northan, Powell, Printer, Robinson, Rose, Smith, Taylor, Whittle, Wood
**Louisa/Luisa/Luesa/Lousa:** Austin, Ayres, Bell, Bellwood, Berry, Boswell, Brazil, Brown, Buckley, Bullen, Bunce/ Bunts, Carter, Chilcott, Clayton, Clouffle, Collins, Colman, Cooper, Davies, Dawson, Edwards, Elliott, Finney, Fletcher, Ford, Foreman, Fuller, Gaskin, Gatehouse, Giles, Gray, Green, Harding, Harris, Heron, Hicks, Hope, Hughes, Ingram, Jeffs/ Jeffrey, Jones, Joyce, Lansdowne, Lee, Llewellin, Lock, Long, Lovell, Loveridge, Mace, Mann, Mathis, McLean, McLeod, Nail, Neale, Newman, Oliver, Orchard, Parker, Pateman, Peat, Penfold/ Pinfold, Pike, Price, Ripley, Robinson, Sadler, Savage, Scamp, Scarrett, Scott, Sherriff, Small, Smith, Stone, Swallow, Synes, Taylor, Thompson, Todd, Wallett, Wheeler, Wiggett, Williams, Wilson, Wood, Young
**Louise:** Boswell, Cook, Gentle, King, Lee, Livermore, Lovell, Mace, Moss, Scamp, Shaw, Smith, Stanley, Stone, Taylor, White
**Loumesca:** Shaw
**Lousa:** Boswell, Nail
**Love:** Boswell, Brown, Cash, Cooper, Gray
**Lovedy:** Stanley
**Lovelace (m):** Wells
**Lovel(l):** Lovell, Loveridge
**Loverin:** Wood
**Lovevinney:** Brown, Smith (possibly a var. on Lavinia)
**Lovey:** See Luvi

**Lovinia/Lovina:** Boswell, Buckley, Chapman, Lee, Perry, Smith. Cp Levina.
**Luander (f):** Heron
**Lucas:** Lee, Lock, Parker, Wood
**Lucca:** Boswell
**Lucia/Lusia:** Boswell, Gray, Penfold
**Lucian:** Ripley
**Lucifer:** Buckland
**Lucinda:** Heron
**Lucina:** Lee, Price
**Lucrene:** Brown, Heron
**Lucretia/Lucrecia/LucetiaLukresia:** Boswell, Faw, Heron, Lee, Rogers, Smith
**Lucy:** Many families
**Ludlow (m):** Watson
**Ludolphus:** Lovell. Co Rudolphus and Adolphus
**Ludwig:** Boswell
**Luesa/Luisa:** See Louisa
**Luidersille:** Pike/ Pikey
**Luill:** Smith
**Lu(i)rena** Boswell, Mace
**Lujer:** Heath
**Luke:** Ball, Boswell, Bull, Carter, Castle, Draper, Falkaad, Ford, Heron, Lee, Price, Ripley, Rogers, Scarrott, Smith, Stanley, Stephens, Young
**Lulu:** Smith
**Lumas:** Smith
**Lumi:** Boyling, Finney, Gray, James, Lovell, Shaw, Smith, Varey, Webb, Wilson. (Derived from Salomi)
**Luni (f):** Lovell, Wilson
**Lunia:** Heron
**Lunvari (m):** Wood
**Luperziah:** Sawyer
**Lura/Luria:** Boswell, Heron
**Lurayni/Lurina/Lurena/Loreni/ Lurini/ Lueareana/ Luirena (f):** Baker, Boswell, Harris, Heron, Lovell, Mace, Ryles, Sherriff, Wood, Young
**Lurvy:** Scamp
**Lusington:** Grice

**Lussha:** Boswell, Cooper, Fleck, Heron, Lee
**Luther:** Sherrard
**Luvi/Lovie:** Gray, Scamp, Smith
**Lwyddn:** Wood
**Lydia/Lydy/Liti:** Bailey, Beaney, Boswell, Brown, Buckland, Buckley, Burrett, Chilcott, Cooper, Deighton, Dixie, Eley, Elliott, Emmett, Evans, Gowan, Gray, Harris, Hart, Heron, Ingram, Jones, Lee, Light, Lovell, Matthews, Nathan, Newbury, Palmer, Penfold, Porter, Radford, Richards, Roberts, Rossiter, Shepherd, Smith, Stroud, Taylor, Webb, Wilson, Wood
**Lyna:** See Lina
**Lynavly:** Willuiams
**Lynda:** See Linda
**Lynette:** See Linette
**Lynn (m):** Boswell
**Lynn (f):** Scamp
**Lyon:** Boswell
**Lysia:** Lovell
**Lyzvia**: Boswell
**Mabel:** Boswell, Bothwell, Fowler, Gray, Lee, Rhodes, Smith, Scarrett, Stewart, Stirling, Wheeler. Cp Maybell
**Macey**: Boswell
**Mackenzie:** Boswell, Buckley, Lee, Thorpe, Young
**Mackintyre:** Boswell
**MacMensye:** Boswell
**Madeleine/Madlyn:** Bonnet, Finch, Gray, Lee, Smith
**Madge:** Faw, Gordon, Greig, Young
**Madia:** Smith
**Madiri:** Heron
**Madoc(k) (m):** Roberts, Willett
**Madon(n)a(h)/Modena/ Medanna/ Modonna:** Boswell, Gibbs, Heron, Lee, Mace, Smith
**Madora:** Smith
**Maeia:** Boswell
**Magarette:** Scott
**Magdaline:** Boswell, Gray
**Magenta:** Cooper
**Maggie:** Carloman, Crittenden, Crosse, Griffiths, Hardy, Holmes, Mills, Mochan, Summers

**Maghelas:** Boswell
**Magnes/Magnis/Magnus:** Boswell
**Mahkedah:** Boswell
**Maia:** Boswell, Smith
**Maieni/Maini:** Boswell, Lee, Shaw
**Maier:** Gray
**Maili:** Rawlings
**Maini:** Shaw
**Maireni/ Myrene/ Myrenny:** Bateman, Heron, Kilsbie, Shaw, Smith, Wood
**Mairik:** Lock
**Maisi (m):** Boswell, Linwood, Taylor
**Maize:** Loveridge
**Maillard:** Ripley
**Major:** Ayres, Black, Boswell, Cooper, Gray, Lee, Lovell, Smith, Taylor
**Makayda:** Boswell
**Makepeace (m):** Lee
**Malalena:** Boswell
**Malcolm/Malc:** Lee, Marshall, Nelson, Scamp, Sherriff, Webb
**Maley:** Coleman
**Malgerus:** Smith
**Malin:** Taylor
**Malinda:** Clayton/Clayton
**Maliva (f):** Pierce, Stanley
**Mallon:** Gray
**Mally:** Johnson, Lee
**Malpass**: Boswell
**Malvina:** Ball
**Manabel:** Heron
**Manafish:** Boswell
**Manauo:** Florence
**Mandi (m):** Booth, Shaw, Smith, Townsend
**Mandra/Mandora/ Mandrew:** Gray, Price, Smith
**Mandy (f):** Scamp, Shaw
**Mandy (m):** Price
**Manessah/ Manassah:** Burton, Loveridge
**Manfri/ Manfred:** Price, Wood
**Manful/Man(s)field:** Boswell, Draper, Heron, Roberts

**Manley (m):** Scamp
**Manni(s): (m)** Connor(s), Conway, Golby, Heron, Jones
**Manoah (m):** Lock
**Manroe/Manroeffe (m):** Florence
**Manso:** Smith
**Mantis:** Buckland, Heron, Lovell
**Manuel:** Beam/Beamy, Boswell, Buckland, Heron, Holland, Ingram
**Maranda:** Wood
**Marbolini/Marbelina (f):** Lee, Lock, Wood
**Marcella**: Boswell
**Marcia:** Scarrett, Shaw
**Mardling:** Loker
**Marella/Marilla:** Draper, Scamp, Smith
**Marenni (f):** Heron
**Maresko/Mariscoe/Muroisco:** Romana, Smith, Winter
**Maretta/Mareti:** Lee, **Scarrett**
**Marey:** Gam. Probably a var. on Mary.
**Marger:** Lovell
**Margaret:** Boswell, Butler, Chapman, Coate(s), Crittenden, Dollan, Drake, Draper, Faw, Finch, Finney, Frankham, Gallagher, Gibson, Graham, Gray, Grice, Harbour, Harper. Harris, Harrison, Heron, Hind, Hobbing, Hodgkiss, Hogg, Holden, Holmes, Hurst, Ironside, Jackson, Jones, Kelbie, Kenny, Kerr, King, Knight, Laidlaw, Lambert, Lee, Lock, Lovell, Mahoney, Marshall, Mason, McCarthy, McCready, McCullock, McIntyre, McKie, McLean, Munday, Myatt, Newbury, Nichols(on), Parker, Peel, Penfold, Pettytt, Rafferty, Ripley, Robinson, Rogers, Romney, Scamp, Scarrett, Scott, Shaw, Shipley, Shepherd, Short, Small, Smith, Sowden, Stanley, Stephens, Stewart, Stone, Swales, Tams, Tapsall, Taylor, Thompson, Thorley, Todd, Valentine, Vaughan, Walker, Watson, Welch, Williams, Williamson,. Wilson, Wood
**Margary**: See Marjerie
**Marger (m):** Lovell
**Margharetti/Margaretta**: Boswell, Small
**Mariag:** Butler
**Maria(h):** Baker, Boswell, Bowers, Bray, Brown, Carter, Closs, Colbert, Collison, Cooper, Davies, Dexter, Dimberline, Dixon, Faw, Fuller, Gray, Hall, Harris, Harrison, Heap, Hedges, Herrick, Heron, Ingram, Johnson, Jones, Knight, Latham, Lee, Lloyd,

Lock, Lovell, Loveridge, McCormick, Mclean, Newsome, Palmer, Parker, Parkinson, Perkins, Petrovna, Podalaze, Ripley, Robinson, Scott, Sherriff, Sivers, Small, Smith, Strange, Tait, Taylor, Teeth, Thaniel, Todd, Tomlinson, Walker, Webb, Wharton, White, Williams, Wood

**Mariam (f):** Rhodes

**Marian(ne)/Mariana:** Boswell, Carter, Heron, Howard, Ladds, Radford, Sa(u)nders, Scamp, Smith, Stanley, Ward, Young

**Marie:** Boswell, Clarke, Cooper, Ford, Heron, Humphrey, Ingram, Lee, Scamp, Scarrett, Smith, Wood

**Marilda:** Smith

**Marilla/Marelli/Mariel:** Draper, Lovell, Small, Smith

**Marina:** Booth, Boswell, Buckley, Heron, Lovell, Shepherd, Sherriff, Small, Smith

**Mario:** Evans

**Marion:** Boswell, Florence, Green, Jackson, vLee, Loveridge, Smith

**Marisko:** See Maresko

**Marja:** Edwards

**Marjerie/ Marjorie/ Marjery/ Marji:** Boswell, Draper, Finney, Griffin, Lee, Lock, Lovell, Mulleyn, Smith,Taylor, Webb, Wood

**Mark (f):** Boswell

**Mark:** Berry, Boswell, Brazil, Campbell, Carter, Cooper, Crittenden, Davies, Douglas, Eley, Gaskin, Gibson, Giles, Gess, Heron, Holland, John(s), Jones, Lee, Light, Lovell, Loveridge, McDonald, Noble, Orchard, Parker, Porter, Ripley, Roberts, Rogers, Scamp, Scott, Shepherd, Sherriff, Sines, Smith, Stevens, Stokes, Swales, Swallow, Tamlin, Thorpe, Turner

**Marki:** Booth, Scamp

**Marlille:** Scamp

**Marmaduke:** Gibson, Petch

**Marrer:** Newman

**Marsala:** Scamp

**Marsay:** Johnson

**Marshall (m):** Latham, Lee, Reynolds, Ripley, Rogers, Round

**Marth:** Boswell, Watford

**Martha/Marthay/Marther:** Many families

**Martin** (m): Boswell, Dee, Drake, Femine, Lee, Lovell, Marshall, Newbury, Scamp, Smith, Stanley

**Martin** (f): Boswell, Newbury
**Marvelles:** Boswell
**Mary:** Most families.
**Maryam/Mariam:** Bird, Martin
**Mary Ann:** Most families
**Maryann/Maryanas:** Bishop, Herrick, Lee
**Maryellen:** Finney
**Mary John** (sic): Brawn
**Marzell:** Boswell
**Masella (f):** Scamp, Smith. Cp Mizelli
**Masey/Masire:** Chapman, Hoskins
**Mason (m):** Wass
**Master:** Heron
**Mather:** Smith
**Mathusalem:** Lee. Cp Methuselah
**Matilda**: Acome, Ayres, Beldorn, Bird, Booth, Boswell, Bowers, Brockless, Brown, Buckland, Buckley, Burden, Burton, Carter, Chilcott, Clayton, Coate(s), Colbert, Collins, Cooper, Davidson, Deighton, Eley, Evans, Finney, Gaskin, Gatehouse, Giles, Gray, Hardy, Harris, Harrison, Head, Heron, Holland, Hughes, James, Jones, Keet, Lamb, Lee, Livermore, Lovell, Newbury, Nixon, Oadley, Penfold, Price, Ripley, Scarrett, Selby, Shaw, Shepherd, Sherrard, Sherriff, Small, Smith, Stanley, Stone, Turner, Vaughan, Waterfield, Welch, White, Williams, Winter. Cp Mitilda.
**Matt:** Booth, Swales
**Mattha:** Douglas
**Matthew(s)** (f): Boswell, Scamp, Smith
**Matthew(s)** (m): Booth, Bowers, Boswell, Butler, Carlton, Clayton, Cooper, Falkad, Fisher, Giles, Graham, Grainge, Gray, Heron, Jackson, Johnson, Jones, Junnix, Keet, Lee, Lock, Loveridge, Mills, Mitchell, Murphy, Perkins, Perry, Powell, Pride, Ripley, Scamp, Scott, Shaw, Smith, Stephens, Sword, Wardle, Watkinson, Williams, Wood, Young
**Matthias**: Boswell, Brown, Clarke, Cooper, Griffiths, Hughes, Lee, Lovell, Mitchell
**Matthro:** Connor
**Matt(i):** Anderson, Cooper, Keet, Griffiths, Lee, Loveridge, Orchard
**Maud:** Ayres, Baker, Boswell, Cooper, Dale, Ford, Gess, Goldsmith,

Holmes, Isaacs, Johnson, Lee, Lewis, Lovell, Loveridge, Miller, Mills, Nichols(on), Penfold, Rowley, Sanger, Scamp, Scarrett, Sloper, Small, Smith, Townsend, Webber
**Mauda/Maudie:** Boswell, Curl, Feltham, Loveridge, Smith, Townsend
**Mauger/Maugerus:** Smith
**Maul:** Rossiter
**Maundrew:** Florence
**Maureen:** Falkener, Finney, Lovell, Price, Scamp, Scarrott, Shepherd, Smith
**Maurice:** Adams, Ayres, Gray, Lock, Orchard
**Maurov:** Florence
**Mausolina:** Heron, Smith
**Mavis:** Lee, Whitham
**Max:** Sheffield
**Maxey:** Boswell
**May (f):** Boswell, Cheeseman, Collins, Fletcher, Heron, Hill, King, Lee, MacDermot, Matthews, Menday, Miller, Price, Recos, Ripley, Rowley, Scamp, Scarrett, Sloper, Smith, Taylor, Thompson, Wilshire, Winter
**May (m):** Ripley, Taylor
**Maybell:** Lee. Cp Mabel
**Mayboth:** Lee
**Mayfield (f):** Booth, **Taylor**
**Mayo:** Boswell
**Mayrick (m):** Lee
**Mayvene:** Lee
**Mayzaia, -iah/ Maysi/ Mazy/ Meso (f and m):** Boswell, Draper, French, Heron, Lee, Scott, Taylor
**Mazella:** See Mizelli
**Mazeppa:** Loveridge
**McCoy (m):** Scarrett
**McGrigor:** Boswell
**McJoy:** Boswell
**McKenzie:** Boswell
**McPherson (f):** Price
**Medanna:** See Madona
**Medina:** Lee
**Medrick:** Smith

**Mehitable:** Boswell, Smith
**Mel:** Smith
**Melanda:** Smith
**Melania:** Heron
**Melanie:** Scamp, Taylor
**Melina (f):** Sherriff
**Melbourne:** Mace
**Melchior:** Boswell
**Melicent:** Boswell
**Melinda:** Boswell
**Melissa:** Lee
**Melita:** Heron
**Mella (f):** Scamp
**Mellie** Jackson
**Mellor:** Wood
**Melvina/Melvinia:** Huggins, Lee
**Melwyn:** Lee
**Memberensi/Membrance:** Boswell, Lock, Palmer, Smith (Form of Remembrance)
**Mena:** Mcfarlane
**Mendoza:** Shaw, Smith, Webb
**Menilla:** Smith
**Mennitha:** Boswell
**Menry(f):** Scamp
**Menty/Menti:** Lee, Ryles, Scamp, Smith. (Sometimes — perhaps always — an abbreviation for Sinamenti.)
**Merack:** Lock
**Meray:** Heron
**Merce:** Gray
**Merchimar:** Smith
**Mercia:** Butler, Elliott, Pierce, Smith, Stanley, Winter
**Mercury:** Boswell
**Mercy (f):** Arnold, Ball, Butler, Carter, Everton, Faw, Gray, Heron, Lee, Loveridge, Ripley, Stanley, Thompson, Wood
**Meredith:** Ingram, Wood
**Merelda/Meralda/Merella:** Joules, Loveridge, Smith
**Meriah:** Lee, Smith
**Meriall:** Gray, Smith. Cp Mirriall
**Meriam:** Boswell

**Merick:** Lock
**Merime:** Scarrett
**Merke:** Boswell
**Meror: (m)** Boswell
**Meriore (f):** Faw
**Mernell (f)@** Sherriff
**Merrily/Merrilla:** Cooper, Joules
**Merrior:** Boswell
**Merry (m):** Draper, Wood
**Merryfield:** Lovell
**Mesala:** Buckland, Smith. Cp Mizelli.
**Meshach;** Gray, Heron, Smith
**Mesi:** See Mayzaia.
**Mesiah:** Smith
**Meskech:** Smith
**Metcalfe:** Boswell
**Methusalah:** Heron, Lee. Cp Mathusalem
**Metraine/Metraina:** Burton, Lee
**Mew:** Childs, Young
**Mexorcon:** Boswell
**Mezelley.** See Mizelli
**Mezi:** See Mayzaia
**Miah:** Boswell
**Michael:** Boswell, Brown, Casey, Chapman, Clayton, Fallard, Ford, Hammond, Hennesley, Heron, Ingram, Jackson, Johnson, Lee, Lovell, McDonald, Norton, Penfold, Quinn, Sanders, Scamp, Scott, Shadlock, Shipley, Smith, Solomon, Stanton, Swales, Watson, Whatnell, White
**Michaela:** Gray
**Michelle:** Gerrard, Scamp
**Mick(y):** Hughes, Mair, Matthews, Whatnell
**Midora:** Lee, Smith
**Mig(n)onette:** Ayres, Lovell, Smith
**Miguel:** Heron
**Mike:** Orchard, Sanders/ Saunders/ Sanderson
**Milan:** Markinkovic
**Mildred:** Lee, Gray, Mclean, Roberts
**Miles (m):** Lee, Powell, Robinson
**Miley:** See Murelly

**Miller (m):** Boswell, Heron
**Millicent:** Boswell, Fearne, Gaskin, Marshall, Smith, Waller
**Millie/Milly:** Ayres, Boswell, Cooper, Gray, Heron, Lee, Pidgley, Pike, Smith, Young
**Millitrana:** Boswell
**Mima/Mimi:** Boswell, Ray, Stokes
**Minam:** Smith
**Minerald:** Taylor
**Minerva:** Boswell
**Mingman:** Gray
**Mini (m):** Heron
**Minit/Minnett:** Smith
**Minna:** Smith
**Minnie:** Adams, Black, Boswell, Chapman, Cooper, Cox, Finney, Gardiner, Golding, Heron, James, Jefferson, Johnson, Lane, Lee, Light, Lovell, Mace, Marshall, Matthews, McLean, Morton, Nichols(on), Penfold, Price, Ripley, Scamp, Scarrott, Small, Smith, Stephens, Stork, Taylor, Waite, White, Wilson, Wood
**Minnow (f):** Heron
**Mira:** Boswell, Scarrett, Smith
**Miranda:** Smith, Stephens
**Mirandra:** Gray, Newbury, Smith
**Miranger:** Lee
**Mirelli:** Chilcott, Smith
**Miria:** Gray
**Miriam:** Boswell, Fleckie, Price, Smith, Swales, Wood
**Mirrelli/Mirriall/Miarial/Meriall:** Draper, Gray, Smith
**Misella:** See Mizelli
**Miseretta:** Boswell
**Missab (f):** Elliott
**Misty:** Brown, Stapleton
**Mitelda:** Lee. Cp Matilda
**Mizeck:** Lock
**Mitzi:** Scarrett
**Mivaniel:** Smith
**Mizelda:** Burton
**Mizelli/er /Mezelley/Misella/ Mazella/ Miziellia/ Myzella/ Mazelia/ Mizi (f):** Boswell, Buckland, Gray, Hiscox, King, Lamb, Lee, Lovell, Loveridge, McCready, Ryles, Scamp, Shaw, Smith,

Stephens, Wilks
**Mizeretta/Mizeretti/Miseretti (f):** Boswell, Elliott, Heron, Pierce, Smith, Winter
**Mizi (f):** Lamb, Lee
**Miz(z)anah:** Adams, Boswell
**M'Kenzie:** Boswell, Young
**Moadi:** Boswell
**Moati:** Boswell, Lovell
**Mochus/Mokius:** Boswell, Heron, Lovell
**Modena:** See Madona
**Modi/Moti/ Motti:** Boswell, Harris, Heron, Lovell, Smith
**Modiven:** Smith
**Moellus:** Boswell
**Mog:** Gibson, Heron, Smith, Steggall
**Mokus (m):** Heron
**Molenda/Silenda:** Smith
**Molia:** Burton, Ryles
**Moll:** Boswell, Smith
**Molly:** Boswell, Heron, Neville, Pierce, Stanley, Vinden
**Molvina:** Heron
**Monchelsea (m):** Wood
**Monica:** Lovell
**Montague/Montegue:** Boswell, Gray, Heron, Lovell, Smith
**Montana:** Steele
**Monteque:** Heron, Smith
**Montgomery:** Scamp
**Montrosseur:** Mace
**Monty:** Boswell, Scamp, Sherriff
**Moody:** Smith
**Moony (m):** Lee
**Moor:** Boswell
**Mora (m):** Boswell
**Mordecai:** Boswell, Wainwright
**Morela (f):** Miley
**Morford (f):** Scamp
**Morgan:** Brown, Jones, Lee
**Mori:** Gray
**Moriah:** Todd
**Morjiana/Morgeanna:** Boswell, Heron, Lee

**Morkea:** Johnson
**Morley:** Boswell
**Morpus:** Heron
**Morrell:** Hall, Morgan
**Morris:** Light, Stokes
**Morselina:** Buckley, Lee
**Mortimer (m):** Scamp
**Mose:** Boswell, Ripley
**Moseline:** Lovell
**Moses**: Baillie, Bird, Boswell, Brazil, Buckland, Cooper, Dixon, Eastwood, Elliott, Emmett, Faw, Finney, Ford, Frankham, Giles, Gray, Green, Gritt, Harris, Heron, Holland, Killick, Lee, Lovell, Loveridge, Marshall, Odell, Orchard, Osborn, Parker, Penfold, Ripley, Rogers, Scamp, Scarrett, Shaw, Sherriff, Small, Smith, Thatcher, Todd, Vaughan, Webb, Williams, Wood
**Mossolenia/ Mossalina:** Lee, Lovell
**Moti:** See Modi
**Mounteque:** Heron
**Mountjoy:** Boswell
**Mountseer:** Boswell
**Mouse:** Boswell, Scott, Shaw. (On occasions, this is used as a nickname. These appear to be uses as a bona fide forename.)
**Mowelles:** Boswell
**Mower:** Gray
**Moysie:** Faw
**Mozania:** Boswell
**Mozella:** See Mizelli
**Mudi:** See Modi
**Muldobriar (m):** Heron
**Mulli:** Lee
**Mullinder:** Heron
**Munro:** Florence
**Muperella:** Smith
**Murdo:** Brown
**Murelly:** Gray, Miley. See Mirelli.
**Muroisco:** See Maresko
**Muriel:** Boswell, Lovell, Scamp
**Murzelli:** See Mizelli
**Musgrove/Musgrave:** Boswell, Waite

**Mush:** Finney
**Mushy/ Mushie:** Taylor. Toogood
**My:** Boswell
**Mybob:** Shaw
**Myfanwy:** Hughes
**Mylyane:** Sword
**Myra:** Burton, Smith, Todd
**Myrack:** Lock, Lovell
**Myre:** Lock
**Myrenee/-renny:** See Mairenni
**Myriall:** Wood. Cp Meriall and Mirrial
**Myrian:** Buckley
**Mythias:** Lee
**Nadine:** Gray
**Nahoma:** Abbott
**Naley/Neli/Naylus/Naylis/Naylie:** Buckland, Fenner, Lee, Lock, Scamp, Sherriff, Shaw, Toogood. An abbreviation for Cornelius.
**Namise:** Loveridge
**Nan (f):** Arnold, Gordon, Heron, Smith, Swales
**Nanc:** Boswell
**Nancy:** Berry, Booth, Brown, Butler, Cooper, Dobson, Edwards, Faiers, Hall, Hogg, Johnson, Lee, Lovell, Miles, Parry, Ripley, Roberts, Robinson, Rogers, Scamp, Smith, Stone, Swales, Taylor, Todd, Wood, Woolley
**Nanny:** Byles, Lee, Smith, Walmsley, Ward
**Nanowley:** Boswell
**Nanus:** Wood
**Naomi:** Agar, Barton, Bateman, Boswell, Doe, Gray, Harris, Hogden, Johnson, Lee, Loveridge, Midmore, Pateman, Penfold, Reed, Ripley, Roberts, Rossiter, Scamp, Shaw, Sherriff, Smith, Stephens, Tann, Taylor, Todd, Webb, Wilson, Wood
**Napolean:** Lee, Scamp
**Naptha:** Boswell
**Narelli:** Boswell
**Naria:** Boswell
**Narissa:** Burton
**Natasha (f):** Scamp
**Nate:** Boswell
**Nathan:** Baildon, Bannister, Bird, Boswell, Buckley, Claydon/

Clayton, Deighton, Fletcher, Gray, Kindon, Lee, Scamp, Scarrett, Shaw, Smith, Steele, Taylor, Wenman, Wood, Youngt

**Nathaniel:** Agar, Barber, Boswell, Chaplin, Evans, Fleming, Johnson, Lee, Little, Lovell, Palmer, Rogers, Scamp, Shaw, Smith, Todd, Wimpenny

**Nation (f):** Buckley, Frankham, Lee, Lock, Smith, Wood

**Natty:** Jones, Wood

**Naughty:** Smith

**Naylor:** Ayres

**Naylus:** See Naley

**Nazi:** Burton

**Neal/ Neil:** Boswell, McLean, Mulleyn, Redpath, Scamp

**Nealus:** Mills

**Nearby:** See Niabai

**Neaty:** Rowland, Smith

**Nebuchadnezzar:** Price

**Ned/Neddy:** Boswell, Buckland, Calladine, Hanneford, James, Jones, Lamb, Lee, Scamp, Shevlin, Smith, Stokes

**Needles:** Price

**Nehemiah:** Austin, Ayres, Ball, Boswell, Cooper, Lovell, Parry/Perry, Smith, White

**Neil:** See Neal.

**Nelda:** Lewis

**Neli:** See Naley

**Nell/Nellie/-ly:** Ayres, Bonnett, Booth, Brines, Cole, Cooper, Dunton, Gordon, Graham, Gray, Heron, Hope, Jamieson, Jeffs/Jefferies, Johnson, Livermore, Lock, Loveridge, Manders, Matthews, MacFee, McFarlane, Newbury, Nicholls, Palmer, Pike, Price, Ripley, Ryles, Smith, Stephens, Swallow, Taylor, Todd, Wood, Wallett, Wright

**Nelson**: Ayres, Boswell, Buckland, Buckley, Cooper, Gray, Green, Gregory, Heron, Herrick, James, Lee, Lovell, Mace, Marney, Murphy, Penfold, Pilcher, Scamp, Scarrett, Scott, Smith, Stanley, Wenman, Young

**Nelus.** See Naley

**Nench:** Smith

**Nenti:** Brazil

**Nepthene:** John(s)

**Neptune:** Ayres, Barber, Loveridge

**Nerelli:** Boswell
**Neriah:** Smith
**Neverfess:** Boswell
**Newbury:** Boswell
**Newcomb(e):** Boswell, Heron
**Newmarch (m):** Lee
**Newton:** Boswell, Gray, Lee, Lovell
**Nezer** Lee
**Niabai/Nearby/Nibby:** Heron, Shadlock. This name is found as both m and f, but more commonly m.
**Niahbella:** Wood
**Nichi:** Taylor
**Nichoalz:** George
**Nicholas/Nicolas:** Allen, Bunyan, Gawino, Gray, Ingram, Johnson, Lee, Mackeig, Morgan, Nichols(on), O'Neil, Scamp, Shipton, Slender, Taylor, Tschuron
**Nicholson (m):** Mason, Rowley
**Nicholson (f):** Rogers
**Nicol/Nicolae:** Sanders/ Saunders/ Sanderson, Taylor
**Nicola:** Scamp
**Nigel:** Scamp, Shaw
**Nigger:** Nichols. Note that in this family, the name is traditionally given to a very dark skinned baby. The name also occurs as a nickname amongst several families for similar reasons, especially amongst Prices. It is never used as a racial insult but rather as a compliment to someone seen as very Gypsyish.
**Nikode:** Jones
**Nigel:** Gray
**Nighti:** Scamp
**Nili:** Buckland
**Nimphaney:** Anchorn, Smith
**Nimrod:** Auger
**Nina(h):** Calladine, Clarke, Lovell
**Ninian:** Faw, Shaw, Stewart
**Nippon:** Smith
**Niptherie:** John(s)
**Nipton (m):** Ayres, Hibberd, Ryles, Smith
**Nisi:** Burton

**Nixi:** Lovell, **Smith**
**Noah:** Ayres, Barney, Boswell, Bowers, Buckley, Burton, Castle, Chapman, Chilcott, Collins, Cooper, Davies, Deighton, Florence, Gatehouse, Gray, Heron, Hilden, James, Jones, Lee, Lock, Lovell, Loveridge, Orchard, Palmer, Parker, Penfold, Ripley, Rogers, Scamp, Shaw, Slender, Smith, Stanley, Taylor, Town(s)end, Webb, Willett, Young
**Nobby:** Gray
**Nobias:** Clayton
**Noel:** Butler, Heron
**Noma:** Coleman
**Nona:** Finch, Lee
**Nona:** Finch
**No-Name:** Heron
**Nooks:** See Nukes
**Nora(h):** Boswell, Buckley, Donovan, Gray, Lee, Mace, Scamp, Smith, Stanley, Tann, Waterfield
**Norma:** Narringer
**Norman:** Boswell, Buckley, Heron, Lovell
**Norna/Nornas:** Boswell, Smith
**Norris (m):** Heron, Wood
**Norrit:** Heron
**Notfaw:** Lawlor
**Nott (f):** Scamp
**Nouris:** Heron
**Nugent:** Lovell
**Nukes/Nooks (m):** Heron, Price
**Nuki:** Heron
**Nuti/Nutty:** Jones, Gray, Ryles
**Oaty/Oti (f):** Boswell, Heron, Sherriff, Smith
**Obadiah/Obed:** Baxter, Boswell, Booth, Cooper, Draper, Gray, Lee, Price, Ridley, Taylor
**Obadiri/Obadeary:** Buckland, Lee
**Obedience:** Boswell
**Obi/Obeh:** Chiclott, Gray, Printer, Williams
**Ocean/Oceana/Ocey/Oceanic (f):** Buckland, Cooper, Doe, Lee, Loveridge, Orchard, Penfold, Scarrott. Cp Oshena.
**Ocey:** See Ocean
**Ochan:** Stephens

**Ochenerey:** Smith
**Ochsha:** Biddle, Scarrett
**O'Connor/O'Conna:** Boswell
**Odar:** Boswell
**Offley (m):** Shaw
**Ogga:** Smith
**Ogus:** Boswell
**Ohers:** Lee
**Oini:** Lee
**Okey/Oki:** Booth, Boswell, Heron
**Olbi:** Boswell
**Oldroyd (m):** Lee
**Olfie (m):** Scamp
**Olfred:** Buckland, Reynolds, Smith
**Oli/Olley (m):** Gray, Heron, Lovell
**Oliphant**: Boswell
**Olive:** Berry, Boswell, Buckley, Butler, Carter, Cooper, Corsey, Harris, James, Johnson, Jones, Lee, Lock, McLean, Meers, Miles, Ripley, Roberts, Scamp, Sloper, Smith, Swann, Taylor, Waterfield, Wood
**Oliver:** Ayres, Black, Boswell, Brinkley, Chapman, Cooper, Davies, Eastwood, Heron, Johnson, Lee, Lovell, Mace, Rogers, Scamp, Scarrett, Sheen, Smith, Turner, Walker, Whatnell, Young
**Olivia:** Bird, Boswell, Lovell, Mace
**Olivis:** Atkinson
**Olothea:** Lee
**Ombate:** Smith
**Omega:** Heron, Huggins
**Omi(e):** Boswell, Crabtree, Gray, James, Lovell, Scamp, Smith
**Omiah/Omea:** Midmore, Smith
**Onan (f):** Robinson
**Onesiphorus:** Buckland, Lamb, Smith
**Oni:** Smith
**Onslow:** Ayres, Smith
**Opi/Ope:** Boswell, Davies, Finney, Lee, Price. Normally the same name as Hope, but Opie etc is only found as a male name.
**Orary:** Gray
**Oratio:** See Horatio
**Orbie:** Smith

**Ordi:** Boswell
**Orferus/Orpherus (m):** Cooper, Heron, Lee
**Orlando:** Boswell, Lee, Morleyu, Smith
**Orpherus:** See Orferus
**Orris:** Horace
**Osbald:** Loveridge
**Osborne:** Smith
**Oscar:** Boswell, Buckland, Gray, Heron, Smith, Young
**Oseri/ Osheri/ Osrey/ Oshie/ Ozeri/ Azariah/Ozrey (m):** Boswell, Buckland, Cooper, Gray, Smith. Cp Osiah
**Oshena (f)/Osheni:** Buckland, Green, Heron.Cp Ocean
**Osim:** Smith
**Ossiwall/ Ossowall/ Ossiwelli:** Wood. Cp Otywell
**Oswald:** Boswell
**Othea/Othi/Oti (f):** Boswell, Buckley, Burton, Gray, Heron, Lee, Printer, Sherriff, Smith. This name also occur as m.
**Otywell/ Ottiwell/ Othiwell:** Lee, Wood. Cp Ossiwall.
**Ouncey:** Boswell
**Ovator:** Boswell
**Owen:** Cooper, Corsey, Heron, Hughes. Jones, Lee, McDonald, O'Neil, Scamp, Smith, Stanley, Wheeler, Wood
**Own:** (spelling correct) Boswell
**Oziah (f):** Taylor. Cp Oseri.
**Ozrey:** See Oseri.
**Paccat:** Boswell
**Pacie:** Staveley. Possibly the same name as Paesie
**Paddy:** Doran, McCreary, Turner
**Paesie:** See Paizenni
**Page (m):** Heron
**Paishter:** Mills
**Paizenni/Paizi/Paesie (f):** Hammond, Heron, Jones
**Paizi (m):** Heron
**Pally:** Jackson
**Palmer (m):** Robinson
**Pam:** Page, Smith, Watkins
**Pamela:** Boswell, Buckland, Hewitt, Scarrett, Smith
**Pamilia/Pamely:** Finn, Smith
**Paneley:** Boswell
**Pannett:** Scott

**Panny:** See Pawni.
**Pansy:** Humphries
**Papita:** Pierce, Stanley
**Paprona:** Lee
**Paradise:** Buckland, Buckley
**Paraffin:** Lee
**Parent:** Lee
**Parnell (f):** Boswell, Newbury. Cp Pawni
**Parkin (m):** Boswell, Ward
**Parren (m):** Stephens
**Parthema (f):** Miley
**Pascal (m):** Scamp
**Pashy:** Powell
**Pasthomas:** Gray
**Pat (f):** Smith
**Pat (m):** Lee, Lovell
**Patience:** Berry, Boswell, Brinkley, Butler, Chapman, Coleman, Collins, Collinson, Corbett, Cooper, Davies, Deighton, Doe, Giles, Gray, Heron, Holland, Hughes, James, Keet, Lee, Oadley, Orchard, Penfold, Pike, Rawlings, Ray, Roberts, Scamp, Scott, Sherriff, Smith, Stone, Turner, Webb, Wenman, West, Wheeler, Wilson
**Patricia:** Lewis, Miller, Pattinson, Scamp, Shaw, Smith
**Patrick:** Faw, Fury, Gray, Heron, Hurley, Kelly, Lee, Maxwell, McCormick, McFarlane, Mochan, Percago, Rooney, Scott, Shadlock, Shaw, Sivers, Smith
**Patsy:** Allen, Lovell, Morley, Rafferty, Stanley
**Paul:** Ayres, Boswell, Colman, Cooper, Faw, Gray, Lee, Price, Rogers, Scamp, Scarrett, Shepherd, Stanley
**Paula:** Price, Scamp
**Paulena:** Carris(s)
**Pauline:** Day, Lee, Scamp
**Pavenit:** Boswell
**Pawni/Pani:** Archer, Boswell, Fenner, Heron, Lee, Newbury, Scamp. Cp Parnell
**Peach (f):** Shaw
**Pearl(y):** Price, Scamp
**Peasy:** Stewart
**Peata:** Boswell

**Peats:** Boswell
**Peato:** Boswell
**Pedlar:** Palmer
**Peggy:** Blyth, Boswell, Buckland, Buckley, Heron, Lee, Lovell, McFarlane, Orchard, Smart, Smith
**Pehanet**: Boswell
**Pelham:** Smith
**Pelify:** Boswell
**Pelslant:** Boswell
**Pembridge:** Lee
**Pen:** Lovell
**Penda/Pender:** Buckley
**Pender(b)ella:** Buckley
**Pendrill (m and f):** Rogers
**Peneli/ Penelly/ Penheli/ Pemili/ Pemella/ Penell/ Penerley/ Penuel:** See Pawni — the name is clearly derived from Penelope
**Penelope:** Ayres, Boswell, Buckland, Cooper, Fenner, Lee, Roberts, Smith
**Peni (m)**: Booth, Boswell, Cooper, Lee, Taylor
**Penilla:** Orchard
**Penny:** Boswell, Cooper, Coyne
**Pentecost:** Lee
**Pentevinny:** Lovell
**Percival:** Boswell, Bothwell
**Percy:** Booth, Boswell, Buckland, Day, Gray, Heron, Lee, Livermore, Lock, Mace, Manning, Myers, Penfold, Scamp, Shaw, Sutton, Swales, Tann, Taylor
**Pero:** Heron
**Per(r)on:** Cooper, Smith
**Perpagellion:** Elliott, Heron
**Perrance:** Scarrett
**Perrella:** Draper
**Perri:** Ripley, Scamp
**Perrin/Perun/Peron (m):** Boswell, Buckley, Cooper, Hamilton, Heron, Lee, Sherriff, Smith, Young
**Perro/Pero:** Heron, Lovell
**Perthia:** Lovell
**Pesulius:** Gray
**Peter:** Ames, Arnett, Booth, Boswell, Brown, Buckland, Buckley,

Butler, Cole, Cook, Cooney, Cooper, Davies, Daws, Dimberline, Douglas, Evans, Farrow, Finney, Fox, Gray, Green, Hames, Harris, Heron, Hicks, How, Hudson, Hutchinson, Ingram, Kelly, Lee, Lovell, McPellen, Meggett, Mercer, Miles, Mulleyn, Newbury, O'Neil, Orchard, Parker, Pellen, Pinder, Rogers, Scamp, Scarrett, Shadlock, Smith, Stanley, Swallow, Tait, Taylor, Varey, Vaughan, Wiggett, Winter, Wood, Wright, Young

**Petterick:** Boswell
**Petulengro:** Lee
**Pharoc:** Lee
**Phebe:** See Phoebe
**Phebia:** Matthews. Variant on Phoebe
**Phelps (m):** Heron
**Phenia:** Ayres
**Phesant:** Cp. Fezanti. Buckland, Pierce, Roberts, Smith
**Philadelphia/ Philladfelia:** Boswell, Carter
**Philie:** French
**Philippa:** Scamp
**Philledis:** Lee
**Phillip:** Bell, Boswell, Carter, Dixie, Eley, Fuller, Gray, Hatseyggaw, Heron, Kelly, Lee, Lovell, Loveridge, Martin, Murphy, Scamp, Skeets, Smith
**Phillips:** Ayres, Boswell
**Phineas/Phinehas:** Ayres, Lee, Loveridge
**Phinnymore:** Lee. See Finnamore
**Phoeba:** Bean/Beaney, **Smith**
**Phoebe/Phebe/Pheby:** Arnold, Ayres, Bean/Beaney, Boswell, Bowers, Brown, Buckland, Buckley, Buggs, Bunce/ Bunts, Campbell, Clayton, Collinson, Cooper, Davies, Dennard, Eastwood, Finney, Ford, French, Fuller, Gess, Gray, Gumble, Heath, Heron, Hicks, James, Johnson, Keet, Lawson, Lee, Lock, Lovell, Loveridge, Matthews, Miles, Mudd, Nunns, Orchard, Pannell, Penfold, Procter, Ransley, Ripley, Roberts, Robinson, Rogers, Sa(u)nders, Scamp, Shaw, Sherriff, Small, Smith, Stanley, Stephens, Stewart, Stone, Tapsall, Taylor, Walker, Watson, Weston, White, Williams, Wingrove, Young
**Phoenice:** Lovell. Cp Phoenix
**Phoenix:** Boswell, Gray, Heron, Lovell, Smith, Taylor. Cp Fennix, Fennik and Phoenice.

**Phvenet:** Boswell
**Phyllis/Phillis:** Bird, Bluett, Boswell, Buttery, Cooper, Eastwood, French, Gibbs, Heron, Hibberd, Inwood, Jeffs/ Jeffery, Lee, Lock, Penfold, Ripley, Smith, Townsley
**Pianapicot:** Boswell
**Pianna:** Lee
**Pickett (m):** Lee
**Piki:** Smith
**Pilaster:** See Plaster
**Pin (f):** Boswell, Gray
**Pine/Pyne (f):** Scamp
**Pinki:** Mace, Reynolds, Smith
**Pinner:** Buckland
**Pipa:** Pierce, Stanley
**Piramus/Pyramus:** Gray
**Pizinnia:** Smith
**Pizzler:** Smith
**Plansina:** Boswell
**Plaster:** Lee
**Plato:** Biddle, Boswell, Buckland, Buckley, Lee, Loveridge, Smith, Taylor
**Pleasance:** Boswell, Shaw
**Plesant:** Buckley
**Plentiness:** Boswell
**Plenty:** Boswell, Lock, organ
**Poddles:** Hanneford
**Pol:** Gaskin, Mair
**Poland:** Levy
**Polenio:** Matthews
**Poley (m):** Gray, Heron, Lock, Mace, Robinson
**Polius:** Heron
**Pollandra:** Scamp
**Polly/Pol (f):** Ayres, Biddle, Boswell, Cooper, Elliott, Fenner, Gray, Green, Griffiths, Harris, Heron, Kelly, Lamb, Lee, Light, Lock, Loveridge, Mace, Orchard, Penfold, Philpott, Powell, Price, Rock, Royal, Sa(u)nders(on), Scamp, Sherriff, Smith, Stanley, Tampsett, Williams, Wood
**Polono:** Heron
**Polovene (f):** Heron

**Polypha:** Boswell
**Pompi:** Lee
**Pony:** Moore
**Poppy:** Boswell
**Posh:** Price
**Postellion:** Gray
**Potamus/Posthumas:** Gray
**Poti:** Gray
**Poultney:** Boswell
**Powers:** Smith
**Praesie:** Jones
**Prettymaid:** Smith
**Price (m):** Jones
**Pricey:** Smith
**Pridy:** Smith
**Prime (m):** Rogers
**Prince:** Miller
**Priscilla/Precilla/Pressilla/ Prisseller:** Bagley, Beaney, Boswell, Bowers, Brazil, Burrett, Campbell, Camfield, Carter, Coleman, Collinson, Cooper, Dale, Dean, Eastwood, Florence, Fowler, Gess, Golby, Halden, Heap, Heron, Hollett, Jones, Lee, Lock, Loveridge, Lowther, Nichols(on), Penfold, Potter, Ripley, Roberts, Rogers, Ross, Sa(u)nders. Scamp, Shaw, Sherriff, Small, Smith, Stone, Tapsell, Thompson, Wells, Welsh, Williams, Wood
**Prissy:** Ball, Friend, Jones
**Pritchard:** Gibben
**Pritharne:** Honour
**Prito:** Smith
**Privalla:** Green
**Providence (f):** Baildon, Beldam, Heron
**Prudence/Prudy/Pru:** Barber, Boswell, Buckland, Chilcott, Heron, Lee, Lock, Loveridge, Rogers, Ryles, Scamp, Smith, Stephens, Tooby
**Prunella:** Archer
**Pulla:** Morgan
**Punch:** Cooper
**Purify**: Boswell
**Purpagilian:** Heron
**Puxon (f):** Heron

**Pyne:** See Pine
**Pyramus:** See Piramus
**Pysanet:** Boswell
**Pythagorus:** Clayton
**Quality:** Butler, Heron
**Queen (f):** Gray
**Queenascony:** Loveridge
**Queenation:** Gostlow, Smith
**Queenesia:** Loveridge
**Queenie (f):** Scamp, Smith, Stone, Wood
**Quinkie:** Lee
**Quinton (m):** Hogg
**Rab:** Marshall
**Rabbi/ Rebbi/ Reby:** Boswell, Gray, Heron, Jones, Lee, Lock, Scamp, Shaw, Sherriff, Smith, Taylor. (Almost always a male name, but very occasionally f)
**Rachel /Rechal/Rachael (f):** Allen, Ayres, Bailey, Blythe, Boswell, Castle, Draper, Heron, Hughes, Ingram, Lee, Lock, McLaren, Orchard, Penfold, Richards, Ripley, Ruthven, Scamp, Smith, Swales, Thomas, Whitaker, Williams
**Rachel (m):** Smith
**Radulphi:** Lee
**Radulphus (m):** Boswell
**Rady:** Cooper
**Rai/Rye/Rhy (m):** Elliott, Evans, Scamp, Taylor. This name is sometimes confused with Ray — they are not the same name
**Raia/ Rhy/ Ria/ Rye/ Ryer/ Ra/ Rhia (f):** Boswell, Bowers, Brazil, Brown, Carter, Chilcott, Heath, Heron, Lee, Lovell, Osmond, Scamp, Scarrett, Sherriff, Small
**Raial:** Boswell
**Raili:** Lovell, Smith. Cp Riley
**Railton:** Weller
**Raisi/Raise:** Evans, Lovell
**Raleigh:** Scamp. Cp Riley
**Ralph:** Allen, Brotherton, Dixon, Gamester, Lee, Leyland, Robinson, Smith, Taylor, Todd
**Ramley:** Boswell
**Ramona:** Scamp
**Ramore:** Scamp

**Rana (f):** Lovell
**Randalus:** Taylor, Wood
**Randle/Randell/ Randol:** Boswell, Heron, Lee, Smith, Taylor, Williams
**Randolph:** Brown
**Ranson:** Lee
**Rany:** Seen Reni
**Ranyeal:** Lee
**Raphael:** Lee
**Raphe:** Boswell
**Raura:** Boswell
**Rawlins:** Heron
**Raney (f):** See Rayney
**Ray (f):** Heron. Jeffries
**Raymond:** Rogers, Scarrett, Woolgar
**Rayni/ Rani/ Rawney/ Rainey (f):** Boswell, Pike, Young. Cp Reni.
**Reade (f):** Boswell
**Reading (f):** Smith
**Rebbi:** See Rabbi
**Rebecca/Rebekah:** Many families
**Rebena:** Vaughan
**Reboam:** Lovell
**Rechabina (f):** Lee
**Rechal:** See Rachel.
**Reconcile:** Smith
**Recrusha:** Buckland
**Redeemus:** Boswell
**Rederick:** Lee
**Redos:** Small
**Redpath (m):** Hogg
**Reeve:** Boswell
**Reg:** Sloper
**Regenda:** Lee, Townsend. Cp Richenda
**Regimen** Scamp
**Reginald:** Miller, Scamp, Smith
**Register:** Smith
**Relia:** Boswell
**Relly/ Reily:** Alexander, Lee, McFarlane, Shearing. Cp Cinderella

**Rena:** Boswell
**Render/Renda:** Bibby, Boswell, Green, Smith, Taylor
**Renetta:** Penfold
**Reni (f):** Boswell, Buckland, Cooper, Deighton, Gray, Heron, Scarrett, Shaw, Sherriff, Smith. Cp Rayni
**Repentance:** Lee, Potter, Randall, Smith
**Repona/Reponia:** Chilcott
**Repronia/Repronia:** Lee
**Reservoir/Resevir/Rizavoi:** Butler, Fletcher, Smith. Cp Rizavoi
**Reuben:** Barton, Bird, Bond, Boswell, Brinkley, Colan, Cooper, Falkener, Gillam, Gray, Hall, Harris, Heron, Hicks, Jones, Lee, Lovell, Mann, Murphy, Musto, Nichols(on), Potter, Price, Randall, Roberts, Scarrett, Shaw, Shepherd, Sherriff, Smith, Taylor, Walker, Wallett, Watson, Wood
**Revance:** Kennedy
**Rex:** Walton
**Reynold(s):** Heron, Smith
**Rhia:** See Raia
**Rhoda/ Roda/ Rhode:** Anderson, Barnes, Barney, Booth, Boswell, Brinkley, Burton, Cooper, Draper, Gray, Green, Johnson, Lee, Lovell, Matthews, McLean, Rossiter, Scamp, Scarrett, Small, Smith, Stanley, Stubley, Taylor, Vaughan, Wells, Young
**Rhodabella:** Ayres
**Rhodi:** Gray, Smith, Stanley
**Rhodian:** Boswell
**Rhona:** Boswell
**Rhonda:** Scarrott
**Rhy:** See Raia
**Ria:** See Raia
**Rial:** Heron
**Rice (f):** Heron
**Richard/Dick:** Many families
**Richelda:** Bagley, Carey, Scamp, Smith
**Richen(ige)nda:** Boswell, Heron, Lee, Townsend, Tribe, Young. Cp Regenda
**Ricky:** Smith
**Ridey:** Lamb
**Riding:** Arnold
**Rifey:** Lovell

**Right Door:** Lee
**Righteous:** Draper, Gray, Lee, Smith
**Right/Righto:** Buckland, Buckley, Smith
**Rigo/Riggy:** Scamp
**Riley:** Beldorn, Boswell, Coats, Eastwood, Jeffery/Jeffs, Lee, Lovell, McLean, Scamp, Sherriff, Smith, Ward. Cp Raili
**Rina:** Boswell, Jones
**Riotus:** Lee
**Rita:** Emmett, Finney, Lee, Lovell, Scamp
**River(s):** Jordan
**Rizavoi/ Reavoi:** Butler, Fletcher, Smith. Cp Reservoir
**Roady (f):** Dinson
**Rob:** Jones
**Robbins/Robbun/ Robin**: Booth, Boswell, Scamp
**Robby:** Carter, Newbury, Newland
**Robert/Bob:** Most families
**Roberts (m):** Lee
**Robin:** Gray, Shaw, Taylor, Todd
**Robina:** Hogg, Scamp, Small, Smith, White
**Robinson (m):** Green, Lee, Stewart
**Robjent:** Boswell
**Rocky:** Price, Scamp
**Roda:** See Rhoda
**Roderic(k(:** Podalaze, Ripley, Scamp, Scarrett
**Rodi/ Rodia (f):** Boswell, Coleman, Elliott. Gray, Heron, Hope, Ingram, Jones, Mochan, Taylor
**Rodney (f):** Smith
**Rodney (m):** Brinkley, Lee, Shaw, Smith, Stone
**Rodolphus**. See Rudolphus
**Rodos:** Small
**Rodsome:** Lock
**Roger:** Boswell, Buckland, Harby, Jones, Lee, Pinkney, Thompson, Tuttle
**Roland/Rowland:** Gabriel, Jackson/Jacques, Johnson, Robinson, Smith, Stephens, Totten, Wood
**Roller:** Smith
**Roma (f):** Scamp
**Romaly:** Hesketh
**Roman:** Taylor

**Romany:** Smith
**Ron:** Worral
**Rona:** Smith
**Ronald:** Bowman, Frankham, Lovell, Scamp, Scarrett
**Ronna:** Small **Ronnie:** Booth, Taylor, Wiggins
**Rosa:** Brinkley, Butler, Foster, Gaskin, Heebef, Heron, Johnson, Levy, Lock, Lovell, Loveridge, Matthews, Mitchell, Potter, Robinson, Rogers, Scarrett, Smith, Thorne, Vanis, Vaughan, Wall, Willett, Williams
**Rosabella:** Chilcott
**Rosaina/ Rosehanna/ Roseana/ Rosanna/ Rosina/ Roseannne/ Roseina/ Rosane/ Rosenna:** Ayres, Boswell, Buckland, Carter, Davies, Finney, Green, Griffiths, Heron, Holland, Kitt, Lane, Lee, Lovell, Loveridge, Mitchell, Penfold, Price, Ray, Robinson, Rogers, Scamp, Scarrett, Small, Smith, Vanis, Wall, Wells, Willett, Williams, Wood
**Rosaline/Rosalina/ Rosalind:** Finney, Lee, Lovell, Scamp, Smith, Stirling, Taylor
**Rosamund:** Boswell, Smith
**Roschille:** Lee
**Rose:** Ball, Beale, Boswell, Brazil, Brinkley, Brown, Buckley, Camfield, Cartridge, Casey, Chappell, Cooper, Crow, Davies, Ellis, Finney, Francis, Fuller, Gatehouse, Glaizier, Godsmark, Gray, Gritt, Hancock, Harris, Hedges, Heron, Johnson, Jones, Keet, King, Lee, Lovell, Loveridge, Maitby, Manning, Marshall, Mitchell, McLean, Mochan, Moss, Nanye, Nichols(on), Phillips, Pike, Porter, Price, Richardson, Ripley, Roberts, Rowel, Scamp, Scarrett, Schooling, Seldon, Selmes, Shaw, Shepherd, Slater, Small, Smith, Stephens, Taylor, Thompson, Turner, Valentine, Wass, Welsh, Young
**Rose(l)la:** Lee, Scamp, Small, Yalden
**Rosemarie/-a/ Rosemary:** Barringer, Childs, Edwards, Scamp, Scarrett, Smith, Taylor, Young
**Rosetta:** Booth, Boswell, Brown, Dale, Hale, Harris, Johnson, Lee, Rowley, Smith, Stephens. Todd
**Rosey/Rosie:** Baillie, Booth, Buckley, Gordon, Gray, Griffiths, Lee,:ight, Lovell, Merrick, Mitchell, Ripley, Rossiter, Scamp, Small, Taylor
**Rosi(a)na:** Beckett, Hiscox, Johnson, Lee, Lovell, Mace, Mitchell,

Rossiter, Scamp, Small, Wells
**Roslyn:** Campbell
**Ross:** Gray
**Rough/Roughie:** Baker, Marshall
**Row:** Lovell
**Rowaras:** Boswell
**Rowena:** Scott, Smith
**Rowland:** See Roland
**Roy:** Sanger, Scamp, Scarrett, Taylor
**Royal (m):** Heron, Lee
**Royl;ance:** Lovell
**Royley:** McLean, Scamp
**Rozieanah:** Mace
**Rubin.** See Reuben
**Ruby:** Scamp, Thomas, Webber
**Rudolph:** Heron
**Rudolphus:** Boswell, Lee, Smith
**Rufus:** Nichols(on)
**Ruhanna/Ruhama:** Boswell
**Rupert:** Smith
**Ruslo:** Lee
**Russell:** Godden, Scamp
**Ruth:** Boswell, Brockless, Butler, Carter, Chilcott, Collison, Crosse, Evans, Finney, Ford, Gaskin, Heron, Joules, Lee, Lovell, Loveridge, Matthews, McLean, Newbury, Penfold, Price, Ripley, Rogers, Rossiter, Shepherd, Small, Smith, Vaughan, Williams, Willson, Wood, Young
**Rye:** See Rai
**Sabarata:** Smith
**Sabatha:** Ford
**Sabina (h)/Sabin/ Sabaina:** Ayres, Boswell, Buckland, Burton, Draper, Gray, Heron, Lee, Lovell, Loveridge, Smith
**Sabra/Saborah:** Hudson, Leatherland, Light, McLean, Smith, Whittle
**Sabraina:** Cooper. Cp Saiberenni.
**Sabrina:** Lovell
**Sacky/Saccy/Saki:** Boswell, Finney
**Sacole:** Femine
**Sady/Sadie:** McCready, Smith

**Safely (m):** Scamp
**Saffery:** Scamp
**Sage (f):** Boswell, Draper, Heron, Smith
**Sagel (m):** Odam
**Sagy:** Heron
**Saiberenni:** Boswell, Draper, Holland, Smith. Cp Sabraina.
**Saibi:** Smith
**Saiena:** See Seni
**Saiera/ Syari/ Syeira/ Syer:** Abbott, Boswell, Bowstead, Buckland, Draper, Heron, Lee, Lovell, McLean, Smith, Taylor
**Saifi:** Lovell, Scamp
**Saiforella/ Syforella:** Price, Roberts, Templeman, Wood
**Saiki:** Heron
**Sailor:** Emmitt
**Saily:** See Seli
**Saini:** See Seni
**Saint Noah:** (Probably the same name as Santania). Boswell
**Sal:** Lee
**Saladin:** Heron
**Salamander:** Scamp
**Salarina/-e:** Heron
**Salathiel:** Boswell
**Salavico/Salavice:** Smith
**Salavena/Salavino/Salvino:** Boswell, Smith
**Saley:** See Seli.
**Salina:** See Selina
**Salissa:** Scamp
**Salloman:** Swales
**Sally:** Anderson, Barnes, Booth, Boswell, Dennard, Drury, Evans, Green, Heron, Hicks, Johnson, Jones, Lee, Price, Ripley, Rose, Scamp, Sherriff, Smith, Taylor
**Salome:** Buckland, Draper, Hedges, James, Smith, Stone. a comon variant on this name is Loomi, which see.
**Salthera:** Loveridge
**Salvester:** See Sylvester
**Sam/Sammy:** See Samuel.
**Samantha:** Lee, Scamp
**Sambriel:** Heron, Lovell
**Sampi (f):** Boswell, Finney

**Samrock:** Lock
**Sam(p)son:** Ayres, Barton, Berry, Blackham, Boswell, Butler, Chilcott, Colbert, Cooper, Gardener, Garey, Green, Harrison, Heron, Holland, James, Johnson, Lee, Light, Loveridge, Nichols(on), Oadley, Palmer, Pilcer, Price, Roberts, Robinson, Rowland, Scamp, Smith, Swales, Taylor, Young
**Samuel:** Most families
**Sanburn:** Boswell
**Sandra:** Brown, Lee, Scamp, Scarrett
**Sandy:** Brown, Lovell, Miller
**Saney (f):** See Seni
**Saniobra:** Boswell
**Sanders:** See Saunders
**Sandi/Sandy:** Barrett, Brown, Faw, Lovell, Miller, Townsley
**Saniobia (m):** Boswell
**Sanpeel (f):** Reynolds
**Sansby:** Deighton, Lee
**Sanspirella/ Sanspareil (f):** Boswell, Heron, Lee, Scamp, Smith
**Sant:** Boswell, Buckley
**Santa:** Thomas
**Santalina:** Buckley
**Santa Maria:** Boswell
**Santania/Santanoa:** Boswell, Printer
**Sapy:** Lovell
**Sarah:** Most families
**Sarahanna:** Rogers, Taylor
**Saraje:** Boswell
**Sary:** Boswell
**Sasparil:** Scamp
**Satchwell:** Arnold
**Sativia:** Smith**Satona:** Finch
**Saul:** Scamp
**Saunders/Sanders:** Boswell, Deighton, Draper, Gaskin, Smith
**Savaina/Savina/Savinia:** Boswell, Gray, Lee, Lovell
**Savery (m):** Scamp
**Sayers:** Gray, Heron
**Sayki:** Boswell
**Sayni:** Boswell, Smith
**Saythi:** Boswell

**Scarrett:** Boswell
**Scott (m):** Boswell, Brown, Scamp
**Scott (f):** Scamp
**Sculian (f):** Draper
**Sean:** Boswell, O'Neil
**Sebastane:** Lawlor
**Sebastian:** Collins, Lawlor
**Sebra:** Lock
**Sebriol:** Lock
**Secelia:** See Cecelia
**Sedinia:** Gray, Heron
**Seely:** Scamp. Cp Seli
**Seji:** Boswell, Gray, Heron, Smith, Williams
**Seki:** Boswell
**Selby:** Ayres
**Selesia:** Lee
**Seli/ Saily/ Saly (f):** Brazil, Price, Robinson, Taylor. Cp Seely
**Selia:** See Celia
**Seliana:** Boswell
**Selina/Seline/Selena:** Ayres, Bean/Beaney, Biddle, Bishop, Boswell, Buckley, Burton, Butler, Camfield, Camp, Campbell, Clifford, Colman, Cooper, Draper, Duck, Eastwood, Elsey, Emmett, Evans, Finney, Green, Hedges, Heron, Hicks, Higgin, Holmes, Hughes, Irving, James, Jones, Knight, Leatherland, Lee, Lovell, Moon, Murphy, Organ, Parker, Peters, Price, Ridlewy, Roberts, Rogers, Scamp, Scarrett, Schooling, Shaw, Sherriff, Smith, Spencer, Stacey, Staff, Steele, Stephens, Taylor
**Selinda:** Elsey
**Selinia:** Staff
**Seliona: James**
**Semania:** Boswell
**Sence:** Smith
**Senentia:** Scarrett
**Seni/Saney/Saini/ Saiena (f):** Boswell, Buckley, Burton, Cooper, East, Florence, Heron, Lee, McLean, Price, Smith, Stephens
**Senimenta:** Buckland
**Sentelina:** Evans
**Sentibel:** Evans
**Sentinia:** Smith

**Sentinius:** Smith
**Sentley:** Loveridge
**Sentman (f):** Marshall
**Senty:** Penfold
**Separ(r)i (f):** Boswell, Heron
**Septimus (m):** Boswell, Cooper, Crosby, Gibson, Stewart
**Septirus:** Boswell
**Sequah (m):** Heron
**Serena:** Collinson, Lee, Townsend
**Servita:** Napolian
**Sesalley:** Lee
**Seth/i:** Boswell, Heron, Lee, Lovell, Rogers, Swales
**Seulian (f):** Draper
**Sevina:** Lee
**Seymour:** Barker, Shepherd
**Shadrack/Shadrick:** Alford, Ayre, Boswell, Heron, Lee, Loveridge, Roberts, Scarrott, Smith
**Shady/ Shedi:** Heron, John(s), Smith
**Shafto:** Boswell
**Shake (f):** Lee
**Shandres:** Camp, Gray, Lee, Scamp, Smith
**Shandrop:** Boswell
**Shandrus:** Boswell
**Shane:** Scamp
**Shani (f):** Fowkes
**Shanni (m):** Baxter, Boswell, Finney, Gray, Phillips, Scamp, Steele
**Shan(n)on:** Cameron, McDonald, McLean, Shepherd
**Shanny (f):** Wood
**Sharleen:** O'Neil (Cp Charlene)
**Sharlott:** Scarrett (Var. On Charlotte)
**Sharnderer (m):** Lovell. Cp Syrenda
**Sharon:** Lee
**Shaunon (f):** Webb
**Shaw (m):** Wilson
**Shawn:** See Sean
**Sheardon (m):** Stephens
**Shearman:** Johnson
**Sheba:** Lock
**Shedi:** See Shady

**Sheila:** Brown, Lee, Scamp
**Shenton:** Lovell
**Shepherd** (f) Boswell, Green
**Sherriff (m):** Baker, Boswell, Johnson
**Shevasanah (f):** Scamp
**Shillingworth:** Boswell
**Shilvaiah (f):** Ingram
**Shippy:** Buckland
**Shipton:** Buckland, Smith, Synes
**Shirley:** Ayres, Jameson, Scamp, Smith
**Shooky/Shuki:** Burton, Lee, Smith
**Shoori/Shuri/Shurensi (f):** Boswell, Chilcott, Heron, Smith, Young
**Shoshoi/Shushi:** Price
**Shotgun:** Price
**Shuki:** See Shooky.
**Shurensi (Shuri):** See Shoori.
**Siaforella:** Wood
**Siah:** Smith
**Siani:** Wood
**Siari:** Boswell, Burton, Draper, Wood
**Siberensi/Sybaranor/Sibereni:** Buckland, Flint, Heron, Smith
**Sibereti (f):** Heron
**Sibi/Sibbie:** Boswell, Doe, Draper, Fletcher, Heron, Smith, West
**Sibil//Sibell(a):** See Sybil
**Sibillene:** Bagley
**Sicily:** Smith
**Sid:** See Sidney
**Side:** Taylor
**Sidnal(l):** Baker, Smith
**Sidney/Sid:** Baker, Boswell, Braham, Brazil, Brinkley, Buckley, Cooper, Dooley, Finney, Fletcher, Heron, Hughes, Jackson, Jones, Kidd, Lee, Lovell, Rogers, Scamp, Scarrett, Shaw, Shepherd, Smith, Stock, Taylor, Todd, Toms, Tyler, Welsh, White
**Siffy:** Smith
**Signet:** See Cygnet
**Siharer:** Coleman
**Silas:** Hughes, Lee, Smith
**Sileby:** Heron

**Silena:** Smith
**Silence:** Boswell, Johnson, McLean, Smith
**Silenda:** See Molenda
**Silethian/Silerthian:** Boswell
**Silvaina/Silvania:** Lovell, Wood
**Silvanus**: Ayres, Boswell, Fletcher, Hicks, Pike, Roebuck, Smith
**Silver (f):** Jones
**Silverthorn:** Smith
**Silvesta (f):** Gray, Smith
**Silvester:** See Sylvester
**Silvia:** See Sylvia
**Silvey:** Carter
**Silvio:** Smith
**Siminta:** Lee. Probably to be connected with Romany *Simenta*, 'cousin'.
**Sim(m)eon:** Boswell, Green, Smith
**Simon:** Biddle, Boswell, Davies, Fraser, Harris, Johnson, Lee, Sherriff, Smith, Sutton, Wilson
**Simonem:** Marshall
**Simphy:** Doe, Smith
**Simpronius Bohemia:** Boswell
**Simson:** Lee
**Sinah:** Boswell
**Sinai:** Boswell
**Sincere:** Lee
**Sinclair (m):** Chapman
**Sinderella:** See Cinderella
**Sinerus:** McLean, Smith
**Sinetta:** Lambourne, Smith
**Sinnamenta:** See Cinamenta
**Sinfai/ Sinfire:** Boswell, Brown, Buckland, Gray, Hazard, Heron, Lee, Lewis, Lovell, Pierce, Slender, Smith, Taylor
**Singi:** Buckley
**Sini:** Buckland, Heron
**Sinti:** Taylor
**Sinurus:** Heron, Smith
**Siobhan:** Page, Spencer
**Siterus (m):** Boswell, Lewis
**Siverency:** Butler

**Sivewella Awswell:** Boswell
**Skipper:** Buckley
**Slack:** Lovell
**Slasher:** Lee
**Slater (m):** Scott
**Smith (f):** Boswell, Scarrett
**Smith (m):** Wells
**Snakey:** Boswell
**Snippy/Snipey:** Brown, Butler
**Snow/ Snow Alley/ SnowEllen/ Snoweli (f):** Boswell, Evans, Gray, Heron
**Snowdon/Snowi:** Evans
**Solena/ Solamina:** Boswell, Smith
**Solinon:** Heron
**Solivaino/ Solavina (m):** Heron, Smith
**Solomon:** Barton, Boswell, Clarke, Deighton, Doe, Draper, Elliott, Gray, Heartless, Heron, Holland, Johns, Johnson, Jones, Keet, Lee, Light, Lock, Lovell, Loveridge, McLean, Penfold, Reader, Robinson, Scamp, Sherriff, Smith, Swales, Taylor, Williams, Wood, Young
**Somerset:** Lock
**Sonia:** Scamp
**Sonny:** Miley, Price, Sherwood, Stone
**Soobi:** Smith
**Soodi:** Lee
**Soph:** Weeks
**Sophia/Sopha**: Arnold, Austin, Ayres, Baglin, Baker, Ball, Booth, Boswell, Buckland, Buckley, Burton, Charlotte, Chilcott, Cooper, Davies, Draper, Gamester, Golbey, Gray, Gregory, Guthrie, Harris, Harvey, Head, Heron, Hicks, Huggins, Hughes, Ingram, Isden, Jones, Kemp, Lee, Lock, Lovell, Manley, McLean, Munro, Neale, Orchard, Pike, Rogers, Rose, Sanders, Sawyer, Scamp, Scarrett, Shaw, Sherrard, Sherriff, Small, Smith, Snelling, Stanley, Stephens, Steward, Taylor, Thurston, Wallett, Welsh, Wood
**Sophie/Sofie**: Boswell, Carter, Godsmark, Heron, Karpath, Lee, Manley, Matthews, Orchard, Penfold, Sa(u)nders(on), Scamp, Shaw, Smith
**Sophrania:** Boswell
**Spam (m):** Scamp

**Spanish:** Lovell
**Spears:** Smith
**Speedy:** Boswell
**Speller:** Boswell
**Spencer (m):** Draper, Lovell, Rainbow, Sherriff
**Spennymoor:** Stephens
**Spicella:** Matchett
**Spicer:** Cooper
**Spider/Spidey:** Bennett, Price
**Spinky:** Huxley
**Spiranna:** Boswell
**Spiratana:** Smith
**Spizzani:** Heron
**Spoati/Spot:** Boswell
**Sportcella/Sportseller:** Boswell, Taylor
**Spring (m):** Small
**Squire (m):** Lee, Thorpe
**Stacey (f):** Lee
**Stacey (m):** Lee, Marshall, Scamp
**Stafford:** Lovell
**Stanbury** (f): Boswell
**Standfield:** Lovell
**Stanley:** Draper, Evans, Higgins, Mason, Scamp, Scarrett, Smith, Vinden, Webb, Wyatt
**Stanney (m):** Shaw
**Stapleton:** Smith
**Star (f):** Booth, Price
**Stari (f):** Boswell, Heron
**Starina/Starini:** Price
**Starkey:** Boswell
**Stella:** Wood
**Stephanie:** Scamp
**Stephen/Steven/Steve:** Adams, Bennett, Boswell, Chambers, Clarke, Clout, Gatehouse, Gobie, Green, Heron, Hewitt, Jones, Lee, Livermore, Lock, Newbury, Palmer, Penfold, Pierce, Pitcher, Richardson, Riley, Rogers, Rossiter, Scamp, Scarrett, Smith, Stone. Taylor, Thomas, Todd
**Stephenson:** Jones
**Steve:** See Stephen

**Stevi:** Loveridge
**Stewart:** Boswell, O'Neil
**Stinki:** Buckland
**Stoker:** Reynolds
**Stollting (m):** Storey
**Storm:** Ellse, Scamp
**Stranger:** Boswell, Heron, Price
**Studivares/Stradiveres:** Boswell, Lovell
**Stumpy:** Heron. Probably a nickname
**Subi:** Evans, Lee, Lock, Smith
**Sudamore:** Boswell
**Sudi (f):** Lee
**Sugar:** Smith
**Sugden (m):** Lee
**Sukey (f):** Heron, Mawbley, Ripley, Shaw
**Sunny:** See Sonny
**Superior:** Harris
**Superly:** Smith
**Surlinda:** Lee
**Surrender:** See Syrenda
**Susan:** Many families.
**Susanna(h):** Many families.
**Sushanah:** Penfold
**Susie:** Boswell, Finney, McCready, Sa(u)nders, Smith
**Suti:** Loveridge, Shaw
**Suvesti:** Gardener
**Swaley:** Buckley
**Swallow (m):** Heron
**Swan (f):** Finney
**Sweetheart:** Heron
**Swithin:** Rose
**Syari:** See Saiera
**Sybil/Sibil/Sybell(a):** Boswell, Draper, Finney, Green, Heron, James, Lee, Newham, Smith
**Sybilla:** Boswell
**Sybaranor/Sybarine:** Heron, Smith
**Sydney:** See Sidney
**Syeira/Syer:** See Saiera
**Syforella:** See Saiforella

**Sylbia/Sylbe:** Ayres
**Sylvania:** Lee
**Sylvanus:** See Silvanus
**Sylvester/Silvester:** Booth, Boswell, Draper, Harris, Jones, Lee, Matthis, Loveridge, Scamp, Smith, Taylor, Thorpe, Webb
**Sylvia/Silvia:** Buckley, Gatehouse, Lee, Scamp, Smith
**Symon:** See Simon
**Symond:** Smith
**Sympathy/Symphy:** Buckland, Draper, Loveridge
**Synay:** Boswell
**Synet:** Hiscox
**Syrenda/ Surrender:** Lovell
**Tabitha:** Boswell, Lee
**Taimi:** Boswell
**Taianive:** Scamp. Cp Tienni etc.
**Taishan:** Boswell
**Taiso:** See Tyso
**Talaitha/Talitha/Tilaithi:** Cooper, Hedges, Lee
**Tam:** Blyth, Faw, Gordon
**Tamar:** Camfield, Lee, Miller
**Tamara:** Toogood
**Tamasine:** Clarke, Scamp
**Tannayha:** See Teannah.
**Tantel:** Loveridge
**Tanya:** Stephens
**Tardy (m):** Lee
**Taresia:** Light
**Tasso:** See Tyso
**Tate:** Boswell
**Taw:** Wood
**Taylor:** Gibson
**Teannah/Teanni/ Tannayha (f):** Cp Tee-eni, Tearnai and Tehenna. Booth, Buckland, Fletcher, Marshall, Townsend
**Teante:** Boswell
**Tearnai:** Boswell. Cp Teannah, Tehenna and Tee-eni
**Ted/Teddy:** Black, Buckland, Butler, Lee, Mahoney, Matthews, Scamp, Sloper, Smith, Stevens
**Tee-eni/Teni/Tienna (f):** Boswell, Buckland, Gregory, Heron, Mullinger, Penfold, Smith, Townsend. Cp Teannah, Tehenna and

Tearnai.
**Teerus (m):** Loveridge
**Tehenna:** Cp Teannah, Tee-eni and Tearnai.    Buckland
**Temperance:** Boswell, Lee, Lock, Lovell, Smith, Vaughan
**Tempest (m):** Lee
**Teni:** See Tee-eni
**Tennant/Tenny:** Buckley, Florence, Lock, Smith
**Ter(r)ence/Terry:** Cavena, Colbert, Heron, Lee, Scamp, Scarrett
**Teras:** See Tiras
**Teresa/Theresa/Terizah:** Flint, Gray, Lee, Marshall, O'Neil, Scamp, Smith, South, Thaniel
**Terey (m):** Stanloey
**Testaner:** Smith
**Tet:** Wood
**Thady:** Chilcott
**Thalias:** Orchard
**Thannie: Data lost**
**Thasia:** Boswell
**Theanetta:** Scamp. Cp Trianetta.
**Thelmy:** Marshall
**Theo:** Boswell
**Theodora:** White
**Theodore:** Baker, Boswell, Heron, Lee, Lovell, Matthews, Scarrett, Vaughan
**Theodosia:** Boswell, Gray. Harding, Heron, McLean
**Theophilus/is/ Theofilus:** Boswell, Clayton, Heron, Lee, Nicklas, Scarrett, Smith, Wood
**Theresa:** See Teresa
**Theusela:** Baxter (? an abbreviation for Methuselah)
**Thilda:** Murphy
**Thinza:** Lee
**Thirza:** See Thurza
**Thomas:** Most families.
**Thomasen:** Boswell
**Thomasine:** Curtis, Wilson
**Thoms**: Boswell
**Thor:** Scarrott
**Thorney:** Boswell, Price
**Thurza/Thirza (f):** Boswell, Lee, Miller, Orchard, Smith,

Stephens, Taylor
**Thust (m):** Small
**Thy (m):** Turner
**Tibby:** Booth, Scott
**Tidi:** Wharton
**Tidli:** Dedman
**Tienni:** See Tee-eni
**Tiger:** Shaw
**Tikla:** Ripley
**Tilaitha:** Cooper, lewis
**Tilda:** Boswell, Fox, Gaskin, Gray, Heron, Lee, Penfold, Smith, Webb, Winter
**Tilly/Tillie/Tilla:** Ball, Booth, Burdon, Cooper, Finney, Lee, Penfold, Shaw, Smith, Wood
**Timewell:** Boswell
**Timothy:** Boswell, Brearley, Buckland, Dailey, Heron, Holland, Ford, Lee, Morgan, Price, Robinson, Thompson, Wild
**Tina:** Brown, Finney, Heron, Lovell, Scamp, Scarrett, Sherriff
**Tini (m):** Mace
**Tinker/Tinkerfield:** Heron, Jones, Loftus (probably only as a nickname)
**Tippin/Tipping:** Boswell
**Tiras/Teras:** Mace
**Tish:** Barnett
**Titsum/Titsi (f):** Lee, Smith
**Titus:** Boswell, Jones, Lee
**Tizzy:** Ripley
**Tobias:** Boswell, Shaw, Smith
**Tobit:** Shaw
**Toby:** Shaw
**Todlin:** See Tudlin
**Tolley:** Smith
**Tom:** Birch, Boswell, Cole, Collins, Cooper, Curlit. Dawson, Draper, Finney, Gray, Gregory, Jones, Lawrence, Lee, Loveridge, McCready, Miley, Moore, Musto, Price, Quinlan, Sayers, Scamp, Sherriff, Turner

---

**NOTE**: Although Tom and Tommy are common abbreviations of Thomas, on these occasions they appear to be names in their own right.

**Tommy:** Boswell, Cooper, Darkus, Downes, Lewis, Olfred, Ross, Young
**Tompsin:** Boswell
**Toni (f):** Scamp
**Tony:** Butler, Finney, Lee, Penfold, Scamp, Stone
**Toodly (m):** Lee
**Tooka (m):** Heron
**Tooter:** Price
**Tootles/Tottles:** Price, Smith
**Tootsy/Toots:** Heron, Price
**Towla:** Baillie
**Townsend (m):** Lee
**Townsey:** Sampson
**Tracey (m)/Tresi:** Boswell, Heron, McCready, Onions, Sherriff
**Tracey (f):** Barnes, Scamp, Smith
**Trafalgar (= Algar):** Boswell, Mace
**Trainette:** See Traynit
**Trainti:** See Traynit
**Tranetta/ Tranette/ Traynit/ Trainette/ Trainti/ Trainet/ Trenet/ Trenetti/ Traienti/ Trianti/ Trinetta/ Trametti/ Tryanti:** Boswell, Boyling, Buckley, Burton, Cooper, Crocker, Finney, Gibbs, Heron, Lee, Love, Lovell, Loveridge, Ryles, Sherriff, Smith. Variant on Trinity. (Note that variations on the pronunciation of this name occur widely from family to family. Some families prefer certain versions. Cp Ferneti.)
**Trayton/Traiton:** Collison, Webb
**Treannia:** Booth
**Treeline (m):** Heron. Possibly a variant on Treli or more likely a nickname, though there is a surname Trelinning
**Treli:** Smith, West
**Tresau/ Treasa/ Treci (f):** Loveridge, Sherriff, Smith. Cp Teresa.
**Trevor:** Lee
**Trezian:** Smith. This name, a variant on Tracy Ann, appears in several records as Crazy Ann.
**Trezor:** Gray
**Trinity:** Boswell, Gibbs, Small. Cp Trainetta etc. Treannia may be another variant on Trinity, but is more likely a form of Tearnai
**Triphena/ Trophane/ Triphi/ Tryphena/ Truffeni:** Boswell, Bowers, Cooper, Dix, Florence, Ford, Loveridge, Smith

**Trissia/Trissie:** Broadway, **Lovell**
**Troath:** Smith. Perhaps a variant on Truth.
**Trosaiah:** Lee
**Trout:** Taylor. (Only ever found as a nickname. Arises from a combination of large feet and consequential fish-slapping sound as the person walks. Said to exist amongst other families, but I have no evidence. There is also a surname Troutt.)
**True:** Williams
**Trussler (m):** Childs
**Tryam**: Cp Tyram
**Tryn:** Davies
**Tryphina/phena/ Truffeni/ Trupphina:** Ayres, Boswell, Bowers, Buckland, Carter, Cole(s), Dix, Green, Leach, Lee, Lovell, Shaw, Small, Smith
**Tryphosa:** Jones, Scarrett
**Tucker (m):** Booth, Burnside, Scamp, Taylor. Generally only found as a nickname.
**Tudlin/ Todlin:** Heron
**Tulmillar:** Boswell
**Turnaper/Turnip:** Buckland
**Turnit:** Buckland
**Turpin:** Wood
**Turtle:** Smith
**Tutti:** Boswell, Brown, Finney, Smith, Worrall
**Tuttus:** Lock
**Tynimere:** Stanley
**Tyram:** Boswell. Cp Tryam
**Tyrone:** Shepherd
**Tyso/Taiso:** Boswell, Heron, Young
**Uazhena:** Buckland
**Ubed:** Jones
**Uden (m):** Clarke
**Ugaria:** Burton
**Umbrella:** Lamb
**Uneti/Unatty:** See Yunetti.
**Union (f):** Bosworth, Chilcott, Draper, Giles, Lee, Lovell, Northan, Wood
**Unity (f)**: Ayres, Boswell, Buckley, Gray, Green, Heron, Lee, Lock, Lovell, Parsons, Payne, Pike, Smith. See also Yunetti.

**Urania/Uraney**: Ayres, Boswell, Buckland, Cooper, Evans, Gregory, Lee, Lovell, Osborn, Smith
**Uri**: See Yuri
**Uriah**: Boswell, Buckland, Cooper, Johnson, Lee, Lovell, Magee, Meyer, Shaw, Sherriff, Small, Smith, Turner
**Uriza (m)**: Gray
**Ursula/ Urseley**: Lee, Newton
**Uster (m)**: Williams
**Uzziah**: Lovell
**Vainer**: Smith
**Vaini**: Boswell, Smith
**Vaino**: Boswell, Cooper
**Vaithi**: Gray, Smith
**Valentine**: Boswell, Draper, Heron, Miles, Rogers, Row, Smith, Stanley, Swales, Wood. Also see Volunteen
**Valentino**: Smith
**Valerie**: Cole, Lee, Scamp, Scarrett. Also see Vollie.
**Valley**: Joules, Stanley
**Vanbeest**: Brown
**Vandeloo**: Carter, Stanley
**Vans(e)lo/Vanslo/Wanslow**: Cooper, Lee, Smith
**Vanci**: See Vansi.
**Vand**: Loveridge
**Vandels**: Carter
**Vane**: Boswell
**Vanlow**: Stanley
**Vanselina**: Smith
**Vansi/Vanci (f)**: Boswell, Charlotte, Lee, Scamp, Smith. (Probably an ` abbreviation of Levancy or Crevancy)
**Vantine**: Smith. (Perhaps a variant on Valentine)
**Vanto**: Small
**Vanus/Vanis**: Ayres, Heron
**Varnum**: Taylor. (Variant of Yarnus and Vernon)
**Varto**: Lee
**Vary (f)**: Ford
**Vashti**: Boswell, Cooper, Lee, Mace, Smith
**Vato:**. Boswell. Cp Veto
**Veenee**: Penfold. Cp Vina and Vine
**Velma**: Smith

**Vensa:** Miller, Smith
**Vera:** Cooper
**Vere:** Boswell
**Verity:** Green
**Vernon:** Gamester, Jones, Lewis, Lock, Smith, Taylor
**Veronica:** Boswell, Shepherd, Wood
**Vesse:** Smith
**Vesta:** Loveridge
**Vesti:** Gray
**Veto:** Boswell. Cp Vato
**Vicmenti:** Draper
**Victor:** Boswell, Gray, Heron, Lee, Scamp
**Victoria:** Cramp, Hicks, James, Lawrence, Lewis, Lovell, Sanger, Scarrett, Sherriff, Smith, Stephens
**Vina:** Gray. Cp Veenee
**Vincent:** Boswell, Kelly, Lee, Sheffield
**Vine:** Smith. Cp Veenee
**Vinere:** Smith
**Violence (f):** Heron
**Violet:** Ayres, Booth, Boswell, Burnside, Chappell, Charles, Gamester, Gardener, Gray, Heron, Holland, Jackson, James, Lee, Lovell, Maitby, Moseley, Ripley, Scamp, Shaw, Smith, Taylor, Webber, Wheatley, Wood
**Violetta**: Atkinson, Boswell, Harrison, Smith
**Violette:** Boswell
**Viraminta/Vira:** Gray, Smith
**Virginia/Virgin:** Holland, Scamp, Scott
**Virtue:** Davies, Lee, Stanley, Stephens
**Vitus:** Boswell, Finney, Varey
**Vivian/Vivien (m):** Lee, Lock, Wood
**Vollie:** Ryles. (Variant on Valley)
**Volunteen:** Rodway, Scarrett. (Variant on Valentine)
**Wacker:** Cooper
**Waddi (f):** Gray, Heron, Printer
**Waddilove (f):** Lee
**Wailliam (sic):** Walker
**Waimore:** Boswell, Heron
**Waini (f):** Boswell, Heron
**Wainus:** Killick

**Wainwright**: Boswell
**Walker (m)**: Bowers, Oadley
**Wallace**: Boswell, Webber
**Wally**: Brinkley, Gaskin, Penfold
**Walter**: Many families
**Walton (m)**: Lee
**Wani, Wauni**: Heron
**Wanslow**: See Vanslow
**Ward (f)**: Smith
**Wash (m)**: Williams, Young
**Wasti (f)**: Gray, Heron, Lee
**Watelo**: Boswell
**Watkin**: Ingram
**Watson (m)**: Boswell, Hogg, Lee, Nichols(on)
**Watson (f)**: Lee
**Watty (f)**: Heron, Young
**Waymis**: Lee
**Wayne (m)**: Johnson, Lee, Price, Scamp, Scarrett
**Webber (m)**: Scamp
**Welba**: Robinson
**Welldon (f)**: Price
**Wellington**: Deighton, Lee, Scamp
**Wendy**: Finney, Manning
**Wenty**: Chilcott
**Wesley**: Boswell, Lovell
**Wesson**: Heron, Lee
**Wessy**: Cooper
**Wester**: Boswell, Lee
**Westley**: Boswell
**Weston**: Taylor
**Whipney (f)**: Elliott, Heron
**White (m)**: Golby
**Whittas**: Gray
**Widlake**: Scamp
**Wiggett (m)**: Mace
**Wiggi (m)**: Lee
**Wigmore**: Boswell
**Wikki (f)**: Gray
**Wilberforce (m)**: Giles

**Wilbur:** Smith
**Wiles:** Boswell
**Wilfed:** Finney, Lovell, Mason, Merrick, Ripley
**Wilfrey:** Roberts
**Wilhelmina:** Boswell, Heron, Rostron, Smith
**Wilkinson (m):** Boswell, Todd
**William/Will/Willy:** Most families
**Williams (f):** Penfold
**Williams (m):** Penfold
**Williamson** Hogg
**Willoughby:** Wood
**Wilson (m):** Boswell, Hogg, McFarlane, Todd
**Wilton (m):** Boswell, Lee
**Windsor:** Boswell, Lovell
**Wingi:** Buckland
**Winifred/ Winefred:** Boswell, Buckley, Heron, Jones, Loveridge, Ripley, Wood, Young
**Winifret:** Smith. (Var. on Winifred)
**Winklus/Winkles:** Buckland, Lock
**Winnie:** Rafferty
**Winto:** Boswell
**Wisby/ Wisbe (f):** Robinson, Smith
**Wisdom:** Boswell, Smith
**Wisenaugee:** Boswell
**Wisey Mentaur:** Boswell
**Witham/ Wythan (m):** Webb. Cp Within
**Within (f):** Oadley. Cp Witham
**Wood (m):** Smith
**Woodfine:** Smith
**Woodington:** Andrews
**Woodlock:** Smith
**Woodvine:** Smith
**Wootton (m):** Taylor
**Worcester (m):** Taylor
**Wright (m):** Boswell, Reid
**Wsane:** Boswell
**Wull:** Ruthven
**Wynder:** Scamp
**Wynie/Wynia (f):** Boswell, Lee

**Wynn(e) (m):** Roberts, Wood
**Wytham/Wythen:** Colbert, Smith
**Xavier:** Smith
**Yarday:** Edwards
**Yarnus:** Taylor. Variant on Vernon
**Yetholm (f):** Faa
**Yetta:** Lee
**Yoben (m):** Boswell, Gray, Heron, Young
**Yoki Diddle:** Boswell
**Yoki Shuri:** Boswell, Heron, Smith
**York (m):** Lee
**Yorkie:** Heron
**Yoshua:** Lee
**Young (m):** Rogers, Smith
**Yourania/Yournia** (f): Boswell, Smith
**Yui:** Boswell, Lovell, Smith
**Yule:** Boswell
**Yunaici (f):** Heron. Probably a variant on Yunetti.)
**Yunetti/Unertie:** Ayres, Boswell, Green, Hamer, Heron, Lovell, Smith. Probably a form of Unity. Cp Yuni
**Yuni:** Lee. Cp Yunetti
**Youregh (f):** Lovell
**Yuri/Ury:** Boswell, Heron, Osmond
**Yvonne:** Gray
**Zachariah:** Boswell, Brownell, Cooper, Lee, Lock, Lovell, Scamp, Smith
**Zacharias:** Boswell
**Zacheus/ Zaochus:** Boswell, Lee
**Zackari/Zachary:** Smith, Stewart
**Zacky/Zack:** Boswell, Finney, Gray, Lee, Miles
**Zaila:** Roberts, Wood
**Zane:** Scamp
**Zany:** Florence
**Zarah:** Shaw
**Zathary:** Harris
**Zazil:** Roberts
**Zealand:** Boswell
**Zebellia:** Mace
**Zebhra:** Mace

**Zebulun:** Lee, Lock
**Zechariah:** Boswell, Lee
**Zedibone:** Lee
**Zeki:** Lock
**Zemiea:** Mace
**Zemlah:** Green
**Zena:** Buckland, Leach, Scarrott
**Zenas:** Lovell
**Zephyrus:** Smith
**Zepporah.** See Zipporah.
**Zepreni:** Heron
**Zibberand (f):** Flynn, Smith
**Ziegel:** Smith
**Zilla(h)/Zilliah:** Allen, Boswell, Gatehous, Lee, Roberts, Smith, Wheatley, Yalden
**Zilpha:** Wiltshire
**Zipporah/Zepporah:** Boswell, Carter, Lee, Loker, McLean, Shaw, Smith
**Zoe:** Wood
**Zouly:** Smith. Cp Zilla
**Zuba:** Boswell, Lovell
**Zusanna:** Harris
**Zylpha:** Heron, Lovell

# Chapter 4 — Scottish Sources

## Introduction

This listing does not claim to cover everything. It rather gives sources for information which seem to provide interesting snippets of information about the history, ideas and activities of particular Scottish families. In recent times, census returns, parish records etc, continue to be better sources for the nitty gritty names.

Instead, I have tried only to give the sources where the genealogist can find further information in this very difficult area of family history. As an aid, I have indicated with the words Minor and Major whether the source gives a mention or little more than that or several pages or, if fewer, particularly significant or useful information about the family. Surnames are given alphabetically, and users are recommended to cross check other surnames which are mentioned. The letters of a reference show the source of the information and are explained in the Abbreviations section.

# Abbreviations

(For full details, see Bibliography. The years indicated are those approximately covered by the source.)

AMWW — McCormick, Tales from the Wild Wood (1900).
AMGG — McCormick — Galloway Gypsies
BOR — Borrow, 1860s.
BWR — Betsy Whyte (Red Rowans... ) (1940s-60s)
BWY = Betsy Whyte (Yellow on...) (1960s-80s)
c — circa (about)
CS — Charles Stuart (1860s)
DBGS — Dawson, British Gypsy Slavery. 16th-17th centuries
DGNGS — Dawson, Gypsy Names. 16th C to 2000.
DNOGD — Dawson, ANew@ Old Gypsy Documents. (1700s)
DON — Dawson Own Notes. 1500 to date. Note that these, which consist of some 25 bulging box files, have been donated to the Romany and Traveller Family History. Society. Ultimately they are likely to be stored at the Rural History Centre at Reading University where they may be consulted by appointment and in person only (contact the Rural History Librarian). At the time of publication, however, these are retained by myself so all enquiries should be referred to Robert Dawson, and SAE is essential.
DW — Donald Whyte (1500-2000)
DYR — Dawson, Yorkshire Romanies (16th C to 2000).
GB — George Borrow (1860s)
IS — Ivor Smullen, (1900).
JON — Alyne Jones (18th C)
LTN — Leighton, published c1890. (No clear indication of years)
LTN2 — Leighton, pubished c1900. (No clear indication of years.)
LUC — Lucas (1800s)
m — married
MSD — MacColl and Seeger, Till Doomsday in the Afternoon. (Mainly 1950s-70s)
MST — MacColl and Seeger. Travellers Songs from England and Scotland. (Mainly 1950s-70s)
McR — MacRitchie (1500-1700)
NEA — Timothy Neat (early and mid 20th C)
P — part

PrC — Prebble (The Highland Clearances) (1792-1860)
RC- Robert Chambers (No clear indication of years)
RTFHS — Journal of the Romany and Traveller Family History Society
SEC — Secretary of State for Scotland (1895)
SIM — Walter Simson (to 1860s)
SMI — Jess Smith (1990s)
STW – Sandy Stewart in Leitch (1988)
TOK — Tokeley (mainly to c1900)
V — Volume
WC — William Chambers — Exploits and Anecdotes (1650-1820)
WC2 — William Chambers — Miscellany (No clear indication of years)
WIL — Wilson. No indication of years
WP — Winifred Petrie, (?1700s)

**MAJOR SOURCE**
Particularly significant or extensive information.

**MINOR SOURCE**
Contain some useful information

# Origins of Scottish Traditional Travellers

There were Travellers in Scotland long before Gypsies arrived there c1480. They were musicians, bards and, using the word in its original sense, tinkers — workers in metal. The population was probably very small and their significance in the overall picture was probably not great, except in the longer term by their laying foundation stones for oral remembering of culture and old Gaelic.

Gypsies changed the situation, but probably mainly in Southern Scotland. The arrival of definite Romany peoples introduced knowledge and new traditions. The surnames they brought were mainly lowland ones.

But the formation of modern Scottish Travellers had two significant inputs which made the Romany and Lowland influences much less and the Highland ones more. These events were the 45 Uprising — Bonnie Prince Charlie or the Young Pretender depending upon your viewpoint (1745) — and, even more importantly, the Highland Clearances.

Perhaps not surprisingly, some of the surnames of those who fought on the side of Bonnie Prince Charlie (1745-6) or the previous Jacobite campaign (1715) are those of modern day Scottish Travellers, including Blythe, Brown, Cameron, Douglas, Gordon, Graham, Johnstone, Keith, Kerr, MacDonald, McGregor, McLean, McPhee, MacPherson, Murray, Reid, Stewart and Townsley, and, from Ireland, Sherridan.

I am not here suggesting that all these became Traveller surnames immediately after the 45 Uprising, some predating the 45 as such, and some not appearing until many years later. However, it is true that the use of these surnames amongst Traditional Travellers became more prevalent after 1745. It is also correct that Tinkers fought on both sides during the uprising (cp Prebble, ) A notable example of the Georgian representatives was Gypsy William Marshall, the highway robber, revolutionary and (subsequently) centenarian, who thereby obtained the king's pardon.

The way in which English and Welsh Gypsies obtained their surnames has been described by me in my booklet on surnames and, in summary, is the following:

1. The names of famous gorjers in order to try to obtain some protection by pseudo-influence.
2. Very common gorjer names, like Smith and Brown.
3. Names of gorjers with whom they intermarried.
4. Names created from forenames.
5. Names which derived from Gypsy words, such as Romana, and Lawlo.
6. Names made by amending an existing name.
7. Names said to have been created from incidents within Gypsy history.
8. Names which derived from misunderstandings.
9. Local names to make it seem that the family had always lived there.
10. Aka names from jokes.
11. Aka names from something happening at that moment.
12. Nicknames which have become surnames.
13. Amalgamations of existing Gypsy surnames.
14. Joke-names at the expense of the enquirer.
15. New surnames created by amending existing names.

All these origins are to be found throughout history amongst Scottish Travellers but the most important single source must be refugees from the Highland Clearances (The Great Sheep) when Scottish landowners deliberately evicted their own people to make room for the greater profits available through sheep. Colossal numbers of people were made homeless. It is true that some benign landowners arranged passage for their people to Canada, in particular, where they could begin new lives, but rarely were they given any help to actually do this. Many were literally dropped on the shore of some remote Canadian peninsular and left to fend for themselves.

The evictions were often done with great cruelty. Within the clan system, there was a natural loyalty to the laird, and his instructions were to be obeyed without question. Suddenly, they were being ordered to become homeless.

From this, inevitably, some people were unwilling to be sent to Canada, or to go to the new fishing villages where others were advised to head. They had no option but to travel about doing their best to make some sort of living. In the process, they met and intermarried with the then Romany/Lowland population, and the modern Scottish Traveller was born.

An excellent example is the McPhee family (spellings vary).

## Scottish Traveller Surnames and Sources for Further Information

Note that the absence of a surname from the following list is an indication only that it has not been found in published sources relating to Scotland, and it should not be assumed that it does not exist either as a Traveller or as a Scottish surname. Note too that a minor reference to a family here does not imply that major references do not occur in England, and the contrary.

**Abercrombie:** Minor: DON
**Allan/Allen:** Major: DON Minor: AMGG, DON, DW, RTFHSV4P1, WIL
**Alli(n)son:** Major: DON Minor: DGNGS
**Alston:** Minor: McR, RTFHSV5P4. Compare Yorkston
**Anderson/Anderton:** Minor: BOR, DGNGS, DON, DW, McR, PrC, SIM
**Andree:** Minor: McR, NEA
**Anstruther:** Minor: DW
**Armstrong:** Minor: DNOGD, SIM
**Ayre(s)/Hair:** Minor: DON, DW, McR
**Baillie/Bailley/Bailey/Bailzow** Major: DBGS, DGNGS, DNOGD, DON, DW, SIM, WC Minor: AMGG, LUCF, McR, RTFHSV5P4
**Baird:** Minor: DON
**Baptiste/Baptista:** Minor: DGNGS, DON, DW, McR, NEA
**Baxter:** Minor: SEC
**Beige:** Minor: DGNGS, DON, DW, LUC, McR
**Bergo:** Minor: DGNGS, DON. Possibly a variant on Virgo.
**Bilton:** Minor: DGNGS, DON
**Birk:** See Burke
**Black:** Minor: DGNGS, DON
**Blewit:** Minor: DW
**Blyth(e):** Major: BOR, CS, DON, DW, GB
Minor: AMGG, DGNGS, DYR, McR, RTFHSV1P1, RTFHSV3P4, SEC, TOK, WC2. See also Faa-Blythe
**Boswell:** Minor: DGNGS, DON
**Brown:** Major: DON, DW, SIM Minor: AMGG, DGNGS, McR, RC, WC

**Burke/Birk/Burk:** Minor: DGNGS, DON, SMI
**Burnet:** Minor: DGNGS, DON, SIM
**Cairns/Kairns:** Minor: McR, SIM
**Cameron:** Minor: BWR, DGNGS, DON, DW, MST, MWSD, NEA, PrC Major: SEC
**Campbell:** Minor: AMGG, DBGS, DGNGS, DON, DW, McR, PrC, RTFHSV4P4, SIM Major: SEC
**Carr:** See Kerr
**Charles** Minor: DGNGS, DON
**Chilcott/Kilthorpe:** Minor: DGNGS, DON
**Clark(e)/Clerk:** Major: DON Minor: DGNGS, DW, LUC, McR, RTFHSV4P1, WIL
**Clinton:** Minor: DW
**Cochrane:** Minor: AMGG
**Collins/Collyne/Colyne:** Minor: DW, McR, SIM
**Cooper:** Minor: DGNGS, DON
**Connor** Minor: DBGS
**Cumming** Minor: SEC
**Cunningham:** Minor: DON, SIM
**Curlit:** Minor: RTFHSV4P2
**Davidson/Davison:** Minor: DON, DW, SIM
**Davies/Davis:** Major: NEA Minor: DW
**Doe:** Minor: DON
**Donaldson:** Minor: SMI
**Donea:** Minor: DON, DW, LUC, McR, SIM
**Douglas:** Major: DON Minor: DW, McR, SIM, TOK
**Drummond:** Minor: DON, DW, MST, SIM
**Duffy/Duffey/Duff:** Minor: DON, but often used as an Aka name for Mcphee.
**Duncan:** Minor: DON
**Elliott:** Minor: DON, NEA, RTFHSVP2, SIM
**Euston:** See Yorstoun
**Faa/Fall/Faw/Farr:** Major: AMGG, CS, DNOGD, DON, DW, DYR, LTN2, LUC, SIM, WC, WIL Minor: BOR, DBGS, McR, RC, RTFHSV1P1, RTFHSV3P4, RTFHSV4P1, RTFHSV4P2, RTFHSV4P3, RTFHSV4P4, RTFHSV4P6, TOK, WC2 See also Faa-Blythe and Compare Haw
**Faa-Blythe:** Major: LUC
**Femine:** Minor: DW, LUC, McR, SIM

**Fenwick:** Minor: DON, DW. Compare Fingo
**Fingo/Finco/Finch:** Minor: DON, DW, LUC, McR, SIM. Compare Fenwick
**Fleckie:** Minor: DON, McR, RTFHSV4P2, TOK, WC2
**Fraser:** Minor: DON
**Gagino/Gawino:** Minor: DON, DW, McR, SIM, TOK
**Gaskin:** Minor: SMI
**Geddes:** Minor: DON, SIM
**George:** Minor: DW, McR
**Gibson:** Minor: AMGG, DON, DW, McR, SEC
**Gordon:** Major: AMGG, AMWW, DON, DW, SIM, WC, WC2 Minor: BOR, CS, LUC, McR, NEA, RC, RTFHSV4P5, TOK
**Gow:** Minor: AMWW
**Graham** Major: DON, SIM Minor: DW, NSD, RTFHSV4P2, SEC, WC2
**Grainge:** Minor: DON
**Grant:** Minor: DON, SIM
**Gray/Grey:** Minor: DW, DYR, SIM
**Greig/Greg:** Minor: AMGG, DON, DW, MSD
**Hair:** See Ayre(s); cp Heron
**Hall:** Minor: DON
**Halliday:** Minor: DON, DW, SIM. Compare Holliday
**Hamilton:** Minor: AMGG, DON, SIM
**Hatseyggow/Hatseggaw:** Minor: DON, DW, LUC, McR
**Haw:** Minor: DON, SIM. Compare Faw
**Henderson:** Major: NEA
**Heron:** Major: DON Minor: LUC, McR
**Higgins:** Major: MSD Minor: BWY, MST, SEC, SCO
**Hilton:** Minor: DON
**Hodgson:** Minor: DON
**Hogg:** Minor: DON
**Holiday:** Minor: DW. Compare Halliday
**Hughes:** Minor: NEA
**Hutchison:** Minor: AMGG, MST, SEC
**Irving:** Minor: DON
**Jackson/Jacques/Jaks:** Minor: DON, DW, McR, SIM
**Jako:** Minor: LUC
**Jamieson/Jameson** Minor: DNOGD, DON, DW Major: SEC, SIM

**Jamphrey:** Minor: RTFHSV4P3
**Jeffrey:** Minor: DW
**Johnston(e)/Johnson(e):** Major: AMGG. DON, DW, SEC, SIM, STW, WP Minor: DYR, McR, NEA, PrC, SIM, SMI, WC, WC2
**Jorisse:** Minor: DON
**Kairns:** See Cairns
**Keith:** Minor: DON, DW, SIM, WC
**Kelby:** Major: SEC Minor: MST
**Kelly:** Minor: MST
**Kennedy:** Major: AMGG, DON, DW, SEC, SIM Minor: AMWW, DW, McR, PrC, TOK, WC
**Kerr/Carr** Major: DNOGD, DON Minor: AMGG, BWR, DBGS, DW, McC, SIM
**Langlands:** Minor: DON
**Lawlor/Lalow/Lawler/Lalour:** Minor: DON, DW, DYR, LUC, McR, SIM. Compare Lowther
**Lee:** Major: LTN2 Minor: DON, RTFHSV4P6
**Lin(d)say/Lindsey:** Minor: BWY, DON, DW, McR, SEC
**Livingstone:** Minor: SIM
**Lovell:** Minor: DON
**Lowrie:** Minor: DON
**Lowther:** Minor: DNOGD. Compare Lawlor
**Lsorson:** Minor: DNOGD
**Lucas:** Minor: MST
**Lundie:** Minor: DW, SIM
**Mace:** Minor: DON
**Maglin:** See MacLaren
**Marshall:** Major: AMGG, DON, WC
Minor: AMWW, DW, JON, McR, MSD, SCO, SIM, WC2
**Martin:** Minor: SEC
**Matskalla/Mouschalla:** Minor: DON, DW, LUC, McR. Compare Maxwell
**Maxwell:** Minor: AMGG, DON, DW, McC, SIM. Compare Matskalla
**MacAlister/MacAllister/McAllister:** Major: SMI Minor: DON, DW, MST, NEA, SEC, STW
**McArthur:** Minor: DON, SMI, STW
**MacCallum:** Major: SMI Minor: DON, MST, SEC, STW
**McDonald/McDonnell:** Major: SCO, SIM, SMI Minor: BWR,

BWY, DON, DW, McC, MST, NEA, PrC, STW
**MacDuff:** Minor: MSD
**MacFarlane:** Minor: DON, McR, MST
**McFee/McPhee/MacPhee:** Major: DON, NEA, SCO Minor: DW, DYR, IS, MSD, MST, PrC, SMI, STW. Also see Duffy
**MacFidum:** Minor: McR
**McGregor/MacGregor:** Major: MSD Minor: AMGG, DON, NEA. STW
**McKames:** Minor: DON
**McKay:** Minor: DON
**Mackenzie/McKenzieL** Minor: BWR, DON, MSD, NEA, STW
**McLean/MacLean:** Major: DON Minor: DBGS, DNOGD, NEA, PrC
**MacLaren/Maglin:** Major: STW Minor: BWY
**McLeod:** Minor: PrC
**MacMillan:** Minor: AMGG, DON, MSD, NEA. Major: SCO
**McNair:** Minor: DON
**McNeeL** Minor: DON
**McNeil:** Minor: DON, NEA, Pr Major: SCO
**Macpherson/MacPherson:** Major: RC Minor: DON, DW
**McQueen:** Minor: BWR
**Merchison:** Minor: DON
**Merrick:** Minor: DON
**Middleton:** Minor: BWR
**Miller:** Major: DON Minor: AMGG
**Minny:** Minor: DON
**Montgomery:** Minor: DON, SIM
**Moore:** Minor: DNOGD
**Morrison/Murison:** Major: SMI Minor: AMGG, DON, MSD, NEA
**Mosroessa:** Minor: DON
**Murray:** Minor: WP
**Nelson:** Minor: SMI
**Newbury/Newberry:** Minor: DON
**Newlands:** Major: DON, SCO
**Neyn:** Minor: DON, DW, McR
**Nichoah/Nichols/Nicholson/Nicholas:** Minor: DON, SIM
**Norris:** Minor: DON, SCO
**O'Connor:** Major: SMI

**Ogilvie:** Minor: DON, DW, SIM
**O'Neil:** Minor: AMGG, NEA, SCO
**Paterson:** Minor: DW, NEA
**Pinkerton:** Minor: DON, DW, McR, SIM
**Power:** Major: SWMI
**Ramsay:** Minor: DON
**Redpath:** Minor: DON
**Reid:** Major: SEC, STW Minor: BWR, BWY, DBGS, DW, NEA
**Richards/Richardson:** Minor: DON
**Riley/Reilly:** Minor: BWR, DW, MST, SMI
**Robertson:** Minor: DW, MSD, MST, NEA, PrC, SIM
**Robinson:** Minor: DON
**Rochester:** Minor: McR
**Ross:** Minor: DON, PrC
**Rowland/Roland/Rolland:** Minor: DW, McR
**Rutherford:** Minor: DON, DW, SCO. Compare Ruthven
**Ruthven/Rivens:** Minor: DON, DW, SIM, WC. Compare Rutherford
**Scott:** Minor: SIM
**Shaw(e):** Major: DON, DYR, SIM Minor: DBGS, DNOGD, DW, LUC, McR, RC, TOK, WC
**Small:** Major: DON Minor: DW, McR, RTFHSV2P3, SIM
**Smith:** Minor: DON, RTFHSV2P3, SMI
**Steedman:** Minor: SIM
**Stewart/Steward:** Major: DON, MSD, NEA, SEC, STW Minor: AMGG, BWR, BWY, DBGS, DW, JC, McR, MST, SIM, SMI
**Stirling/|Sterling:** Minor: DON
**Storey:** Minor: DNOGD
**Tait/Tate:** Major: DON, DW, SIM Minor: AMGG, BOR, DBGS, IS, McR, SCO, TOK
**Thompson:** Minor: BWR, MSD, MST
**Torrie:** Minor: DON
**Townsley:** Major: SCO, STW Minor: DBGS, DON, MSD, NEA
**Trotter:** Minor: DON, McR
**TurnbullL** Minor: RTFHSV3P4
**Tweedy:** Minor: DON
**Valentine/Vallentyne:** Minor: DON
**Walker:** Minor: DON, DW
**Wallace:** Minor: DON, DW

**Wann:** Minor: DON, McR
**Watkins:** Minor: DON
**Watson:** Major: DON Minor: AMGG, DW, SCO
**Welsh:** Minor: McR
**Whyte/White:** Major: BWY, DON, RTFHSV4P2, SCO Minor: BWR, BWY, DC, MSD, MST, STW
**Wilkie:** Minor: DON, DW, SIM
**Williamson:** Major: NEA, SCO Minor: DBGS, DON, DW, MSD, STW
**Wilson:** Major: DBGS, DON, DW, SIM
**Wilson:** Minor: AMGG, DYR, IS, McR, MSD, SCO, WC
**Winter:** Minor: DBGS, DW, LUC, McR, RTFHSV4P1, WIL
**Winterup:** Minor: DW
**Wiper:** Minor: DON
**Wood:** Minor: DON, LUC
**Yorstoun/Yorkstone/Euston/Yowston:** Major: SIM Minor: DBGS, DON, DW, McR, RTFHSV5P4, SIM. Compare Alston
**Young:** Major: DBGS, DON, DW, SMI
**Young:** Minor: DYR, McR, RTFHSV4P5, SCO, SIM, TOK, WC, WC2

# Chapter 5 — Wayside Burials

## Acknowledgements

I acknowledge with gratitude the help given to me in information for the writing of this by the following in the locating and recording of Gypsy wayside burials:

Siobhan Spencer (a direct descendent of the Romany patriarch Abram Wood).

David Spencer (descended from Romany Spencers and Griffithses).

Coun. Ian Whyles of Whitwell.

Joy Thrower, Derby and Derbyshire Traveller Education Service, and her husband Clive.

Whitwell Local History Society

Comfort Booth (a descendent of some of the most distinguished Romany families in Britain).

The Derbyshire Romany Smiths

The Romany Shaw, Lock and Jones families.

Ruth MacDonald (a descendent of Romany Smiths and MacLeans).

Dr. William Lockwood, Department of Anthropology, University of Michigan

Liz Hewitt, Rotherham Traveller Education Service

Mr. Ralph Lord

Numerous other Romany people whose snippets of remembered family history gave me so many valuable clues.

## Introduction

The existence of graves of Romany people other than in official church or public cemeteries is an area which has been barely touched upon in the available literature. Brian Vesey Fitzgerald refers to a grave at Strethall; George Borrow to ones on Mousehole Heath; Trigg to unofficial burials in general; Simson to several in Scotland; T.W. Thomson to several unofficial burials in general terms.

The extent to which graves exist is doubted by Alan McGowan of the Romany and Traveller Family History Society. He states in the Society Journal (Vol 3, p 284), "It is likely that some unofficial Gypsy burials did take place, but I have yet to be convinced that they account for more than a small percentage of the total."

My own interest in Gypsy graves came about through two incidents: As a boy, I was once shown the grave of a dead Gypsy and, being a boy, I went back when no-one was about to investigate and did indeed find bones. I then returned the soil and worried for some time after about being haunted by the bones. The grave is still there.

The second incident occurred many years later when, as a head teacher, I gave a talk to Whitwell Local History Society in NE Derbyshire, and was approached afterwards by a member who told me of visits to the locality by a Gypsy called Shadrack (Isaac) Boswell, apparently soon after World War 2, to three separate locations in the vicinity where he placed flowers. I subsequently found a human bone at two of these locations, one in a mole hill, and the other on the surface (both sites had been ploughed).

Subsequently, I learned through Joy Thrower of interesting graves at Sheldon and Bakewell.

The Bakewell grave quickly proved crucial. There was considerable evidence for its existence and for the reasons it was there in the first place. By a lucky coincidence, the circumstances of this site were elaborated in the correspondence of George Henry Sherriff, a Romany who learned to read and write in prison and whose mother and baby sister are buried at the wayside. This is only one of two wayside burials which can be dated in the 20th century, all the others predating the century.

I then discovered more about local graves from Gypsies who travelled Derbyshire, and from other independent evidence.

The oral tradition for graves is often thin. This is because travel patterns have changed, and most of the graves are beside very old travelling routes no longer in use. This will be returned to. At one time, people on foot or in wagons would comment to others, "Some of our breed's buried over there," or words to that effect. Details were probably always thin. In addition, of the two burials occurring in the 20$^{th}$ C, neither was in the second half, so wayside burials in very recent times are extremely unusual.

Oral tradition itself is often a good indicator, but does have its pitfalls and vagaries. To take as oral examples, traditions from my own family which have been passed down over numerous generations:

In the **Wars of the Roses** (1455), two Dawsons, one from Lancashire and one from Yorkshire, found themselves on opposite sides of a battlefield. (Impossible to prove. There are no records of who was in each battle, except for the leaders, but at the time of the War, there were Dawsons living in both Lancashire and Yorkshire who were closely related to each other.)

In 1745, James Dawson (an ancestor) took part in the **'45 Rebellion**, joined Bonnie Prince Charlie, was taken as traitor and hung drawn and quartered. (Proved correct. He was executed in 1746, but I am descended not from him but from another of his family.)

From this it is clear that oral tradition can range from 'could be true' to 'unquestionably true, and almost totally accurate' and traditions of each wayside burial should be seen as lying somewhere between these positions.

What has emerged is that, in the cases of graves where a good deal is known, the primary reason for such burials of adults or older children has been for the protection of other Gypsies, in one way or another. This point, and the circumstantial evidence for it, will be returned to. In addition, there is considerable oral evidence for numerous burials of stillborn babies, or very young infants.

Excluding still-born burials, almost 30 have been identified, the evidence ranging from thin to massive. A total of ten possible pieces of evidence have been found from which it is possible to identify a grave.

# Evidential hierarchy from which to identify graves

1. Near a traditional stopping ground
2. Marked with stone
3. Near cross roads or other landmark perceived as permanent.
4. Marked with thorn trees/shrubs
5. Oral tradition of the burials — Gypsy
6. Oral tradition — gorjer
7. Written record, eg estate records, parish records etc
8. Evidence of artifacts, eg broken pottery
9. Evidence of human bones
10. Partial or Full identification of occupants

Clearly, the more of these 'clues' which can be attributed to a specific location, the stronger is its authentication, and the further down the hierarchy the clues occur, the more likely it is to be bona fide. I regard some evidence from 6 to 10 as essential.

# The Graves

Each grave has been identified with a series of three letters and a number, the letters indicating the County. Although the number of graves is heavily weighted to Derbyshire, this should be regarded as only because I happen to live there, and therefore have better access and sources. It is to be hoped that others will follow-up this booklet in their own areas.

Pottery has been found at some, in confirmation of the known standard Gypsy custom of destroying any of their belongings (other than a few valuables buried with the deceased), which always included pottery.

Descriptions of the graves have been grouped by area or by family or other historical ties which will become apparent. Because of the known Gypsy practise to bury some valuables with a person, exact locations are not given so as to deter ghoulish treasure seekers but are known to others apart from me. Researchers with a legitimate need for it will be given precise geographies where known.

# North East Derbyshire: Graves DBY1, 2, 3, 4 and 5

These graves are all situated in the Whitwell, Derbyshire area, in a chunk of land bordered to the north by South Yorkshire and to the East by Nottinghamshire.

There are a number of traditional stopping places in the area, including Whitwell common itself, Gypsy Lane and Belph Common. Several of the 'old' families regularly stopped here, especially Derbyshire and Yorkshire Smiths, Boswells and Herons. Surrounding parishes contain several baptismal records, including children of the infamous Riley Bosville and his family. There are very few burial records.

Whitwell parish itself — the main one in the area — has traditionally been the living of a rector, and, also traditionally, was occupied by clergy who were destined for promotion to dean and even bishop. They were often staid in their ways and conservative in outlook. It is unlikely that Gypsies would have received much of a welcome in the life of a church all too often associated in the past with prejudice and persecution.

Belph Common was a very important stopping ground, now destroyed by a large spoil heap from quarrying. It was an idyllic place, with plenty of fresh water and a variety of wild life. There was an abundance of fuel for the fires, and numerous types of wood to allow for cooking a variety of dishes, and for making pins, skewers, pegs, flowers and, of course, the all important tent poles. It was near small towns/large villages useful for hawking, including Worksop, Clowne, Creswell, Bolsover and Renishaw, and perhaps Shirebrook, and the area was full of farms for casual work. For instance, in the 1920s-40s, Hodthorpe Primary School, half a mile away, regularly took in Gypsy children during the summer months.

Two distinct parts of the Common were used for stopping. In one place, Herons traditionally stayed, and the other families in the other. For reasons which are not now known, the two groups kept apart, though the Herons and Boswells intermarried quite frequently. At one time,. Herons were regarded as being 'not quite nice' and bearing in mind that some of the Yorkshire Smiths especially regarded themselves as an elite group, this might explain the stand-off, but this is pure speculation.

Information about the three Belph graves came to me from a local historian and I was subsequently told, independently of each other, by Locks and Jones that the graves contained Boswells, Smiths and Edwardses. Both the Locks and Jones family frequently married with Edwardses and Boswells. Both families also told me that one of the graves contained an Edwards family, who had (it was said) been wiped out by TB and consumption.

This grave is probably DBY1. When I first saw it (it has since been ploughed) it was a raised mound which had been heightened by digging a ditch round much of it. Presumably, the sheer number of bodies needed extra soil, as about 18" (45 cms) below soil level there is a huge magnesium carbonate rock throughout the district and above it a layer of shale, all of which would have been very difficult to penetrate. The grave is next to a public footpath and near a hedge, and hawthorn trees of about the right age for a Victorian grave had been planted on it. There are mid-Victorian pottery pieces round. After ploughing, I found the pelvic bone of a child with an estimated age of about 3 and a black clay bead from a child's necklace There were also two bones from a young pig, pork being a favourite of Gypsies, and it may originate from the post-burial feast. (I found almost the whole skeleton of a young pig, minus the head, at 'The Half Moon', an ancient stopping ground about two miles to the north.)

Three distinct Edwards families can be identified:

1. Formed by the union of Nancy Wood of the Welsh Romany Woods to a gorjer (non-Gypsy), John Edwards. This is generally regarded as the principal Edwards family.

2. A second Welsh Romany family formed by the union of another Welsh Gypsy (name not known) to a gorjer, or possibly simply an obscure branch of the 'A' Edwardses.

3. A union between the Nelson and Davies families which renamed itself Edwards.

A photo of Gypsies taken at Longton, STF, near the railway line, was identified as members of the extinct Edwardses, but this cannot be the case, because this was taken in 1904 and all three graves predate this. Rather, the photo shows either Edwardses who survived or, more likely, "A" Edwardses, in which case the vanished Edwardses are "B".

Grave DBY2 is situated on private land at the opposite end of the village approaching Whitwell. It was originally mounded, next to a hawthorn hedge between two fields, and marked by six large hawthorn trees, suggesting it was of older date than DBY1. During the miners' strike, the trees were cut down and burned for fuel.

Once again, there is ample evidence of pottery, though some caution must here be used, as it is also fairly close to an old rubbish dump and it is not impossible that some of the pottery was dropped on the way to that. All the pottery in the area of the grave appears to date from early Victorian times and included a funeral urn for holding flowers.

Soon after ploughing, I visited it and in a mole hill found a bone identified for me as a humerus. This bone was 21.3 cms long. There is a very approximate ratio between the length of a humerus and the height of a person, (multiplying by 5.33), though the thigh bone is a much better indicator. Thus, the human known to be buried there was roughly 114 cms (45 inches) tall. Clearly, it was a child, and by modern standards one aged about 6. However, the probability is that these children would have been malnourished, so it is reasonable to assume that the child was a little older, perhaps about 8 or 9 years.

Oral tradition identifies the occupants of this grave as Smiths and Boswells.

Grave DBY3 is more problematic. It is in the middle of a field and the gate is wired up with razor wire. Access is therefore not possible, and it is only possible to note its presence, but no good evidence other than the Shadrack Boswell tradition and a very obvious smallish hawthorn can be assigned to it.

The Clowne Lane (DBY4) grave contains the body of one George Booth, who probably died in 1947. His great niece, who witnessed the burial when aged about 7, said she was told that he was buried there to stop him falling into the hands of the gorjers, as he had been wanted by the police for many years. This sounds more to me like a 'fob off' version to hide another reason for a wayside burial as late as 1947, since by then there was no good reason to avoid a proper cemetery internment.

Although its location was described to me, I have found two possible places and am unsure which it could be. Both have hawthorns near; in one place there is a large stone and in the other, brambles. I favour the stone site. My informant cannot remember if the grave was marked, and naturally her description is that of a seven year old remembering it. She never returned to it.

Local tradition has it that Gypsy Lane (DBY5) was a regular stopping place in the distant past, and both gorjer and Gypsy tradition places graves there. I have examined the lane carefully, and though there are possibilities, I have not been able to find any sites which I could authenticate.

## Newton Wood, DBY6

Again, the exact location of this grave is not known and it seems likely that it has ceased to exist. It was situated along a lane at Newton, Alfreton, and said to be near an ancient and traditional stopping ground used by Derbyshire Smiths, Booths and Taylors at the now disappeared Newton Wood, almost opposite the Wood End pub. The site is almost certainly exactly where the M1 motorway ripped through the area: bones were found there during the construction, but after examination were decided as not forensically suspicious, and too old to warrant investigation anyway.

## Tansley, DBY7

The Derbyshire Romany Smith family state that some of their forebears are in wayside graves at Tansley, near Matlock. I have checked the village as far as possible, and can find none, but it is very much a needle in a haystack search. Certainly the village was used very considerably as a stopping ground by Smiths and Booths. Both families are well represented in the churchyard, and this is confirmed by numerous entries in parish records since 1820. Experience from other grave sites now suggests that I was not looking in the right place, and that I should have searched on Tansley Moor.

# Pilsley, Bakewell, DBY8

This is unquestionably one of the most important burial sites to be found, because so much is known about it.

*Kanna Mandi sas a Tarno chavo* (When I was a young boy)
In an account thus headed, George Henry Sherriff, who whilst serving a prison sentence sent about 400 pages of letters to a lawyer friend, describes the death of his mother, Eliza.

Before I knew of the existence of these letters, I made a discovery myself.

In about 1995, a former gamekeeper, Mr. Ralph Lord, kindly showed me a wayside grave off a lane near the Baslow-Bakewell road (the A619) near Pilsley, Derbyshire. Mr. Lord told me of local tradition that in about 1919, a Gypsy caravan slipped off a narrow bridge into a tributary of the River Derwent and an adult and child drowned. The two were buried nearby, beside a lane.

Soon afterwards, Siobhan Spencer, secretary of the Derbyshire Gypsy Liaison Group, and her husband David, met an elderly man who called himself Monty Sherriff. Monty — he was, of course, George Henry (known as Henry) — explained more of the death of the adult and her burial nearby. On his death soon after, he had hoped to have his ashes scattered on his mother's grave, but at the time the two matters were not connected. He was not aware of the death of a child.

Henry sent an account of the matter to Richard Wade in about 1962. Henry was under the impression that his mother died in Matlock, but in fact it was in Bakewell. Henry says they were stopping at The Dimple in Matlock, a site below hydro pump houses. He may be confused here. The place they were staying at they colloquially called Long Lane, though they were below two pump houses..

Smedley's Hydro was where the chairs to be mended were. It became part of the Matlock Teachers Training College and is now part of the County Council's offices.

David was not the baby who was born following the incident. David was about 4 years old when it happened, and Henry about 7. The baby itself was stillborn. Clearly, this must be the baby buried near Eliza. David's adoptive family, the Carters, according to local Gypsies, were fairground people, or somehow connected with fairs.

Subsequently, I traced and met Henry's nephew Arthur Sherriff, in Retford, and Arthur Sherriff confirmed this.

At the same time each year and over several decades, a woman (whose name is known) camped in a bender tent on a hillock near the site of the tragedy every year for several decades and put flowers on the grave. Judging from what Henry reports of the last encounter between his mother and this woman, she may well have felt some guilt. This could also be a factor in Eliza not being buried in an official cemetery.

Henry writes:

*When I was a young boy about eleven, we were stopping at Matlock in Derbyshire. My Dadus (father) had the contract for reseating the cane and rush chairs at Smedleys Hydro The manager's name was Captain Douglas. We were the only Romany folki (Gypsy people) that was allowed to camp on the Bakewell Road because of my fathers contract with the Hydro. Inspector Kennedy was in charge of the police at the time, he was a friend of my father's. Near where we were atchin (stopping) was a steep hill up to the Hydro; at the back of our Bow topped waggon was the river Derwent.*

*There was a flood at the time my mother was in bed with confinement. My father stuck the kettle iron as far in the ground as he could, and then fastened a chain to that and the waggon wheel, so as the flood would not move our Vardo (wagon). The pipes at Smedleys Hydro burst, and the water came rushing down the Dimple, that is the name of the hill, the water went over our waggon front board and into the waggon and to the bed where my mother was laying.*

*The Gorgio folki (local people) got my mother out of our waggon and they took her to Darley hospital. She had a boy, my youngest brother David. With getting wet through in the flood she had Pneumonia. In two day she died. They said it was the flood water that had killed her. We buried my mother and burned the waggon. I went back then to live with my poori folki (grandparents). My father, who had never drunk a glass of beer in his life started to drink heavy.*

*My other brothers and sisters were taken by my different uncles and Aunts, all but one, Hope, he stayed with my Dadus. My Uncle*

*Hope Sherriff and Aunt Rebecca, she was a Clayton, were stopping with their waggon at Ringing Lows. Ringing Lows is just on the moors outside of Sheffield My Uncle Hope had very little money so he walked from Ringing Low to Matlock and had blisters on his feet. He took to my sister Trainett. My Uncle Uria took to my brother Fred.*

*My youngest brother David is now a Captain in the Koorramengroes (soldiers), The Royal Artillery. A Bauri Rei ta Rauni (a great gentleman and lady) called Carters at Bakewell, Derbyshire had him staying with them as a bitti chavi (little boy). They finally adopted him with my father's consent. He was sent to college and has had a fine Education. He uses the nav (name) of the people who brought him up, Herbert David Carter.*

*If you are ever in Matlock and talk to any of the old folki you will be able to hear this story as it was talked about a bit.*

*About two weeks before my mother died, (here Henry names a woman) came to our waggon at Matlock and ordered my mother out to fight. My mother had a good fight with her but lost, the only reason was because she was pregnant.*

*My brothers and sisters are all doing well and happily married thank God. My Dadus (father) died at eighty odd years of age.*

*Patser mandi, meero pooro Dei shumas a latcho Duveleski trashava monishni. Yoi pend laki monya sorkon rarti katar moro Duvel. Duvel kom laki sorkon chairus.* (Thankfully, my old mother was a good God-fearing woman. She said her prayers every night to God. God love her for ever.)

Elsewhere, Henry refers to people being buried unofficially *dre the puv* (in the field). It is clear from Henry's account that the death of Eliza followed the beating she received at the woman's hands, and that, heavily pregnant, she was lying in the wagon when it was flooded. Already ill from the beating, the cold from the water and the soaking, with probably no dry clothes as they would all have been soaked too, she succumbed.

Naturally, the family would have felt very vulnerable. In 1904 three of Eliza's brothers were arrested and jailed for the killing of a policeman. The culprit — actually Jack Sherriff — did not confess and they were jailed in connection with the death and not with murder as the three stuck together to avoid seeing Jack go to the gallows. Thus the family had already had one traumatic brush with a murder investigation, and must have feared an investigation into Eliza's death. Therefore, they put about the story of the wagon crashing over the narrow bridge and Eliza drowning to account for the injuries she had received. That, too, is why they buried her dre the puv instead of in a churchyard — it avoided more awkward questions!

## Beeley, DBY 10 and 11

There originally appeared to be three separate graves at Beeley, but the grave originally numbered DBY9 has been eliminated.

DBY9 is a patch of graves situated on the moors above the village, which forms part of the Chatsworth Estate. The graves concerned are situated next to a very old and now disused roadway across the moors and are mounded and easy to see, though hard to get to. In the Estate records they are described as Paupers' Graves.

I now believe these are too early to be Gypsy as they probably date from the 15th century, before the generally accepted date for the first record of Gypsies in England. Not surprisingly there is no independent Gypsy tradition of these.

The evidence for DBY11 is also weak. Although it is claimed as such by local Romanies, no exact location has been reported.

Though much stronger, the evidence for DBY10 is not conclusive and I have not personally seen it, being unable (from a health point of view) to get to it.

On the steep and winding road leading from Beeley to Chesterfield, there is a field on the right hand side, just above the last of the houses. This has been a traditional stopping place for a great many years. At one time, they pulled over this field along a track which then existed and stopped about a mile along this lane next to a wood.

The use of this place ceased before the end of wagon time, reputedly because it is a spooky place. This suggests superstition, of course, but the superstition must be relatively recent. Hence the claim by local Gypsies that it must be a burial site.

## Hathersage, DBY12 and 13

Whilst searching for DBY12, I inadvertently found a second grave at the opposite end of the village. The DBY12 grave is North-west of Hathersage on the A625 (Sheffield-Whaley Bridge) road, beside a little road junction, and is marked with a small stone. According to the local Gypsies, it contains the body of one of the Derbyshire Smiths who had died earlier in a migration, and who was carried to the spot and buried clandestinely. Its location and existence is very well known by most of the older Gypsy families who frequent the area.

Grave DBY13 is in the verge near the entrance of a little lane, South-west of the village and off the same road as DBY12. Nothing is known of its history, but it has been marked with a very ancient gravestone (the inscription is part buried) which must have been dragged or carried from the local cemetery.

## Chapel en le Frith, DBY14

Sadly, the exact location of this most important mass grave is not known to me. I first found clues to its existence in the parish records of Chapel en le Frith, where two references appear of stillborn Gypsy babies being dug up and 're-interred in the Boswell Graves' in the 18th century

Although several burials of Romany Boswells appear in the registers, the clear impression given is that 'The Boswell Graves' lie elsewhere than in a churchyard. A local historian told me he knew where the graves were, and that they lay between Chapel en le Frith and Glossop but nearer to the former (ie, somewhere near the A624) but the information was never forthcoming. I have searched the area by car to no avail, though it is worth noting that there are a number of very minor roads in that area which would have been typical Gypsy routes pre Wagon Time.

## Sheldon, DBY15A and B

There are two graves here, one in a lane (DBY15A) and the second in the church yard (DBY15B) — but the second is not a normal burial. Technically, the wayside grave (15A) is that to be considered here but the circumstances of 15B are so unusual and so illustrative of attitudes to Gypsies that they are worth giving in full.

Knowledge of the presence of 15B is attributable to Mr. Lord, though the Rev Clive Thrower had already alerted me to a very odd burial at Sheldon, and a fascinating story emerged.

The story was that a Gypsy called Smith died in Wheal Lane and was carried to the churchyard. He was buried in the churchyard by the family and villagers but the then incumbent, Revd James Coates, refused to have anything to do with it except for allowing the burial to take place.

Thomas was the first internment in the new graveyard, near a recent pile of shale from graves and the compost heap. In a horizontal snowstorm I took photos, which are indistinct and with white assegai spears across. (Apparently, it only snows MOST days at Sheldon).

Talking to the warden and villagers, the tradition is that the man died at a local stopping ground and was carried into the village to be buried. For many years since, certainly throughout the 19th and into the 20th centuries, villagers have put flowers on the grave to mark it.

It all began to fit into place, and I remembered the tradition that the soul of the first internee in a new churchyard belongs to the devil. So this poor chap was the devil's sacrifice and the villagers, with something of a conscience, had been trying to make amends with their flowers ever since.

In Wheal Lane, Taddington, I examined the old stopping ground. There was a bizarre patch of heather (growing on limestone!), clearly the remains of someone's private patch for bikinning the bokty ling.

New age travellers had stayed there in the 1990s, and had won over the locals. A second group of New Agers had left piles of rubbish and proved a nuisance, leaving after only a couple of weeks because it was 'too cold' (and I agreed). The atching tan is near a Greenway and on an old Gypsy migratory route which ran from Wales, through Staffordshire, Derbyshire, Cheshire and into Lancashire.

The Sheldon Parish Records show the graveyard opened in 1853 with the first recorded burial on 19th March of a local man, but in

Grave No. 2. So where was the Gypsy? But I realised that if the vicar had refused to have anything to do with the burial, it wouldn't be recorded. I had wanted to find his name and cursed my ill luck.

Then I struck gold. On February 29th, 1856, was buried, aged 41, "Sarah Heron, the daughter of Thomas Smith". Her abode is given as Manchester. I have checked — neither Heron nor Smith (fortunately) are Sheldon names. And, indeed, no Thomas or other Smith appears anywhere in the records.

Now to the next problem. Presuming that Thomas was one of the Smiths known to travel into this area — ie a relative of Woodfine — I am unable to tie him or Sarah into a known family. Several other Gypsy Thomas Smiths are mentioned in records — one was arrested in 1884 (age 28) for theft at Bakewell, another for theft in Chesterfield in September 1852 for pickpocketing, another in 1853 at Matlock for theft, one at Pentrich in 1853 (age 16) for theft, a fifth (age 40) for passing counterfeit coins at Derby in 1851, a sixth for vagrancy in Derby in 1815 and for poaching in 1819 (the most likely candidate).

Several Smiths and Herons are buried at Derby All Saints, and Constance, daughter of Thomas Smith, was baptised there in 1751.

Also promising, in that they seem to be probable relatives of the Sheldon Thomas, is John, son of Thomas Smith out of the parish of Chorley baptised February 1773 at Brailsford and William, son of the same Thomas, buried May 1781.

This leads me to DBY15A which is at the top of Wheal Lane, near the junction of the lane with the main road. It is situated at the base of an old tree and marked with snowdrops. It is not unreasonable to assume that it contains the body of a child, probably of the same Smith family.

## Ladbybower Reservoir, DBY16

There is considerable oral tradition amongst Derbyshire Romany Smiths, Worralls, Quentins, Gaskins and Booths that a burial place exists here. It is an idyllic spot, and walkers pass by it very frequently.

Sadly, I have been unable to find the exact location, though the description given to me fits several places. It is reported to be on the hillside above the dam made famous as the location of the filming for the Dam Busters film and to be marked with stone(s).

Stone is a not uncommon feature of the landscape, however, which from a Gypsy point of view was an advantage for camouflage. It ought to be easy to find, as its nearness to the dam was clearly a major marker for them to find and visit it, but there must have been another landmark which would produce the exact spot. There is no firm information as to who or how many are there, but it seems likely that they/he/she are/is Derbyshire Smith(s).

## YKS1 — Laughton Common, YKS4, 5, and 6

Laughton Common is situated near the village of Laughton in South Yorkshire. The church graveyard contains several extremely interesting graves including Booths, Smiths, Prices and others. In particular, two of the Price tombs are especially fine, one having a family verse, and both some exceptionally good carving.

This has been an area long visited by Gypsies over many centuries. The existence of unofficial graves on the Common (YKS1) was described to me by members of the Booth family and are thought to contain Smiths. The Common is partly built on and the rest quite inaccessible. Though I have done my best to search the area which remains, I could not find them.

The same family told me of other graves at Anston (YKS4), a dozen miles away, but no details were forthcoming.

Graves are reported in two locations at or near Sheffield (YKS5 and 6) but no details are known.

## YKS2 and 3 — Gilstead, YKS

Gilstead is a small village set on the hills above Bingley. At one time, a particular spot at the bottom of Gilstead moor was used during wagon time, but ceased to be used by about 1957. It was inaccessible to standard motors.

There is little suitable grazing there, and the only spot with grass of any use was that used by Gypsies at the village end of the moor. Most of the moor, including the location of Grave YKS3, has thin topsoil with sedimentary rocks, which are easily broken, and harder sandstone underneath. In the 1950s, the families mainly found there were Smiths and Booths, and I met one of the latter, then an old lady, almost 40 years later in Derbyshire.

Grave YKS3 is situated at the base of a hawthorn: it is unclear whether the hawthorn was planted specially, or whether the grave was placed next to the hawthorn to mark it. I favour the second option. There are stones embedded in the ground around but it is impossible to say whether they were placed deliberately or accidentally. Adult human bones have been found there, about 30 cms below the surface.

Grave YKS2 is reported by George Clarke of Sheffield as having contained the body of a stillborn child. The grave was discovered, and the mother prosecuted. Therefore the grave no longer exists.

## Sale, CHS — CHS1

Publicity for this site was given in the *Daily Mail* of November 7, 1977. The grave is situated in what is now a garden in Church Lane, Sale, and what the paper did not say was that the tree marked the burial place of a daughter of Mrs. Johnson. In fact the tree was planted before 1780, and though Mrs. Johnston was not born in 1780, as tradition implies, I cannot identify her or her actual year of birth.

## Market Drayton — SAL1

No details at all of this site are known.

## Mousehole Heath, NFK1

These are the graves referred to by George Borrow. It is unclear whether they are still there: I believe the heath has disappeared so presume not.

## LEI1 — Leicester

This site has been reported to me by members of the Booth family, but I have no precise location.

## ESS1 — Strethall, Essex

Driving through Stretton, DBY, one day with Romany friends, two of them Shaws, one suddenly exclaimed, "This is our village. Half our breed's buried here."

In fact she was confusing Stretton with Strethall, a wayside burial site described by Vesey Fitzgerald on information obtained by T.W. Thomson, the great Anglo Gypsy scholar.

In c1830, one Squire Nehemiah Parry married a Gypsy girl, Sarah Shaw. Parry despised her family to such an extent that three years into the marriage, three men attempted to murder him. Unfortunately (to take the Gypsy viewpoint) he shot them first but was subsequently acquitted of murder.

In the meantime, members of the Shaw family were buried in one of the squire's fields and it was this event to which my friend was referring. Skeletons were later found there. But in 1909 when Thomson investigated the burials, he could find no oral tradition.

This is not necessarily an indication that the oral tradition did not then exist. The Shaw branch concerned had spent several generations in fairgrounds, returning to the Gypsy community in the 1950s. Therefore, he may simply have been asking the wrong people.

I have not visited this site, which obviously does not now contain the bodies, but if my friend had obtained the knowledge from her own family rather than by a chance discovery of Vesey Fitzgerald's book (from a library, say) it is a good indication of the longevity of oral memory.

## BKM1, Quainton, and Bierton, BKM2

Information about both these graves has been published in Romany Routes, the Journal of the Romany and Traveller FHS, Volume 2, pp 127-28 and 131.

BKM1 is a grave marked with a large stone in Carters Lane, near where Gypsies commonly camped. The stone is dated to 25$^{th}$ March 1641 (new calendar) and five days before were executed at Aylesbury one Edward Bozwell, 'a strolling Gypsy and called King of the Gypsies' for horse stealing, and one 'Edward Smyth for robberie on the highway.' Doubtless the grave is that of one or both of these men.

In 1863, eight skeletons apparently dating from a long time before, were found in a field frequented by Gypsies at Bierton (BKM2). At least two generations were identified, and the bodies are probably those of Bartons and Bucklands.

## LIN1 — Lincoln

No details are known — reported by Derbyshire Smiths and Taylors.

## Fole, STF — STF1

Little is known about this site except its location. It is visible from the A50 Uttoxeter to Stoke on Trent road on the right hand side when going towards Stoke. It is near a small lane and consists of a mounded grave marked with a tree. It is said to contain Smiths.

## Other English Gypsy Wayside Graves

Other Gypsy graves have been reported at: Stewkley Dean; between Fenny Stratford and Simpson; Crowmead; Towersey (all Buckinghamshire)

## Algona, Iowa, USA — USA1

I am obliged to Dr. Bill Lockwood for the following, which appeared in the Des Moines Register (Sunday Magazine Section) of March 11, 1923.

## *Iowa Boasts Only Gypsy Cemetery Known in United States*
## *by Ruth E. Triben*

"Cross my palm, Maaster!"

"Cross weeth silver. Hear 'bout pas', presen' an' future! Beautiful lady an' dark bad stranger. Cross ma palm. Lots money comin' to kind Maester!"

What do you know about Gypsies?

Probably the only gypsy cemetery in the United States is located just six miles north of Algona, Ia.

This cemetery is a shrine — the sacred destination of annual pilgrimages conducted by the Gutzell gypsies. It is cared for each year. Farmers living near, who know the gypsies, say the cemetery is the Gutzell's pride.

A half hour's fortune telling by the seventh daughter of a seventh daughter will not tell you a word of the romantic moving life. Yet it constitutes average knowledge of the race.

In Algona they do know about the gypsies.

The gypsy smiles with sealed lips and baffling eyes. The cards tell only about you — not of Madriga, Alonzo, Josef and their queen. Not of young love in the moonlight or old age around the camp fires. Yet of the carefree roaming existence of wild and lawless adventuring.

The caravan moves over the hill. Good Iowans continue their farming, buying, selling and trading.

The flash of black eyes, merry red lips, the jangles of earrings and the tambourines' clash is only a memory. That is — in most places after a gypsy visit, only the memory remains. The Gutzell gypsies who visit Algona left a shrine, a tradition. It has come to be an anchoring place in their wandering, nomadic life.

This is the story of the Iowa gypsy trail.

In August 1896 the Gutzells, a tribe of typical gypsies travelling in covered wagons, trading horses and finding their living as they went, arrived in Algona. They made their camp about five miles north of the city.

On the second night, the farmers of the neighbourhood were awakened by loud noises. It sounded as though someone had been injured and was crying out for help. At times the voices joined in a long drawn wail. Dogs barked and the commotions continuous.

Morning came and W.W. Annis, whose farm is about three miles west of where the gypsies' camp was pitched, paid a visit to the gypsies. He discovered the cause of the previous night's demonstration. Alonzo Gutzell, son of the gypsy queen, had died. He had been ill with tuberculosis for months.

The singing, dancing and feasting of the night was the departed soul to the world beyond.

Now that the funeral dance was over, the fires were dying and all the tribe busy making preparations to leave.

The brown-skinned youngsters and the women were already in the wagons, while the men were busy with the horses. None of the group seemed at all interested in the body of their companion. It lay carelessly thrown to one side.

"What are you going to do with that man?" demanded Mr. Annis of one of the drivers.

"Oh, it's all right there," came the answer. The wagon started on.

"Who is the head of this concern?" demanded Mr. Annis.

Several of the children pointed to the queen who was reclining in a nearby vehicle.

Mr. Annis approached the queen.

Her majesty was non too amicable after the night's festivities. A shower of unintelligible gestures was her answer. When the volley was exhausted Mr. Annis continued firm:

"You cannot leave that man there."

"What shall we do with him?" asked the royal prince beside his mother.

"Why, bury him of course."

A council was held and the matter discussed. To the gypsies everything necessary had been done. The funeral ceremonies had been observed with the singing and dancing. Only the mere shell — the body — was left and the spiritual being had already been cared for. Why bother further!

The lessons of experience had taught them fear of authorities, however.

When the gypsies learned that city officials would certainly be called out if preparation for burial were not made immediately, they agreed to adopt the customs of the country in which they were travelling, They would bury the body.

The tribe had originally been Catholic. Because of their wandering habits and carefree disposition they had fallen from the good graces of the church. Permission to bury the gypsy prince in the catholic cemetery was therefore refused.

It was hard to convince the lawless queen that action must be taken at once. Finally a private cemetery at some distance was mentioned. The idea pleased the queen. She said she would, like to have the body rest near the woods which Alonzo had loved in life.

The lot was purchased and the burial of Alonzo Gutzell, gypsy prince, took place with simple rites.

Farmers nearby forgot the incident. Weeds grew high over the unmarked grave. Large bands of the wandering folks continued in their carefree way. In the early spring, the caravans of covered wagons came north. When they reached Algona they drove to their burial ground.

A few days later, passers-by noticed that the weeds had been cut away and the grave decorated with flowers. The gypsy band moved on after a week.

With the coming of fall, the Gutzell tribe again returned to their shrine. They were en route for the sunny southland where they spent the winter. Various gypsy bands travel more or less regulated ways. The Gutzells moved from Ortorville, Minn., down to Mississippi, Alabama and sometimes east to Florida in winter. Other gypsy bands move east and west. Still others stay mainly in the eastern states.

In July 1911, the tribe of the Gutzells returned to Kossuth county to bury Oliver, brother of Alonzo. The entire band made the trip in order that the two princes might rest side by side. Again the lot was cleaned up and plants and shrubs planted.

Since that time the tribe has continued their annual pilgrimage to the cemetery. On the trip north during the spring, they stop, clear away the winter's debris and plant flowers for the summer. In the fall they stop and pay homage to their dead companions.

Another lot was purchased to provide adequate space for all the tribe who wished to be buried there. The whole space has been enclosed with a low white marble wall. Seven cedar trees were planted within the enclosure.

Then the queen mother died and was buried in the gypsy cemetery.Among the monuments standing there is one for Albert Jeffrey, a younger member of the tribe. The stone reads:

ALBERT
Son of H and E Jeffrey
Feb 24 1902 — Oct 1 1912
"Asleep in Jesus."

*The names of Albert's father and mother are given in a way which is curious and unlike traditional customs, though the image of a lamb on top of the stone and the monument itself is exactly like those for boys who are not gypsy princes.*

*The visitor will notice curious shells and wooden carvings lying near the markers. These are the trinkets which the individual collected and prized during his or her lifetime. The gypsies always bury all possessions of the dead when they inter the body.*

*With the exception of the old queen, the tribe has proven itself especially law abiding. The Jeffreys own a farm near Ortonville, Minn. After the crops have been harvested in the fall the family starts south to spend the winter. With the first signs of spring they return north.*

*They never omit their visit to the Gutzell shrine.*

*A curious story is told of the old queen, who ruled her tribe with iron authority.*

*The tribe was camping north of Algona and the queen approached a farmhouse.*

*"Can I borrow a little shortening for my biscuit?" she asked the farmer's wife. The article was given to her.*

*Two minutes later, the queen returned. "Could you let me have a little milk for my biscuit?" she inquired. The milk was produced.*

*Another short interval and the royal lady appeared again. She needed flour "to make her biscuit." The gypsies ate biscuits that evening for supper.*

*The Gutzell tribe has grown smaller with the years. Perhaps the semi domesticated life they have adopted, farming for the summer months, has something to do with it. Mr. Annis, who has had many dealings with the roaming race, says they are not bad people to deal with. They trade horses as other traders do and people of the neighbourhood do not find them dangerous in any way.*

*Perhaps the establishment of their shrine has had something to do with taming their wild brood...*

*At any rate it stands — the only gypsy burial ground known in the country — just six miles north of Algona, Ia.*

Cutting away the hype and romanticism from this report, the bare bones are a situation where Gypsies created their own cemetery having initially intended to simply abandon the body of their deceased relative (though abandonment is contrary to every piece of evidence I have ever found with Gypsies.)

The name Gutzell is not English Gypsy, but Jeffrey certainly is. The family mainly travelled round Oxfordshire, Hampshire and Hertfordshire and some migrated to the USA probably in the early 1880s: in 1884 an English Gypsy queen called Jeffreys was buried at Dayton, Ohio, and in 1899 a Gypsy Henry Jaffrey, aged 19, born in England, caused a hue and cry in Ohio when he went missing. They intermarried with English Gypsy Stanleys (some of whom also claimed to be royal) and several of whom also ended up in the USA, and this group intermarried with Russian Gypsies — perhaps the Gutzell element. Or was Gutzell just a typical English Gypsy joke at the locals' expense? Or could it, even, have been a simple alias — I am aware of Taylors in Wales in c 1905 and later in the USA in the 1920s who alleged they were 'Hungarian' Gypsies. They used a bizarre 'Hungarian' surname.

Notice that the Algona graves exhibit almost all the features we have come to expect from wayside graves, only the final proof of human bones being actually discovered there being missing (but hardly deniable).

## Stillborn and Infant Burials

It is very clear that considerable numbers of wayside burials of stillborn babies and young infants occurred and my impression from talking to older Gypsies is that this continued to be the case well into the 20th century.

I want to mention two particular cases, which appear in the Journal of the Gypsy Lore Society where they are described as two unrelated incidents, as I have had the opportunity to hear the Gypsy version from people who, though not present at the time, heard about the incidents from their own families. I should emphasise that it was only after hearing what had happened, that I found these in print, and that I have been told of numerous others which have not thus appeared.

It appears that in April 1917, a group of Smiths and Booths, one of whom was Okey Booth, were travelling through Haxey, LIN, when, with very little warning, one of the women gave birth to a dead child. There and then, they buried the body in a barn where several stillborn babies were already interred. Unfortunately, they had no sooner resumed travelling than a second woman, Bess (or Liza) Booth had a stillborn child actually on the roadside. In the night, Liza took the child to a cemetery and, though unable to read, spotted a gravestone with the name *Elizabeth* on it. She was convinced that someone with the same name as her would protect the child, but as she dug into the head of the grave near the stone, local people saw her and called the police.

She was arrested on suspicion of murder, giving the police the name Mary Ingram (which is one appearing in JGLS). However, it transpired that the baby had been born dead and the mother was released after a severe warning. But police are always police, as far as Gypsies are concerned, and word came to them that there had been a prolonged stay in a local barn. The police found the newly dug grave and arrested a second member of the party. Again, it was found that the baby had been stillborn and they were released. The bodies of the other babies in the barn were not discovered and are presumably still there. (I remember an incident in about 1966 when ten or twelve babies bodies were found in a barn in North Derbyshire — not related to this incident, of course.)

## Check list of known Romany burials

Below appears a summary table of most of the known burials. Note that in addition to the criteria listed below, almost all the burials are on or near commons, moors or on land which was used for this purpose before development occurred.

## Key to column lettering

A   near a traditional stopping ground and/or close to a major Gypsy centre of history
B   Marked with stone

C  Near cross roads or other landmark perceived as permanent.
D  Marked with thorn trees/shrubs
E  Oral tradition of the burials — Gypsy
F  Oral tradition — gorjer
G  Written record, eg estate records, parish records etc
H  Evidence of artifacts, eg broken pottery
I  Evidence of human bones
J  Partial (P) or Full (F) identification of occupants
Y  this feature present
?  appears to be present, but unsure

<u>Note</u> Several known graves are mounded, but this appears to be a feature of the type of land and structure of the grave rather than a deliberate intention.

| Ref | Location | A | B | C | D | E | F | G | H | I | J |
|---|---|---|---|---|---|---|---|---|---|---|---|
| DBY1 | Belph Common, DBY (Welbeck end) | Y | Y | Y | Y | Y | Y |  | Y | Y | P |
| DBY2 | Belph Common, (Whitwell end) DBY | Y | Y | Y | Y | Y | Y |  | Y | Y | P |
| DBY3 | Belph Village, DBY | Y | Y | Y | Y | Y | Y |  |  |  |  |
| DBY4 | Whitwell Common (Clowne Lane) DBY | Y | Y | Y | Y | Y |  |  |  |  | F |
| DBY5 | Whitwell Common (Gipsy Lane) | Y |  |  |  | Y | Y |  |  |  |  |
| DBY6 | Newton (Newtonwood Lane), DBY | Y |  |  |  | Y | Y |  |  |  | P |
| DBY7 | Tansley, DBY | Y |  |  |  | Y |  |  |  |  | P |
| DBY8 | Pilsley, Bakewell, DBY | Y | Y | Y | Y | Y | Y |  |  |  | F |
| DBY10 | Beeley Village (Chesterfield Rd), DBY | Y |  | Y | Y | Y |  |  |  |  |  |
| DBY11 | Beeley Village proper | Y | Y | Y | Y | Y |  |  |  |  |  |
| DBY12 | Hathersage (N), DBY | Y | Y | Y | Y | Y |  |  |  |  | P |

| Ref | Location | A | B | C | D | E | F | G | H | I | J |
|---|---|---|---|---|---|---|---|---|---|---|---|
| DBY13 | Hathersage (S), DBY | Y | Y | Y | Y | | | | | | |
| DBY14 | Chapel en le Frith, DBY | Y | ? | ? | | Y | Y | | | | P |
| DBY15 A | Sheldon Moors, DBY | Y | Y | Y | Y | | Y | Y | | | P |
| DBY16 | Banking overlooking Ladybower Reservoir dam, DBY | Y | ? | Y | ? | Y | | | | | |
| YKS1 | Laughton (Common), | Y | | Y | Y | Y | | | | | |
| YKS2 | Gilstead, YKS | Y | | | | Y | | Y | | Y | |
| YKS3 | Gilstead, YKS | Y | Y | Y | Y | Y | Y | | Y | Y | P |
| YKS4 | N. Anston, YKS | Y | ? | Y | | Y | | | | | ? |
| YKS5 | Sheffield | Y | | | | Y | | | | | |
| YKS6 | Sheffield | Y | | | | Y | | | | | |
| CHS1 | Sale, CHS | Y | | Y | Y | Y | Y | | | | |
| SAL1 | Market Drayton | | | | | Y | | | | | |
| LEI1 | Leicester | Y | Y | Y | Y | Y | | | | | |
| NFK1 | Mousehole Heath | Y | | | Y | Y | Y | | | | |
| ESS1 | Strethall | Y | Y | Y | Y | Y | Y | Y | | Y | Y |
| BKM1 | Quainton, Buckinghamshire | Y | Y | | | | Y | Y | | | Y |
| BKM2 | Bierton, Buckinghamshire | Y | | Y | | | Y | | Y | | |
| LIN1 | Lincoln | Y | | | | Y | | | | | |
| STF1 | Fole, STF | Y | Y | Y | Y | | Y | | | | |
| USA1 | Algona, Ia. | Y | Y | Y | Y | Y | Y | Y | | | F |

## How to find graves

When a suspected grave is found, use the hierarchy on page 4 to decide how likely it is to be one.

To assist, the likelihood of each of the criteria is shown below, but where the percentage is under 100, it is almost always because of lack of data and not because the criteria is not present.

100% are near a traditional stopping ground and/or close to a major Gypsy centre of history
94% have some Gypsy oral tradition of the burials.
63% are near cross roads or other landmark perceived as permanent.
63% are marked with thorn trees/shrubs
63% are within 2.5 metres of a boundary hedge or wall.
52% have some gorjer oral tradition of the burials
48% are marked with stone
42% have some identification of the occupants
19% have evidence of human bones
16% are mentioned in written records of some kind
13% have evidence of artifacts, eg broken pottery

## Why we need to know

Wayside graves need identifying for four reasons:

1. Such sites contain relatives of people alive today.
2. The sites need to be protected from grave robbery or destruction (as with ploughing).
3. For archaeological and historical reasons which, in years to come, will provide people with valuable information as technological, forensic and pathological expertise develops, especially DNA techniques.
4, From a genealogical viewpoint, an explanation of why there are fewer churchyard burials than baptisms, as far as Gypsies are concerned.

5. The locations of burials along the travel routes gives increased knowledge of parishes where people searching their relatives can then search the official records for other kin.

6. Last, but not least, the reason for wayside burials is largely because of severe persecution or prejudice by non-Gypsy people in the past, and it is therefore we who should take some responsibility to make amends.

## Conclusion

Graves do exist and there are probably a lot more than we currently realise. They were marked, not for religious reasons (as in Trigg) but to protect them and help them be found in years to come. Of course, not all wayside graves are of Gypsies. Many more graves have yet to be found.

# References, Bibliography and Further Reading

Anon,. Gypsy Stone, Carters Lane. In *Romany Routes, Journal of the Romany and Traveller Family History Society*, 1996, **2**, p131.

Borrow, George. Lavengro. London, John Murray 1904.

Borrow, George H. Romano Lavo Lil. London, John Murray, 1919.

Chaix, R, *et al*. Vlax Roma History: what do coalescent based methods tell us? In *European Journal of Human Genetics*, 2004, **12**, pp285-292.

Chambers, Robert. *Domestic Annals of Scotland*. Chambers, Edinburgh, 1885.

Chambers, William. *Exploits and Anecdotes of the Scottish Gypsies*. Edinburgh. William Brown, 1886 (reprint of 1821 edition).

Chambers, William. *Chambers' Miscellany*. London, Chambers, c1890.

Craig, David. *On the Crofters' Trail: In Search of the Highland Clearances*. London, Jonathan Cape, 1990.

Dawson, Robert. *Yorkshire Romanies*. Bishopdale, Jean Kington, 1995.

Dawson, Robert. *Gypsy Names for Genealogists. Volume 1: Surnames*. Blackwell, Robert Dawson, 2000.

Dawson, Robert. *Gypsy Names for Genealogists. Volume 2: Surnames*. Blackwell, Robert Dawson, 2000

Dawson, Robert. *"New" Old Gypsy Documents*. Blackwell, Robert Dawson, 2000.

Dawson, Robert. *British Gypsy Slavery: The Caribbean and Americas*. Blackwell, Robert Dawson, 2001.

Dawson, Robert. Rest in Unofficial Peace. In *Romany Routes, Journal of the Romany and Traveller Family History Society*, 1994, **1**, pp 31-35.

Dawson, Robert. Thomas Smith — Sacrifice to the Devil. In *Romany Routes, Journal of the Romany and Traveller Family History Society*, 1995, **2**, pp 7-9

Dawson, Robert. Wayside Graves. In *Romany Routes, Journal of the Romany and Traveller Family History Society*, 1998, **3**, pp 283-284.

Dawson, Robert. Own Notes. Housed in 25 box files. At the time of writing this (2005) housed at publishing address. Due to be given to R&TFHS as part of the Robert Dawson Romany

Collection and due to be housed at Reading University's Rural History Department.

Floate, Sharon Sillers. *My Ancestors were Gypsies*. London, Society of Genealogists, 1999

Gresham, David et al. Origins and Divergence of the Roma (Gypsies). In *American Journal of Human Genetics*, **69**, 2001, pp 1314-1331.

Johnstone, James. *A Memoir of the Forty-Five*. London, Folio Society, 1958.

Jones, Alyn. *Travelling People and the Tinkler Gypsies of Galloway*. Galloway Tryst Archive, 2000.

*Journal of the Gypsy Lore Society*, especially 3rd Series

*Journal of the Romany and Traveller Family History Society*, Volumes and Parts as stated

Leighton, Alexander (Reviser) *Wilson's Tales of the Border*. Manchester, Brook and Chrystal, c1900.

Leighton, Alexander. *Wilson's Tales of the Borders*. London, Walter Scott Publishing, c1890.

Leitch, Roger (Ed). *The Book of Sandy Stewart*. Edinburgh, Scottish Academic Press, 1988.

Lucas. *The Yetholm History of the Gypsies*. Kelso, J. and Rutherford J.H., 1882.

MacColl, Ewan, and Seeger, Peggy. *Till Doomsday in the Afternoon*. Manchester, Manchester University Press, 1986.

MacColl, Ewan, and Seeger, Peggy. *Travellers Songs from England and Scotland*. London, Routledge and Kegan Paul, 1977.

MacRitchie. *Scottish Gypsies under the Stewarts*.

McCormick, Andrew. *Words from the Wild Wood*. Glasgow, Fraser Asher and Co, 1912.

McCormick, Andrew. *The Tinkler-Gypsies of Galloway*. Dumfries, J. Maxwell and Sons, 1906.

McGowan, Alan. Starting Out in Gypsy Family History, Part 3. In *Romany Routes, Journal of the Romany and Traveller Family History Society*, 1997, **3**, p156.

McGowan, Alan. Alan McGowan Comments. In *Romany Routes, Journal of the Romany and Traveller Family History Society*, 1998, **3**. pp 284-5.

McGowan, Alan. *On the Gypsy Trail — Sources for the Family History of Gypsies*. South Chailey, Romany and Traveller FHS,

1998.

Morar, Bharti et al. Mutation History of the Roma/Gypsies.. In *American Journal of Human Genetics*, Oct 2004, **75** pp 596-609.

Neat, Timothy. *The Summer Walker*. Edinburgh, Birlinn Ltd, 2002.

Ni Shuinear, Sinead. Inventing Irish Traveller History. In *History Ireland*, **12** No 4, Winter 2004.

Oldfield, Stephen. Woodman Brian braves curse of gipsy tree. Article in *Daily Mail*, November 7, 1977.

Petrie, Winifred. *Folk Tales of the Borders*. London, Thomas Nelson, 1950.

Prebble, John. *The Highland Clearances*. Harmondsworth, Penguin Books, 1971.

Prebble, John. *Culloden*. London, The Folio Press, 1996.

Secretary of State for Scotland. *Report of the Departmental Committee on Habitual Vagrants, Beggars, Inebriates and Juvenile Delinquents*. Edinburgh, HMSO, 1895.

Simson, Walter. *A History of the Gipsies*. London, Sampson Low, 1865.

Smith, Jess. TRILOGY: *Jessie's Journey; Tales from the Tents; & Tears for A Tinker*, Mercat Press, Edinburgh, 2003/2005

Smullen, Ivor. *The Cave Dwellers, in Countryman*, June/August 2000.

Stuart, Charles. *David Blythe: The Gipsy King*. Kelso, J. and H. Rutherford, 1883

Tokeley, A.V. *The Kirk Yetholm Gypsies*. Borders Family History Society, 2002.

Triben, Ruth E. At the End of the Gypsy Trail. Article in *Des Moines Register*, Sunday Magazine Section, March 11, 1923.

Trigg, E.B. *Gypsy Demons and Divinities*. London, Sheldon Press, 1973 Vanstone, Sue. Antiquarian Discoveries in Bierton (extracts). In *Romany Routes, Journal of the Romany and Traveller Family History Society*, 1996, **2**, No. 3, pp 127-128

Vesey Fitzgerald, Brian. *George Borrow*. London, Dennis Dobson, 1953.

Vesey Fitzgerald, Brian. *Gypsies of Britain*. London, Country Book Club, 1951.

Whyte, Betsy. *The Yellow on the Broom*. London, Futura, 1991.

Whyte, Betsy. *Red Rowans and Wild Honey*. Edinburgh, Canongate, 2000.

Whyte, Donald. *Scottish Gypsies and Other Travellers.* Blackwell, Robert Dawson, 2001.
*Wilson's Tales of the Borders.* London, Ward Lock, c1890.

# Useful Addresses

1. Romany and Traveller Family History Society, 6 St. James's Walk, South Chailey, East Sussex, BN8 4BU.

2. By all means contact me. I don't normally charge. But I emphasise the need for SAE. I won't answer any letters without. At the least, I can usually put you on the track to find your own people. I may even be able to introduce you personally. I have listings of virtually every Gypsy surname in Britain and of all the typically Romany first names. I also know a great many Romanyes nationwide, and there's always a good chance. My address — Robert Dawson, 188 Alfreton Road, Blackwell, Alfreton, Derbyshire, UK. DE55 5JH.

The following organizations may then be able to help but several stress that their only specialism is circus (not Gypsy/Fairground/Bargee etc). SAE or IRCs are normally essential:

3. The Circus Friends Association, 20 Foot Wood Crescent, Shawclough, Rochdale, Lancs, OL12 6PB.

4. The Sanger family: Julie Goddard, 11 Chandos Road, Newbury, Berks. RG14 7EP.

5. The Entertainers Index, Mrs. Marjorie P.Dunn, 2 Summer Lane, Sheffield, S17 4AJ.

6. EFECOT (the European Federation for the Education of the Children of Occupational Travellers), Guimardstraat 17, B-1040, Brussels. This organization is essentially one concentrating on education of fairground and circus children but might be able to guide some people with non-British circus forebears.

7. The booklets of Brian Jones — Index of Indexers. 6 volumes listing specialists in a host of areas, many relevant to Romany and Traveller genealogy. Brian Jones, 32 Myers Avenue, Bradford, Yorks. BD2 4ET.